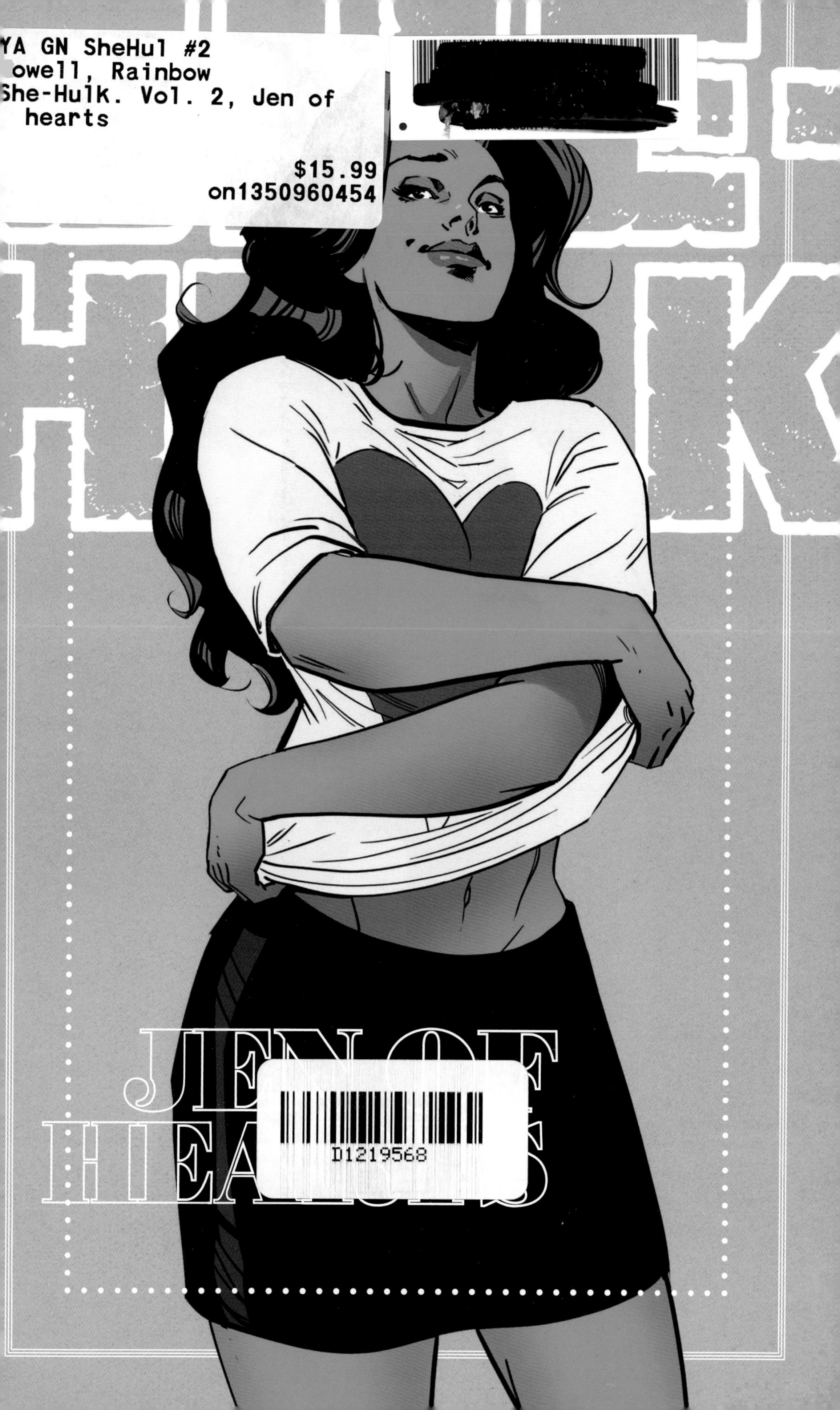
JEN OF
HEA

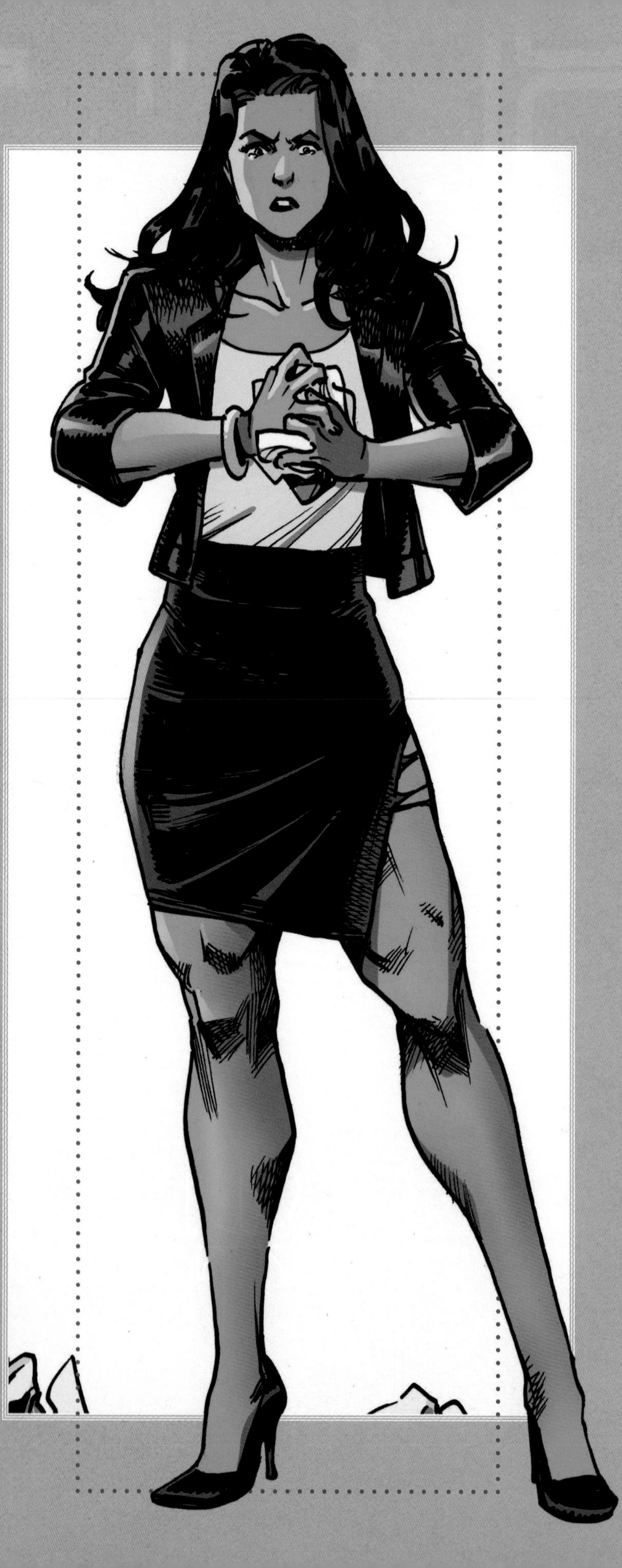

JENNIFER WALTERS — OTHERWISE KNOWN AS **SHE-HULK** — HAS LEFT THE AVENGERS AND RETURNED TO **LAWYERING**. SHE NOW WORKS FOR HER FORMER ADVERSARY **MALLORY BOOK**, WHO HAS A STRICT "NO SUPERHUMAN CLIENTS" POLICY. THINGS WERE GOING WELL FOR JEN — UNTIL SOMEONE UNEXPECTED CRASHED BACK INTO HER LIFE: FRIEND, FELLOW AVENGER AND PREVIOUSLY PRESUMED-DEAD **JACK OF HEARTS**. BUT SOMETHING HAS PUT A DAMPER ON JACK'S POWERS, AND HE STRUGGLES TO PARSE THE FRAGMENTED MEMORIES OF HIS SURVIVAL. FEELING A STRANGE CONNECTION TO JACK, JEN AGREED TO HELP HIM UNRAVEL THE MYSTERY.

SHE-HULK

JEN OF HEARTS

RAINBOW ROWELL
WRITER

LUCA MARESCA (#6-7) &
TAKESHI MIYAZAWA (#8-10)
ARTISTS

RICO RENZI
COLORIST

VC's JOE CARAMAGNA
LETTERER

JEN BARTEL
COVER ART

LINDSEY COHICK
ASSISTANT EDITOR

NICK LOWE
EDITOR

JENNIFER GRÜNWALD
COLLECTION EDITOR

DANIEL KIRCHHOFFER
ASSISTANT EDITOR

MAIA LOY
ASSISTANT MANAGING EDITOR

LISA MONTALBANO
ASSOCIATE MANAGER, TALENT RELATIONS

JEFF YOUNGQUIST
VP PRODUCTION & SPECIAL PROJECTS

ADAM DEL RE
BOOK DESIGNER

JAY BOWEN
LEAD DESIGNER

DAVID GABRIEL
SVP PRINT, SALES & MARKETING

C.B. CEBULSKI
EDITOR IN CHIEF

SHE-HULK BY RAINBOW ROWELL VOL. 2: JEN OF HEARTS. Contains material originally published in magazine form as SHE-HULK (2022) #6-10. First printing 2023. ISBN 978-1-302-94796-5. Published by MARVEL WORLDWIDE, INC., a subsidiary of MARVEL ENTERTAINMENT, LLC. OFFICE OF PUBLICATION: 1290 Avenue of the Americas, New York, NY 10104. **Printed in the U.S.A.** KEVIN FEIGE, Chief Creative Officer; DAN BUCKLEY, President, Marvel Entertainment; DAVID BOGART, Associate Publisher & SVP of Talent Affairs; TOM BREVOORT, VP, Executive Editor; NICK LOWE, Executive Editor, VP of Content, Digital Publishing; DAVID GABRIEL, VP of Print & Digital Publishing; SVEN LARSEN, VP of Licensed Publishing; MARK ANNUNZIATO, VP of Planning & Forecasting; JEFF YOUNGQUIST, VP of Production & Special Projects; ALEX MORALES, Director of Publishing Operations; DAN EDINGTON, Director of Editorial Operations; RICKEY PURDIN, Director of Talent Relations; JENNIFER GRÜNWALD, Director of Production & Special Projects; SUSAN CRESPI, Production Manager; STAN LEE, Chairman Emeritus. For information regarding advertising in Marvel Comics or on Marvel.com, please contact Vit DeBellis, Custom Solutions & Integrated Advertising Manager, at vdebellis@marvel.com. For Marvel subscription inquiries, please call 888-511-5480. **Manufactured between 3/17/2023 and 4/18/2023 by SEAWAY PRINTING, GREEN BAY, WI, USA.**

10 9 8 7 6 5 4 3 2 1

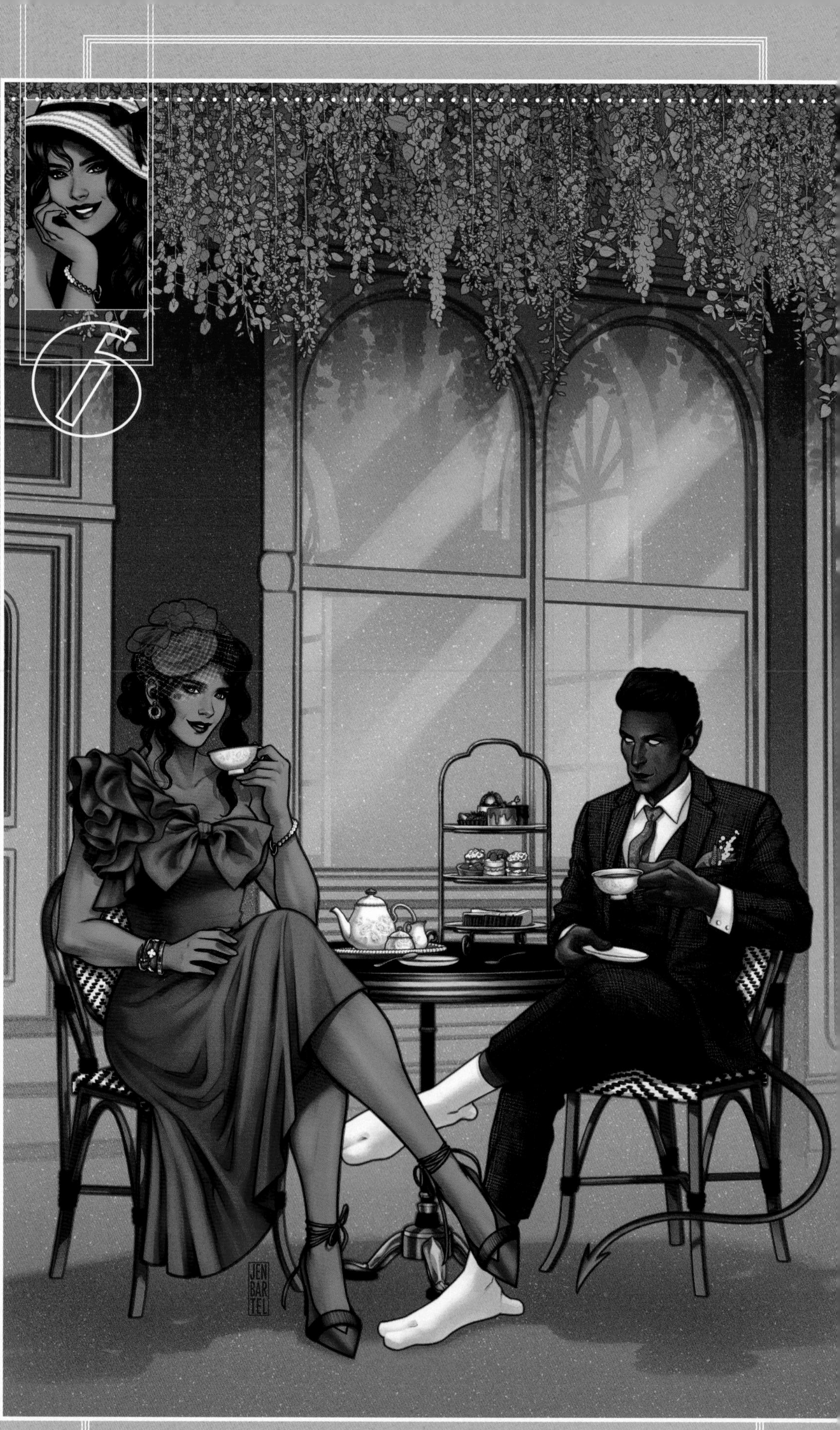
6
JEN
BAR
TEL

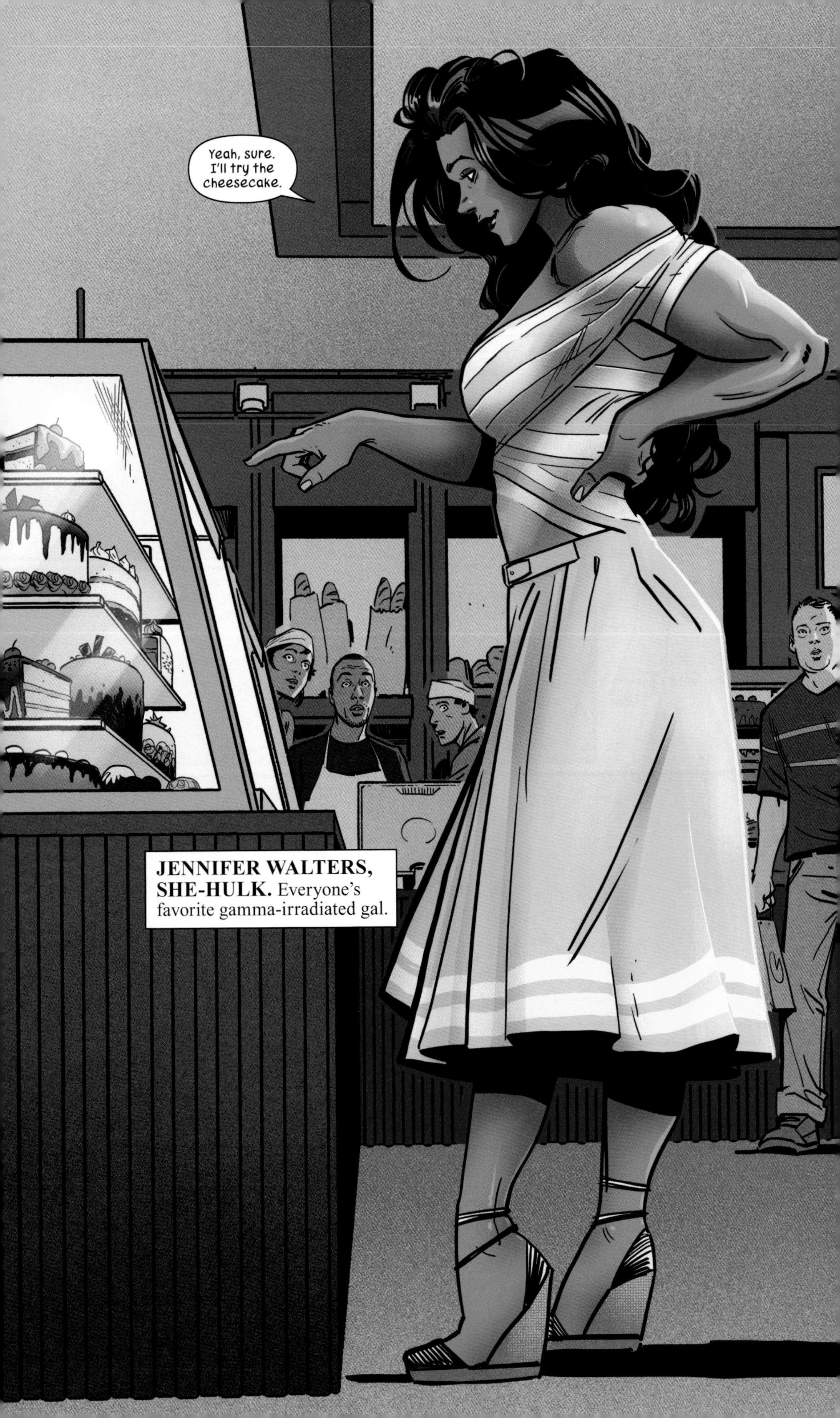
Yeah, sure. I'll try the cheesecake.
JENNIFER WALTERS, SHE-HULK. Everyone's favorite gamma-irradiated gal.

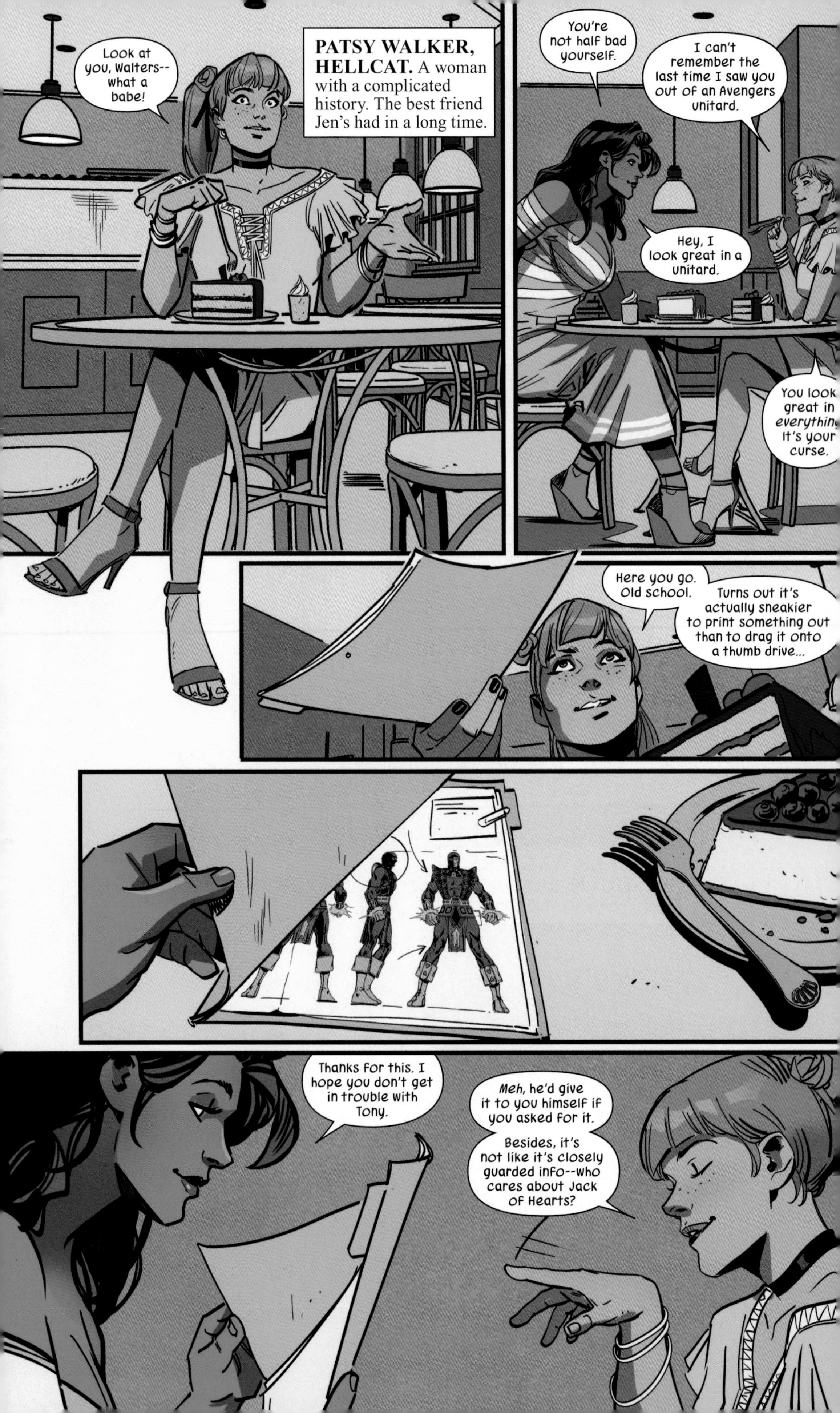

Look at you, Walters--what a babe!
PATSY WALKER, HELLCAT. A woman with a complicated history. The best friend Jen's had in a long time.
You're not half bad yourself.
I can't remember the last time I saw you out of an Avengers unitard.
Hey, I look great in a unitard.
You look great in everythin It's your curse.
Here you go. Old school.
Turns out it's actually sneakier to print something out than to drag it onto a thumb drive...
Thanks for this. I hope you don't get in trouble with Tony.
Meh, he'd give it to you himself if you asked for it.
Besides, it's not like it's closely guarded info--who cares about Jack of Hearts?

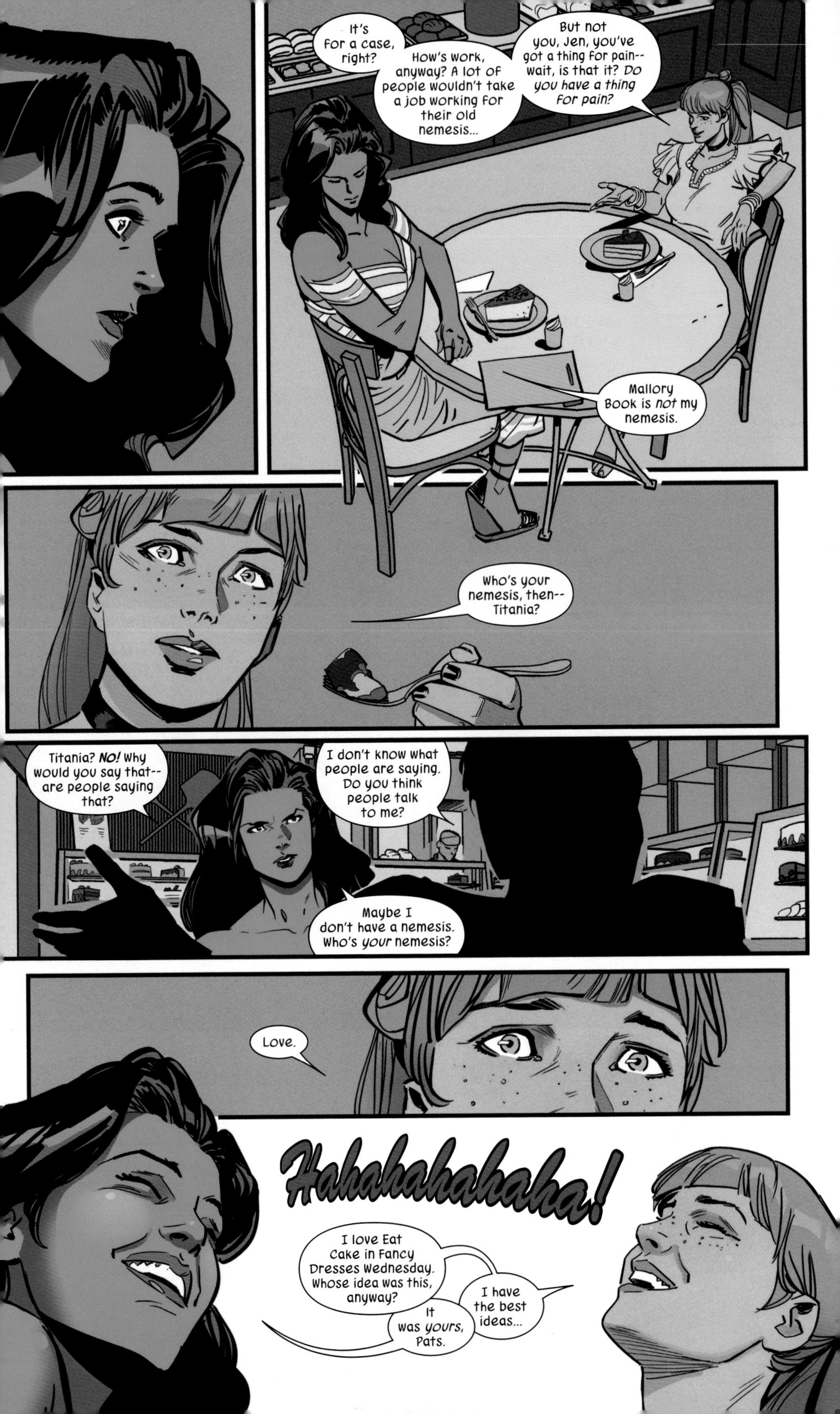

It's for a case, right?
How's work, anyway? A lot of people wouldn't take a job working for their old nemesis...
But not you, Jen, you've got a thing for pain--wait, is that it? *Do you have a thing for pain?*
Mallory Book is *not* my nemesis.
Who's your nemesis, then--Titania?
Titania? ***NO!*** Why would you say that--are people saying that?
I don't know what people are saying. Do you think people talk to me?
Maybe I don't have a nemesis. Who's *your* nemesis?
Love.
Hahahahahaha!
I love Eat Cake in Fancy Dresses Wednesday. Whose idea was this, anyway?
It was *yours*, Pats.
I have the best ideas...

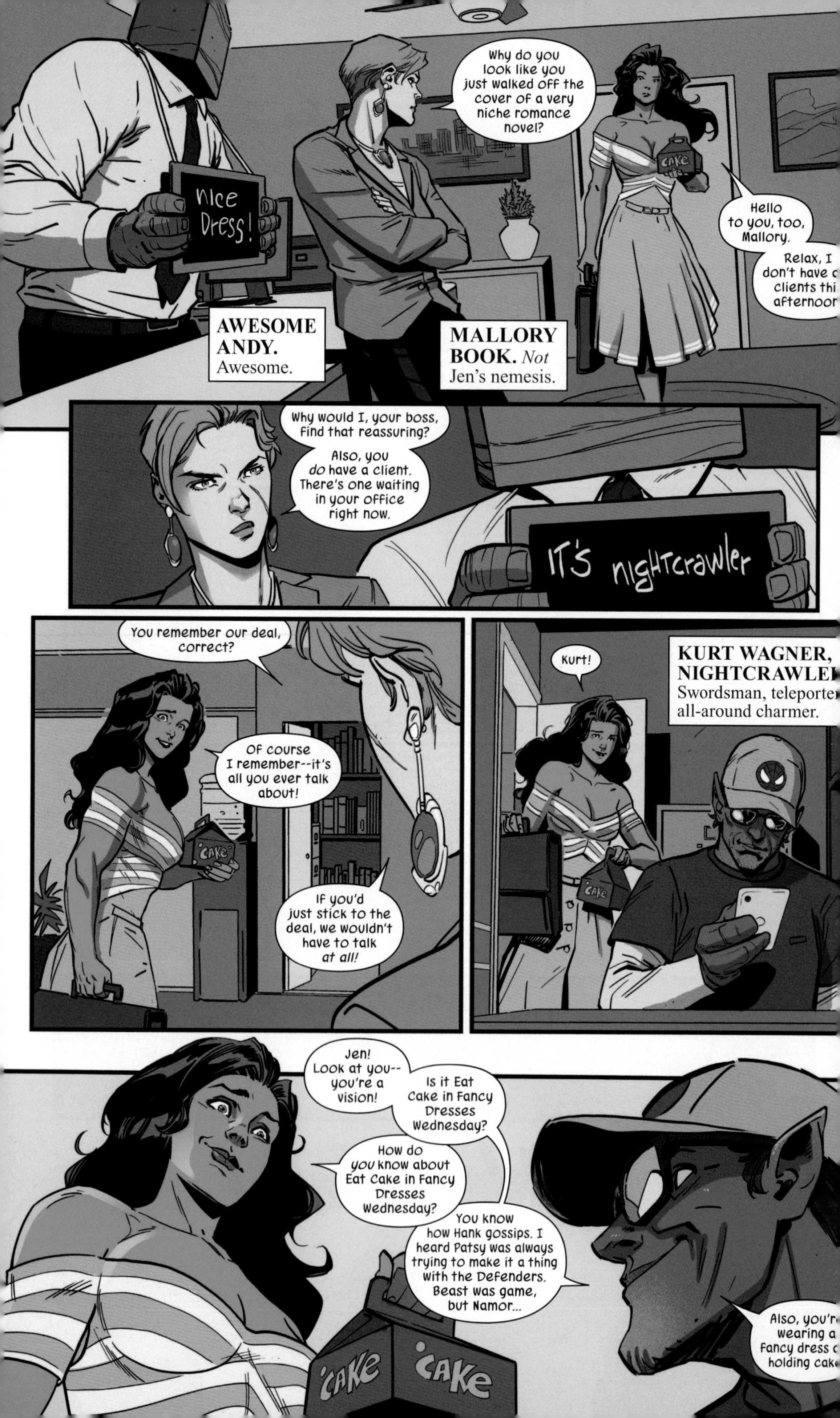
Why do you look like you just walked off the cover of a very niche romance novel?
nice Dress!
AWESOME ANDY. Awesome.
MALLORY BOOK. Not Jen's nemesis.
Hello to you, too, Mallory.
Relax, I don't have clients thi afternoor
Why would I, your boss, find that reassuring?
Also, you do have a client. There's one waiting in your office right now.
IT'S nightcrawler
You remember our deal, correct?
Of course I remember--it's all you ever talk about!
If you'd just stick to the deal, we wouldn't have to talk at all!
Kurt!
KURT WAGNER, NIGHTCRAWLE
Swordsman, teleporte all-around charmer.
Jen! Look at you-- you're a vision!
Is it Eat Cake in Fancy Dresses Wednesday?
How do you know about Eat Cake in Fancy Dresses Wednesday?
You know how Hank gossips. I heard Patsy was always trying to make it a thing with the Defenders. Beast was game, but Namor...
Also, you'r wearing a fancy dress holding cak

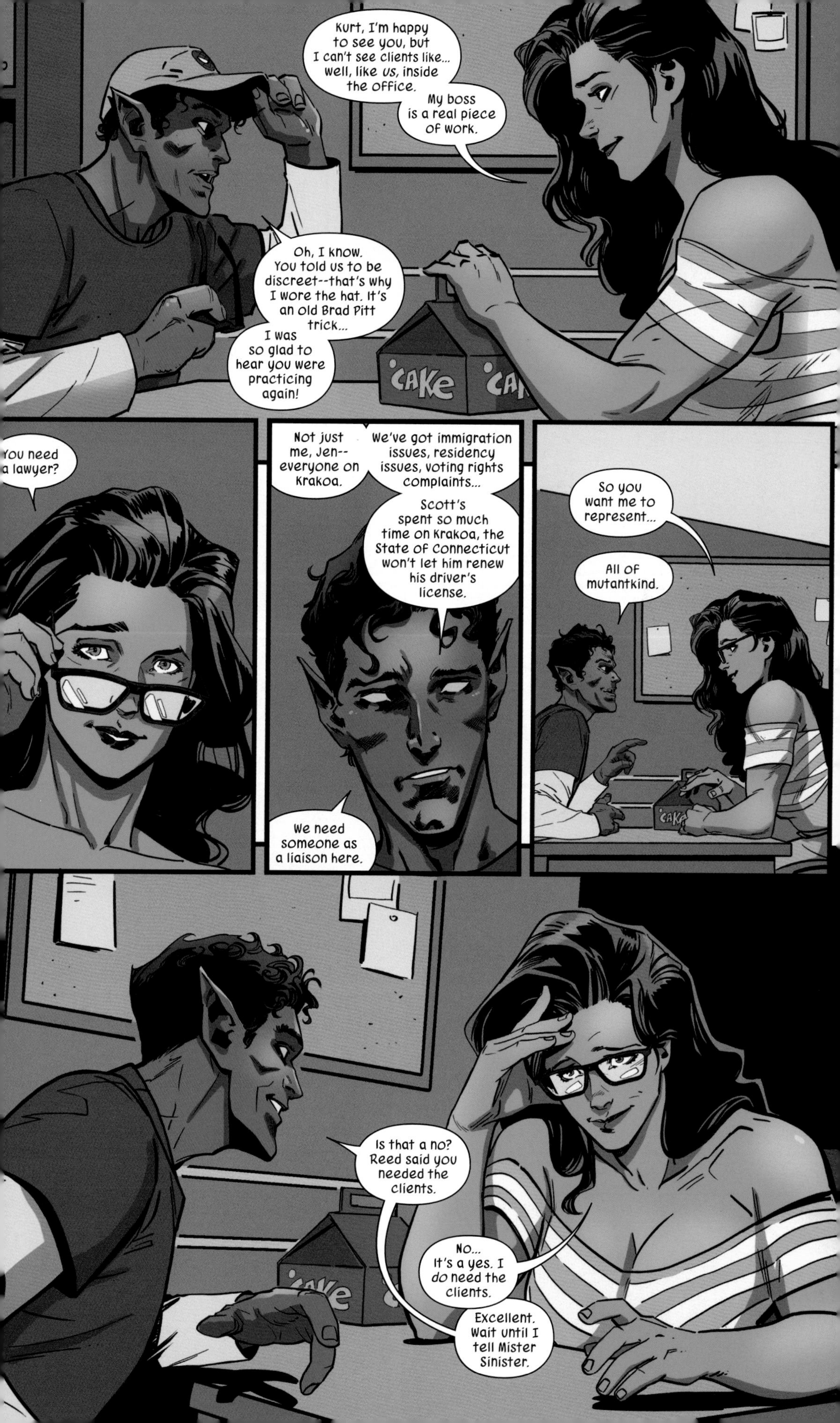

Kurt, I'm happy to see you, but I can't see clients like... well, like *us*, inside the office.
My boss is a real piece of work.
Oh, I know. You told us to be discreet--that's why I wore the hat. It's an old Brad Pitt trick...
I was so glad to hear you were practicing again!
CAKE
You need a lawyer?
Not just me, Jen-- everyone on Krakoa.
We've got immigration issues, residency issues, voting rights complaints...
Scott's spent so much time on Krakoa, the State of Connecticut won't let him renew his driver's license.
We need someone as a liaison here.
So you want me to represent...
All of mutantkind.
Is that a no? Reed said you needed the clients.
No... It's a yes. I *do* need the clients.
Excellent. Wait until I tell Mister Sinister.

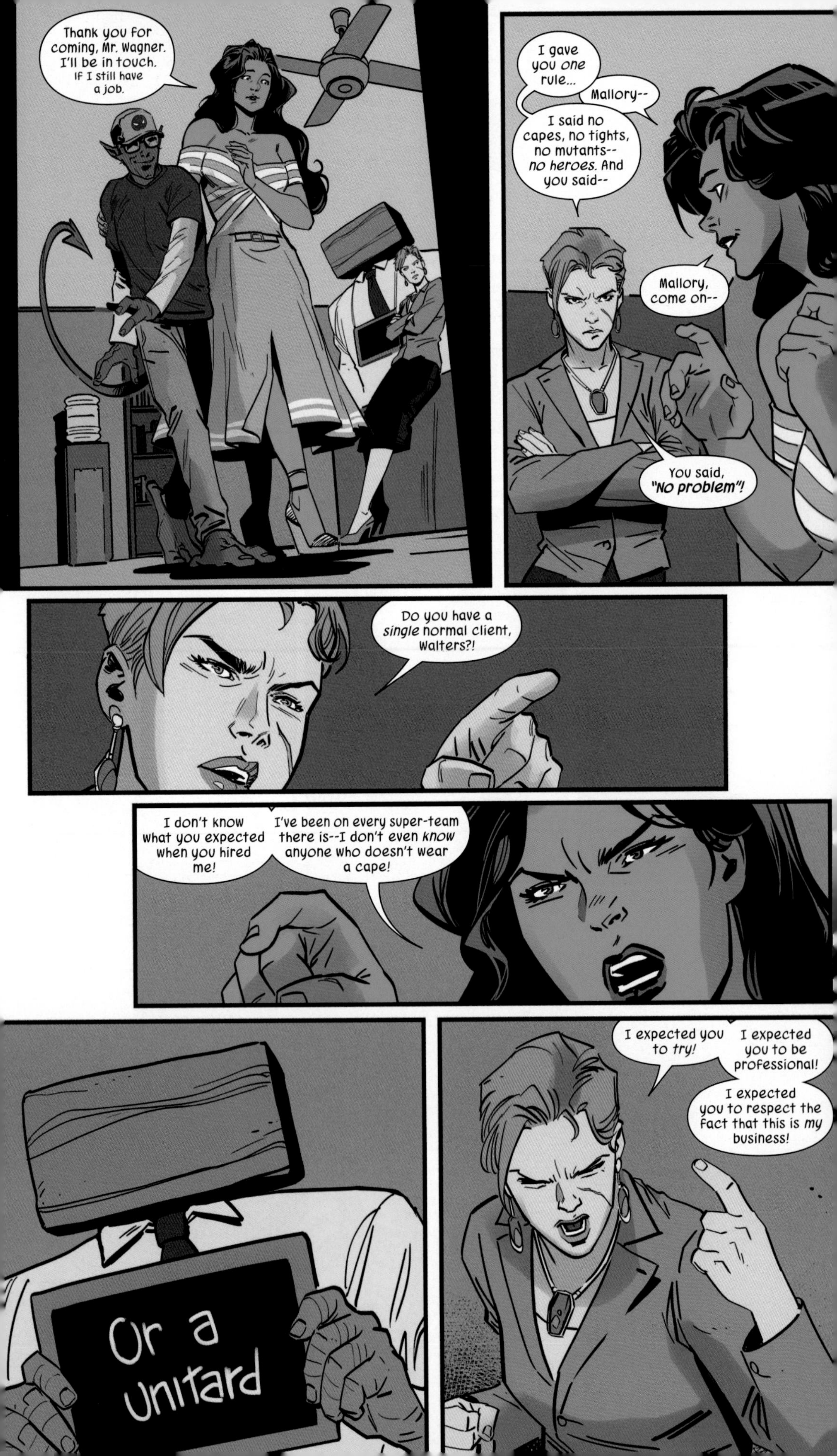
Thank you for coming, Mr. Wagner. I'll be in touch. If I still have a job.
I gave you *one* rule...
Mallory--
I said no capes, no tights, no mutants-- *no heroes.* And you said--
Mallory, come on--
You said, **"No problem"!**
Do you have a *single* normal client, Walters?!
I don't know what you expected when you hired me!
I've been on every super-team there is--I don't even *know* anyone who doesn't wear a cape!
Or a Unitard
I expected you to *try!*
I expected you to be professional!
I expected you to respect the fact that this is *my* business!

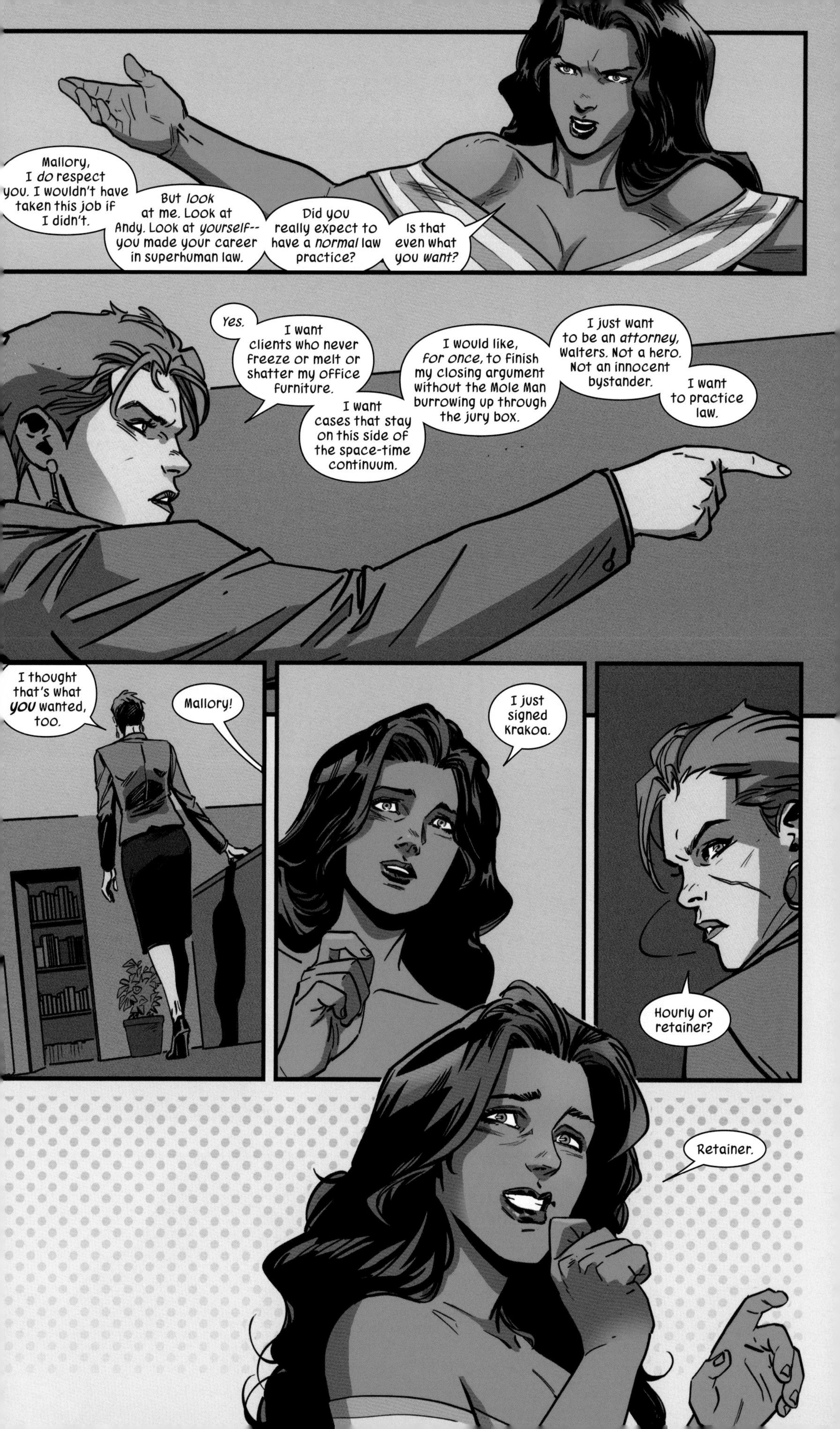
Mallory, I *do* respect you. I wouldn't have taken this job if I didn't.
But *look* at me. Look at Andy. Look at *yourself*-- you made your career in superhuman law.
Did you really expect to have a *normal* law practice?
Is that even what you *want?*
Yes.
I want clients who never freeze or melt or shatter my office furniture.
I want cases that stay on this side of the space-time continuum.
I would like, *for once,* to finish my closing argument without the Mole Man burrowing up through the jury box.
I just want to be an *attorney,* Walters. Not a hero. Not an innocent bystander.
I want to practice law.
I thought that's what ***YOU*** wanted, too.
Mallory!
I just signed Krakoa.
Hourly or retainer?
Retainer.

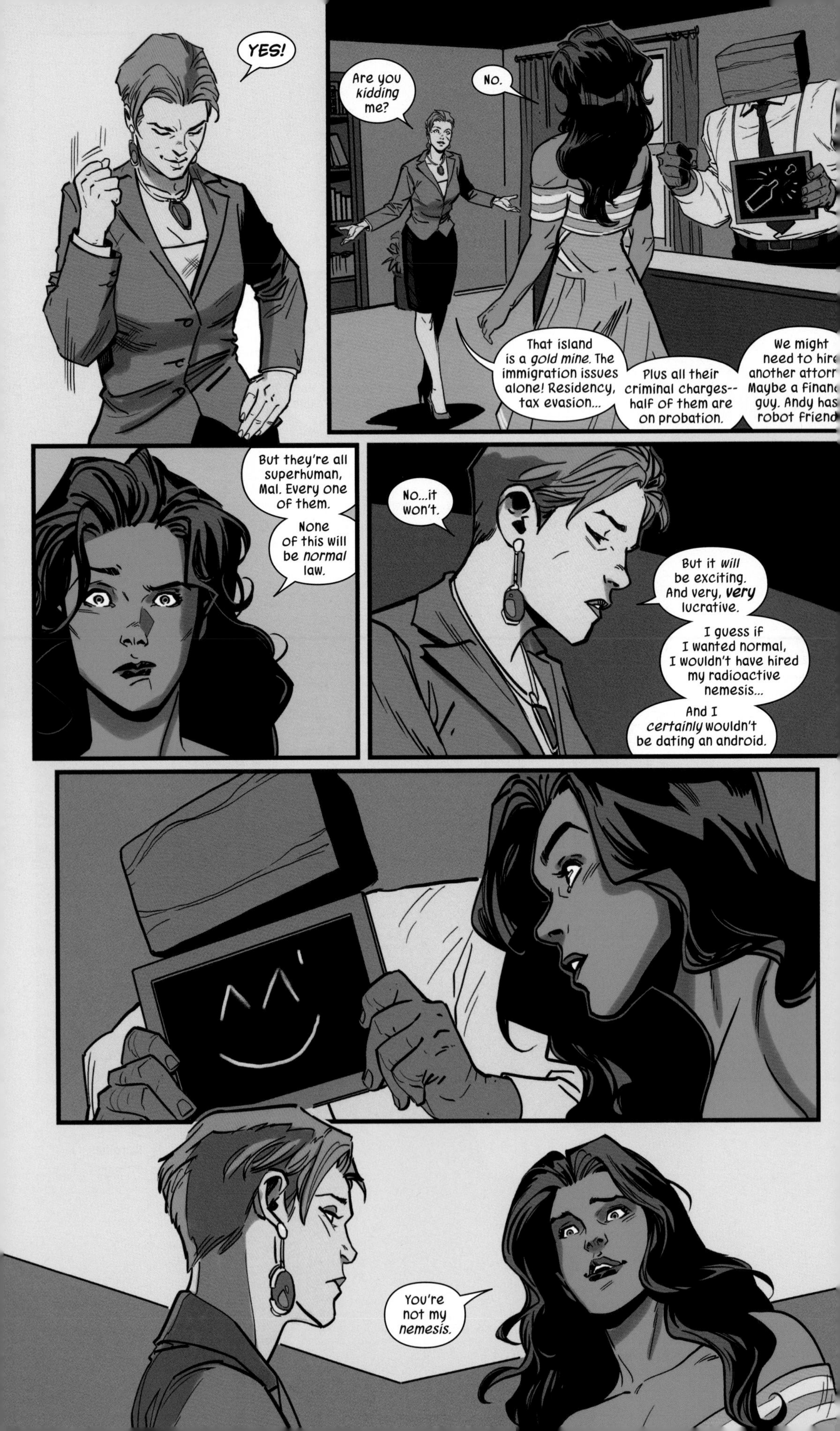
YES!
Are you kidding me?
No.
That island is a *gold mine.* The immigration issues alone! Residency, tax evasion...
Plus all their criminal charges-- half of them are on probation.
We might need to hire another attorn Maybe a financ guy. Andy has robot friend
But they're all superhuman, Mal. Every one of them.
None of this will be *normal* law.
No...it won't.
But it *will* be exciting. And very, ***very*** lucrative.
I guess if I wanted normal, I wouldn't have hired my radioactive nemesis...
And I *certainly* wouldn't be dating an android.
You're not my *nemesis.*

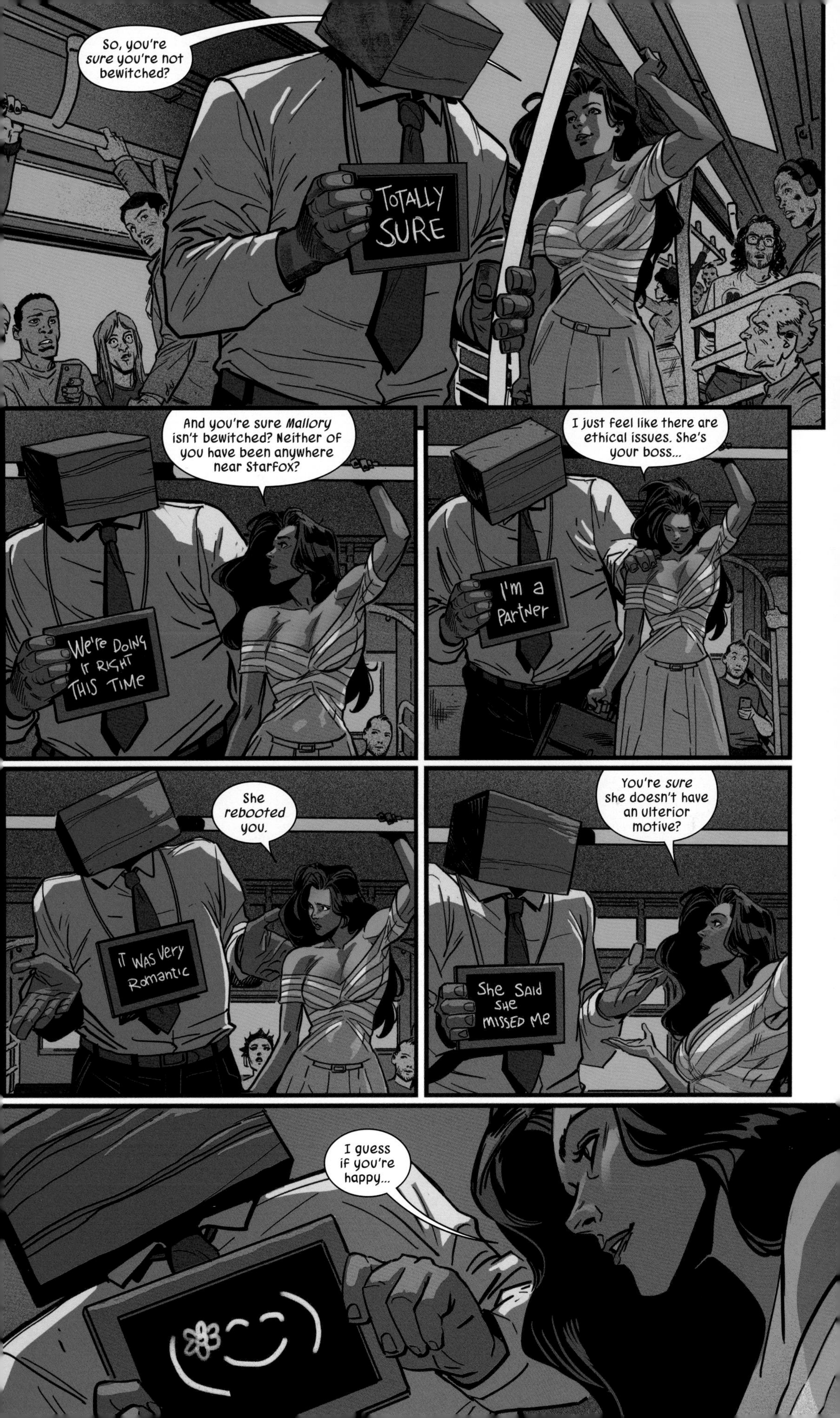
So, you're sure you're not bewitched?
TOTALLY SURE
And you're sure Mallory isn't bewitched? Neither of you have been anywhere near Starfox?
We're DOING IT RIGHT THIS TIME
I just feel like there are ethical issues. She's your boss...
I'm a Partner
She rebooted you.
IT WAS Very Romantic
You're sure she doesn't have an ulterior motive?
She Said SHE MISSED ME
I guess if you're happy...

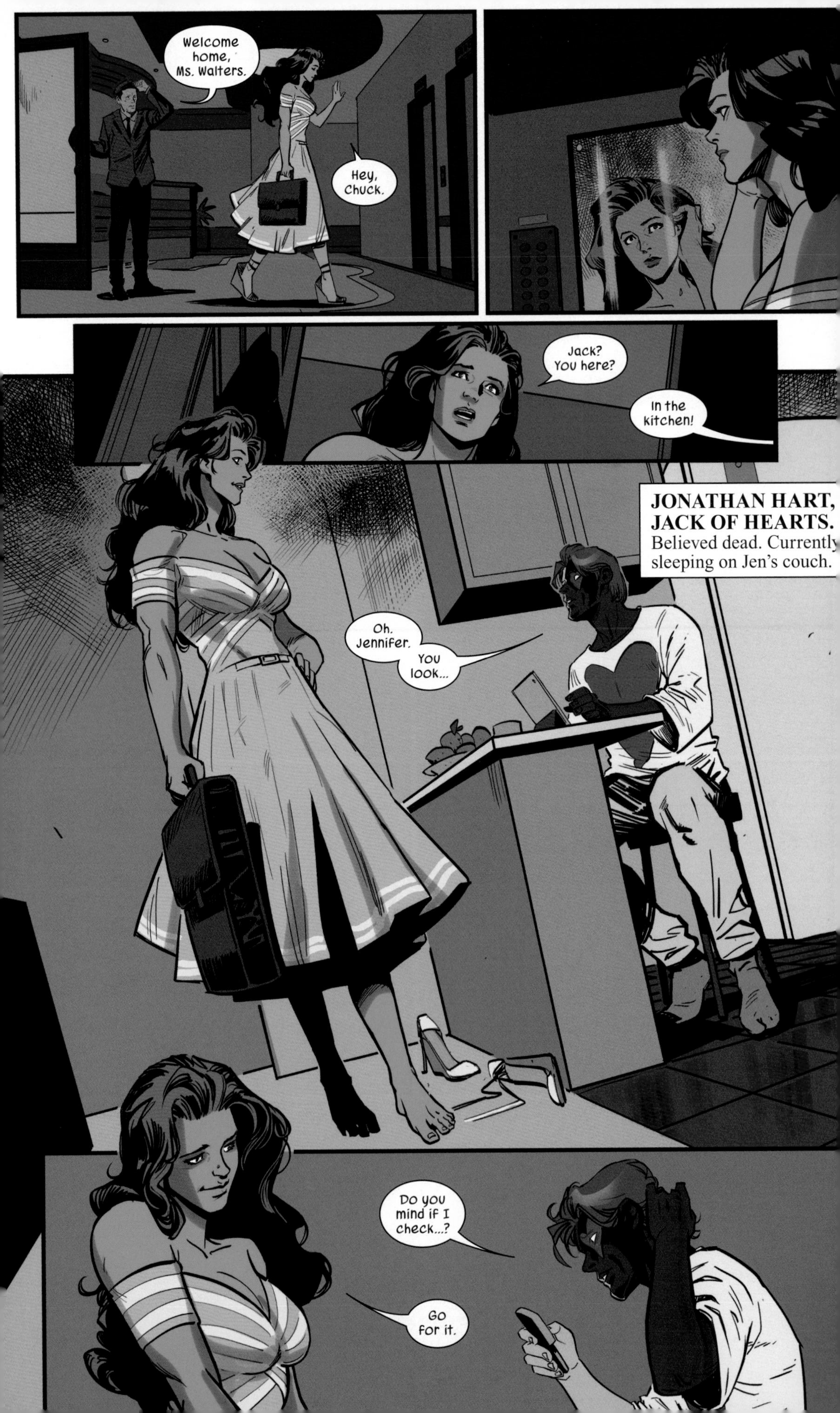

Welcome home, Ms. Walters.
Hey, Chuck.
Jack? You here?
In the kitchen!
JONATHAN HART, JACK OF HEARTS.
Believed dead. Currently sleeping on Jen's couch.
Oh. Jennifer.
You look...
Do you mind if I check...?
Go for it.

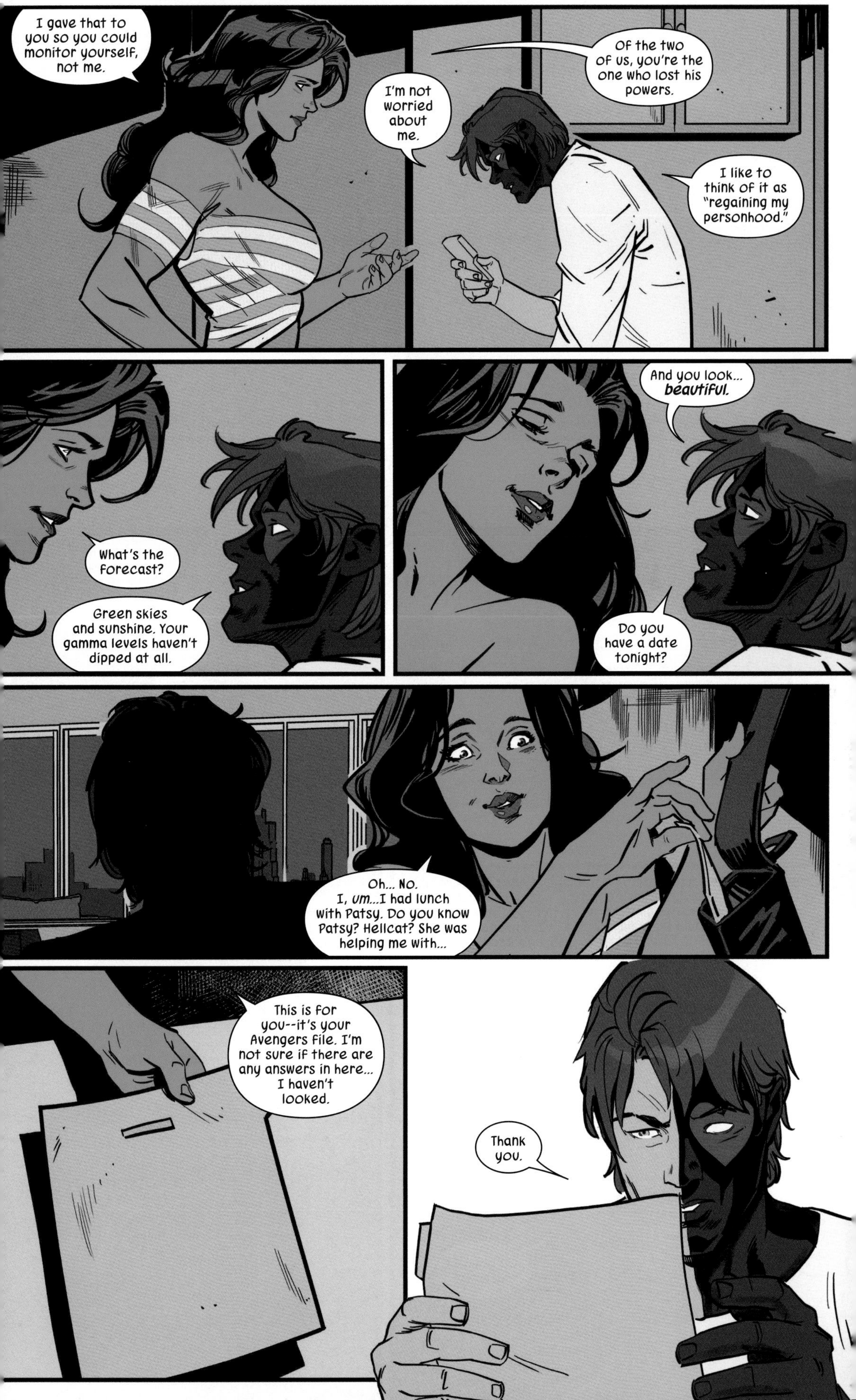
I gave that to you so you could monitor yourself, not me.
I'm not worried about me.
Of the two of us, you're the one who lost his powers.
I like to think of it as "regaining my personhood."
What's the forecast?
Green skies and sunshine. Your gamma levels haven't dipped at all.
And you look... *beautiful.*
Do you have a date tonight?
Oh... No. I, *um*...I had lunch with Patsy. Do you know Patsy? Hellcat? She was helping me with...
This is for you--it's your Avengers file. I'm not sure if there are any answers in here... I haven't looked.
Thank you.

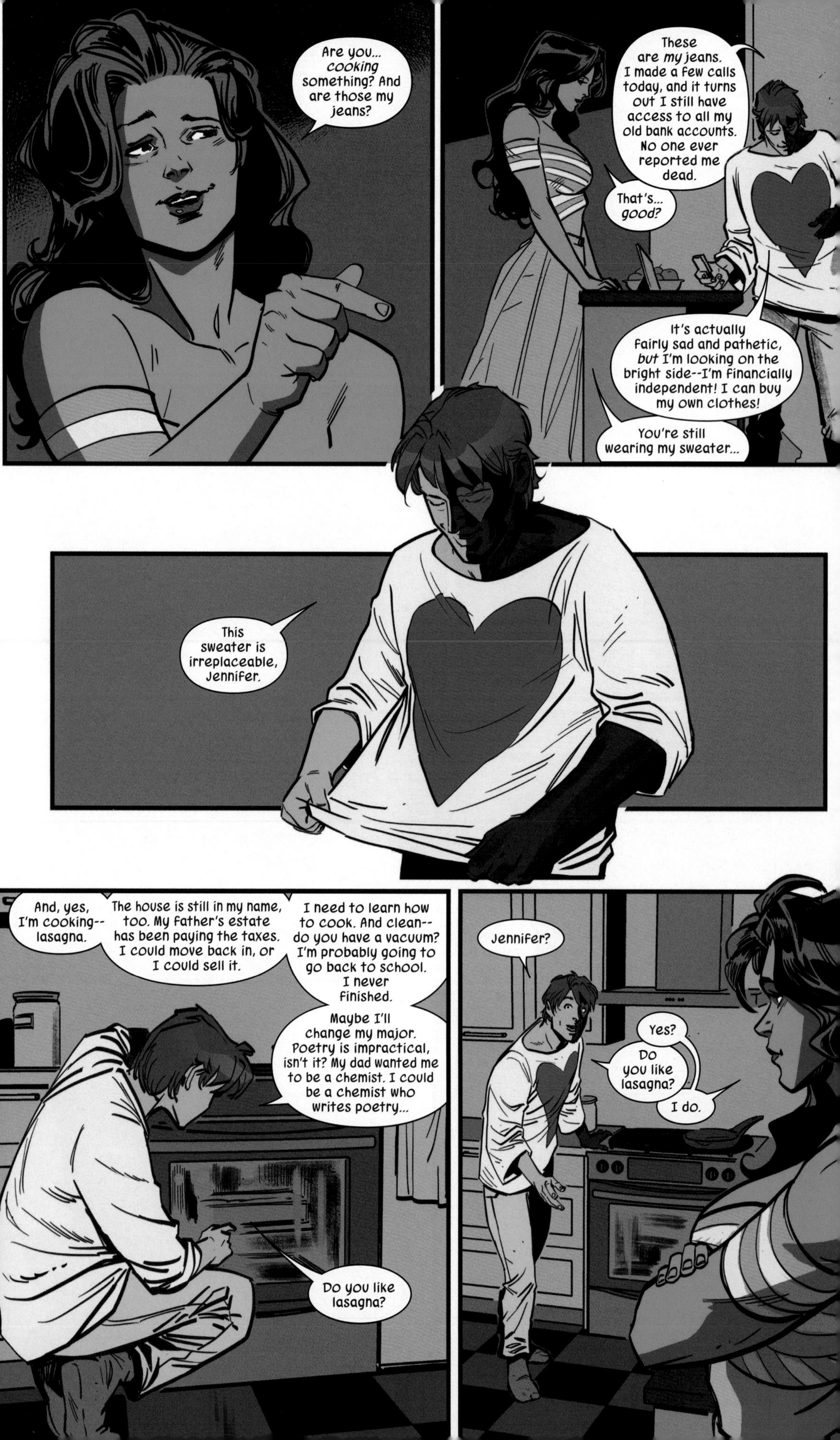

Are you... cooking something? And are those my jeans?
These are *my* jeans. I made a few calls today, and it turns out I still have access to all my old bank accounts. No one ever reported me dead.
That's... *good?*
It's actually fairly sad and pathetic, *but* I'm looking on the bright side--I'm financially independent! I can buy my own clothes!
You're still wearing my sweater...
This sweater is irreplaceable, Jennifer.
And, yes, I'm cooking--lasagna.
The house is still in my name, too. My father's estate has been paying the taxes. I could move back in, or I could sell it.
I need to learn how to cook. And clean--do you have a vacuum? I'm probably going to go back to school. I never finished.
Maybe I'll change my major. Poetry is impractical, isn't it? My dad wanted me to be a chemist. I could be a chemist who writes poetry...
Do you like lasagna?
Jennifer?
Yes?
Do you like lasagna?
I do.

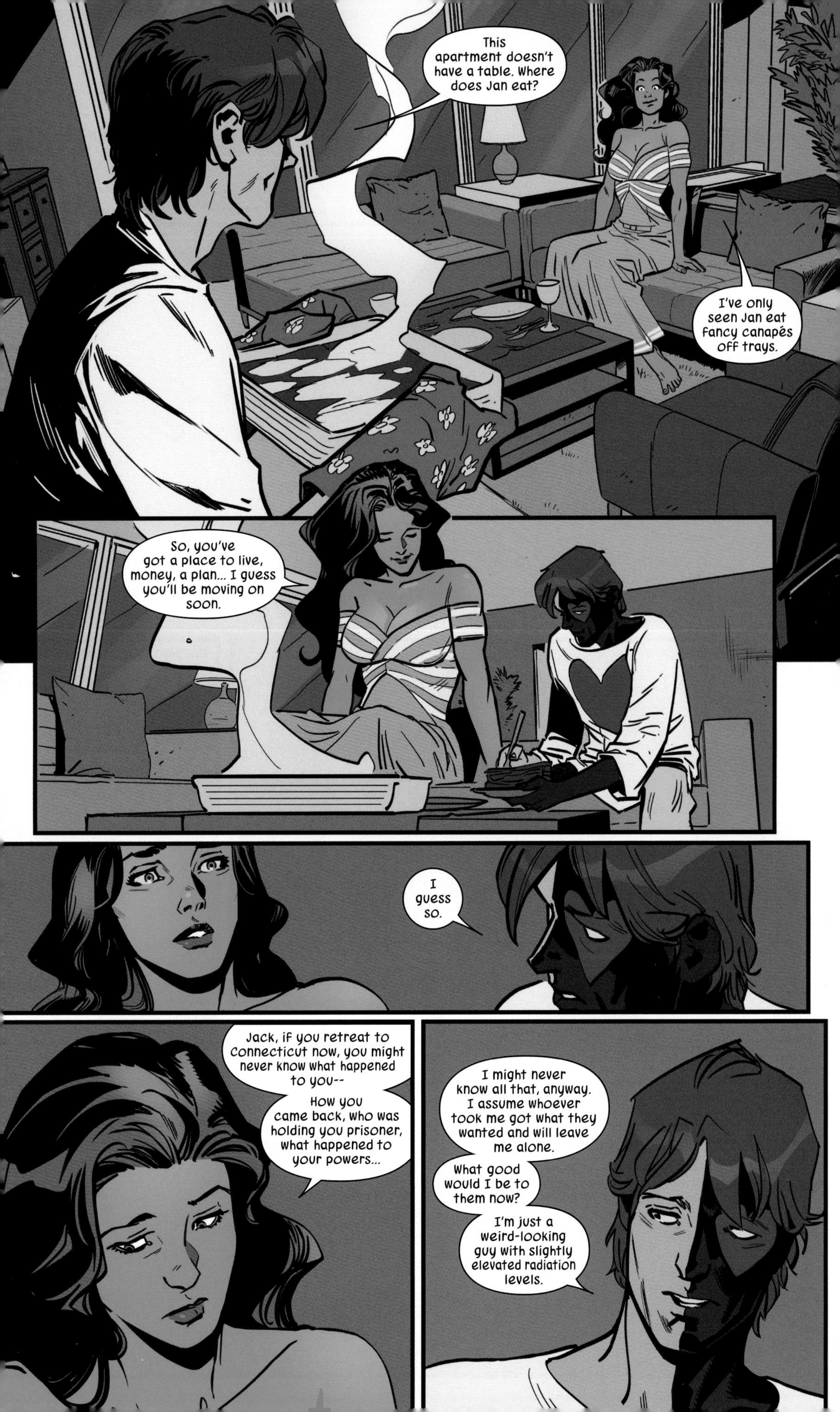
This apartment doesn't have a table. Where does Jan eat?
I've only seen Jan eat fancy canapés off trays.
So, you've got a place to live, money, a plan... I guess you'll be moving on soon.
I guess so.
Jack, if you retreat to Connecticut now, you might never know what happened to you--
How you came back, who was holding you prisoner, what happened to your powers...
I might never know all that, anyway. I assume whoever took me got what they wanted and will leave me alone.
What good would I be to them now?
I'm just a weird-looking guy with slightly elevated radiation levels.

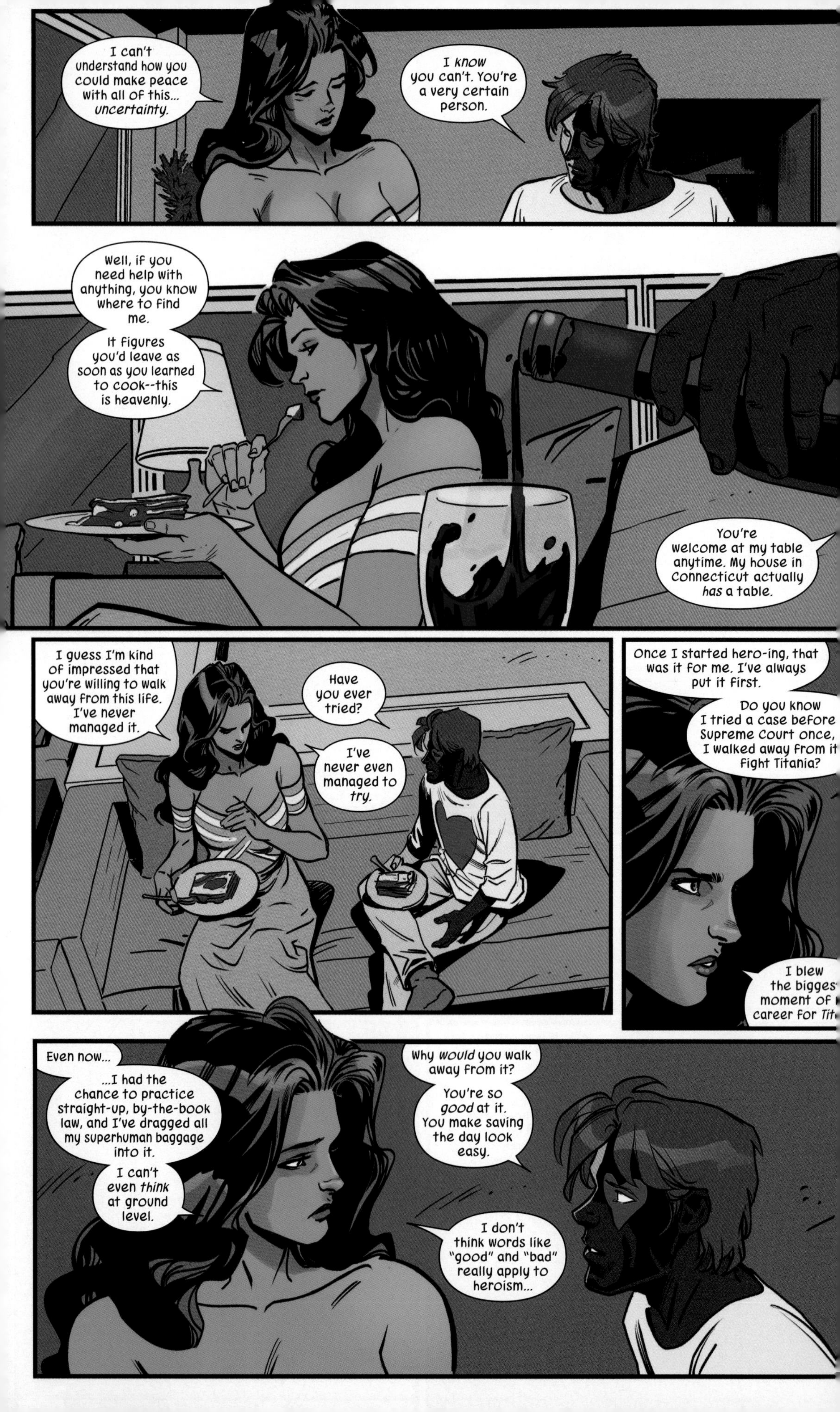

I can't understand how you could make peace with all of this... *uncertainty.*
I *know* you can't. You're a very certain person.
Well, if you need help with anything, you know where to find me.
It figures you'd leave as soon as you learned to cook--this is heavenly.
You're welcome at my table anytime. My house in Connecticut actually *has* a table.
I guess I'm kind of impressed that you're willing to walk away from this life. I've never managed it.
Have you ever tried?
I've never even managed to *try.*
Once I started hero-ing, that was it for me. I've always put it first.
Even now...
...I had the chance to practice straight-up, by-the-book law, and I've dragged all my superhuman baggage into it.
I can't even *think* at ground level.
Why *would* you walk away from it?
You're so *good* at it. You make saving the day look easy.
I don't think words like "good" and "bad" really apply to heroism...

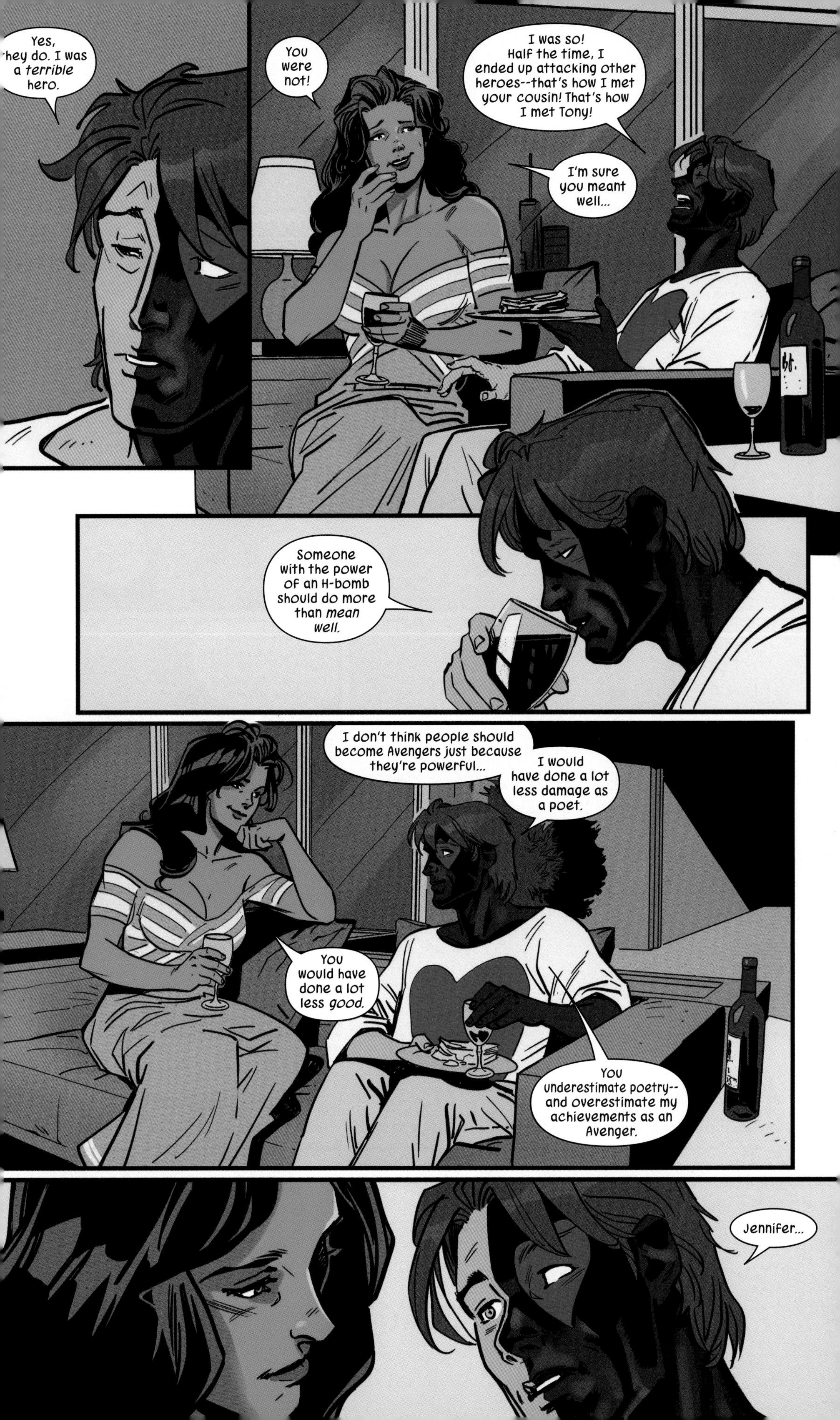
Yes, they do. I was a *terrible* hero.
You were not!
I was so! Half the time, I ended up attacking other heroes--that's how I met your cousin! That's how I met Tony!
I'm sure you meant well...
Someone with the power of an H-bomb should do more than *mean* well.
I don't think people should become Avengers just because they're powerful...
I would have done a lot less damage as a poet.
You would have done a lot less *good*.
You underestimate poetry--and overestimate my achievements as an Avenger.
Jennifer...

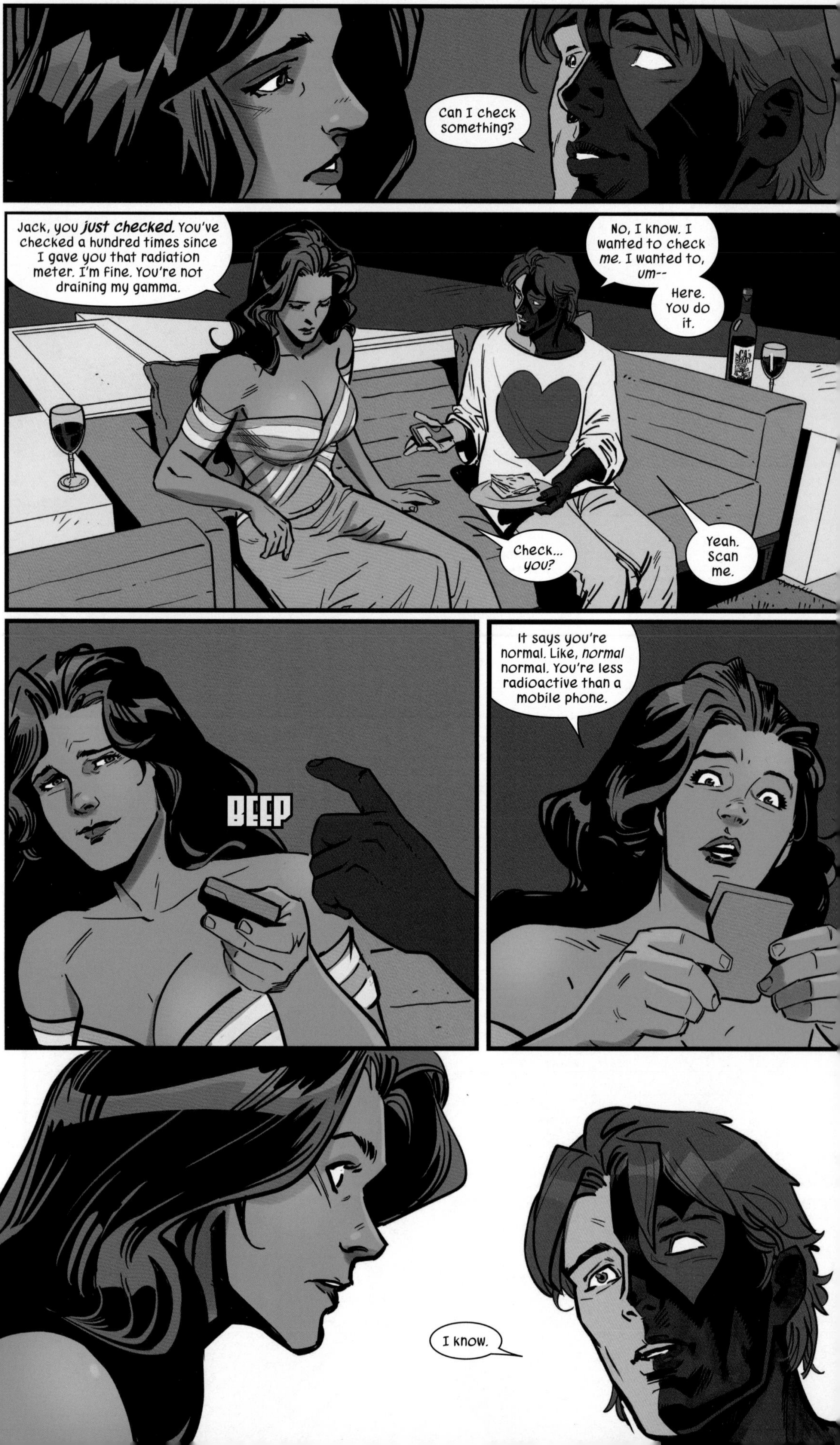
Can I check something?
Jack, you *just checked.* You've checked a hundred times since I gave you that radiation meter. I'm fine. You're not draining my gamma.
No, I know. I wanted to check *me.* I wanted to, um--
Here. You do it.
Check... *you?*
Yeah. Scan me.
BEEP
It says you're normal. Like, *normal* normal. You're less radioactive than a mobile phone.
I know.

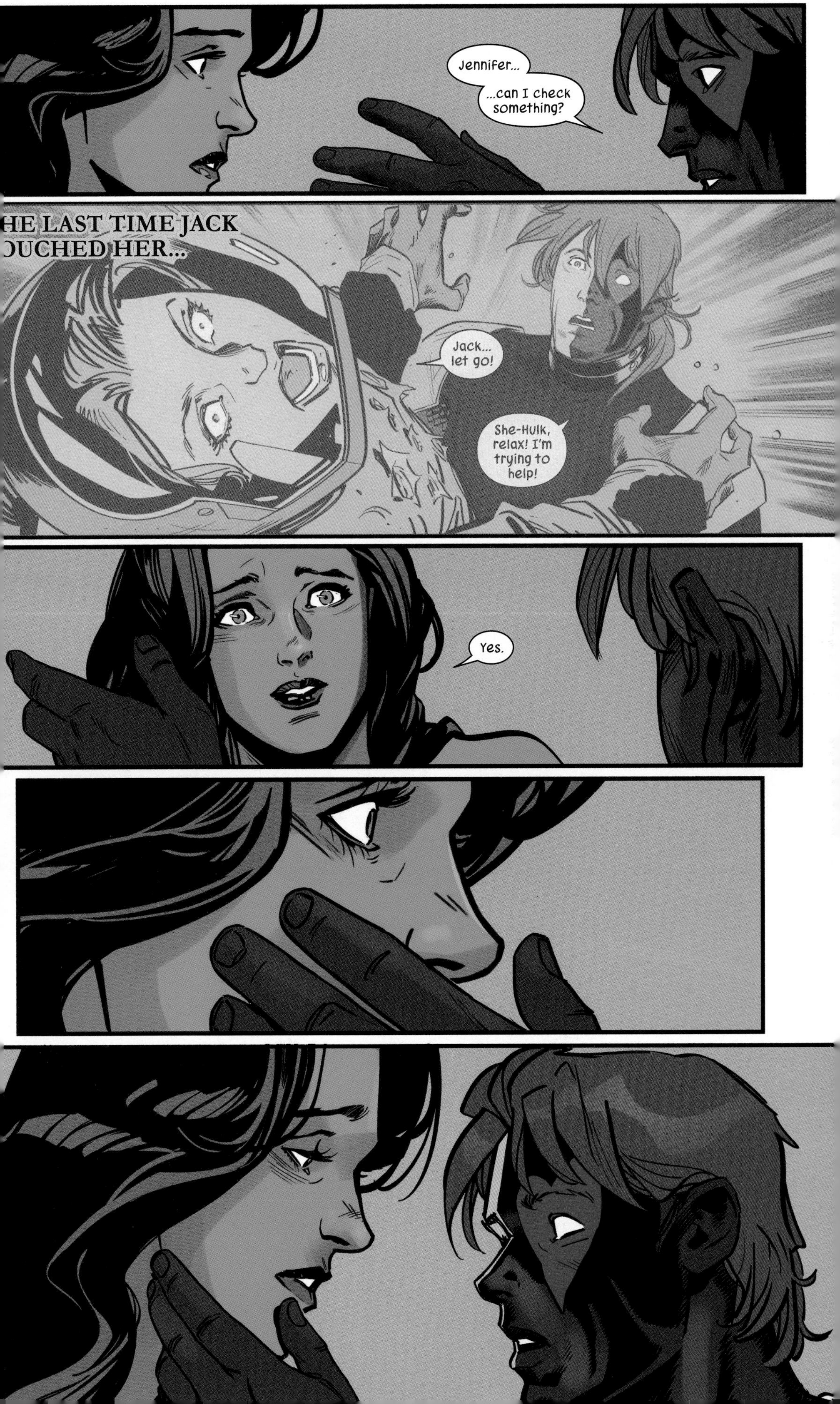
Jennifer...
...can I check something?
HE LAST TIME JACK
OUCHED HER...
Jack... let go!
She-Hulk, relax! I'm trying to help!
Yes.

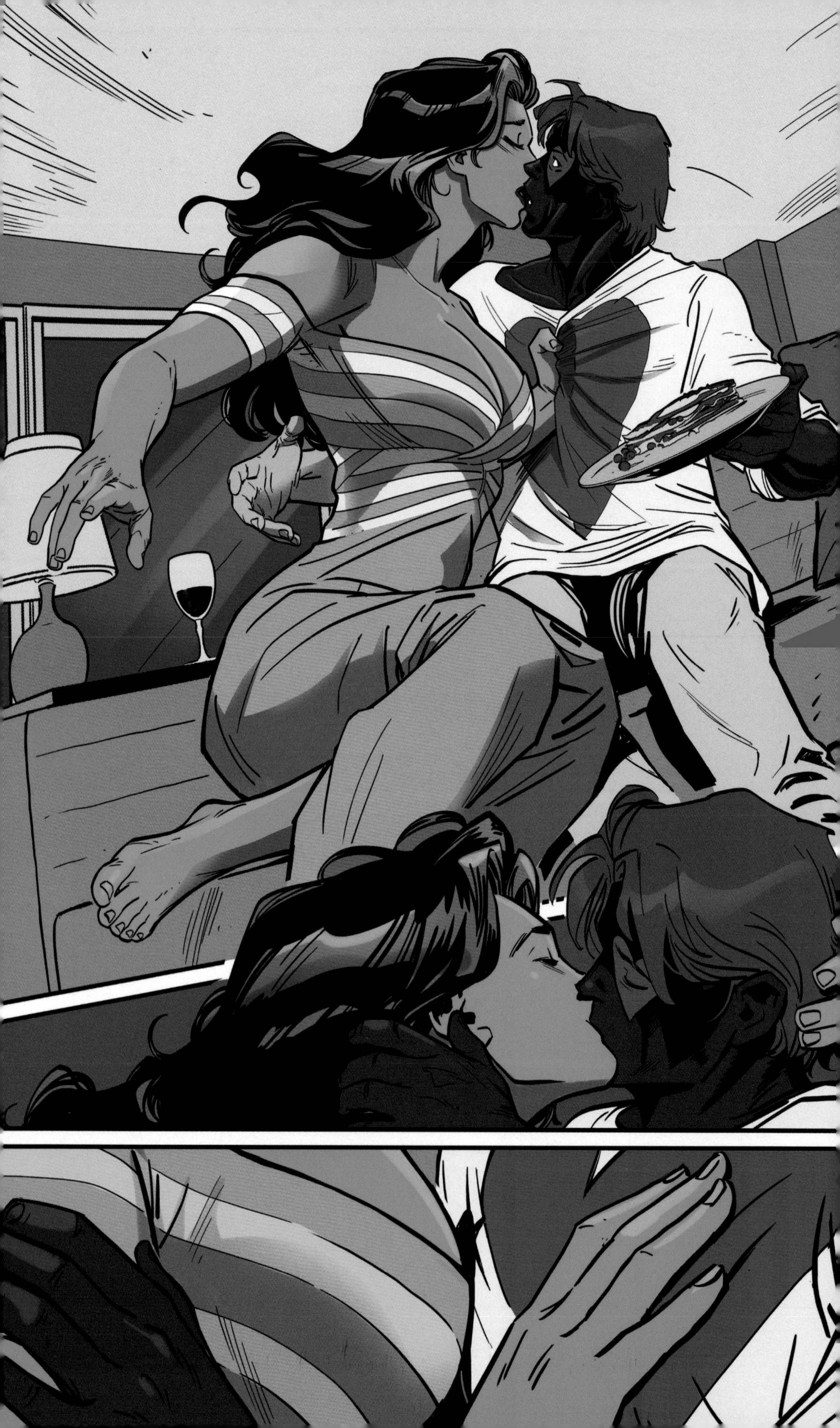

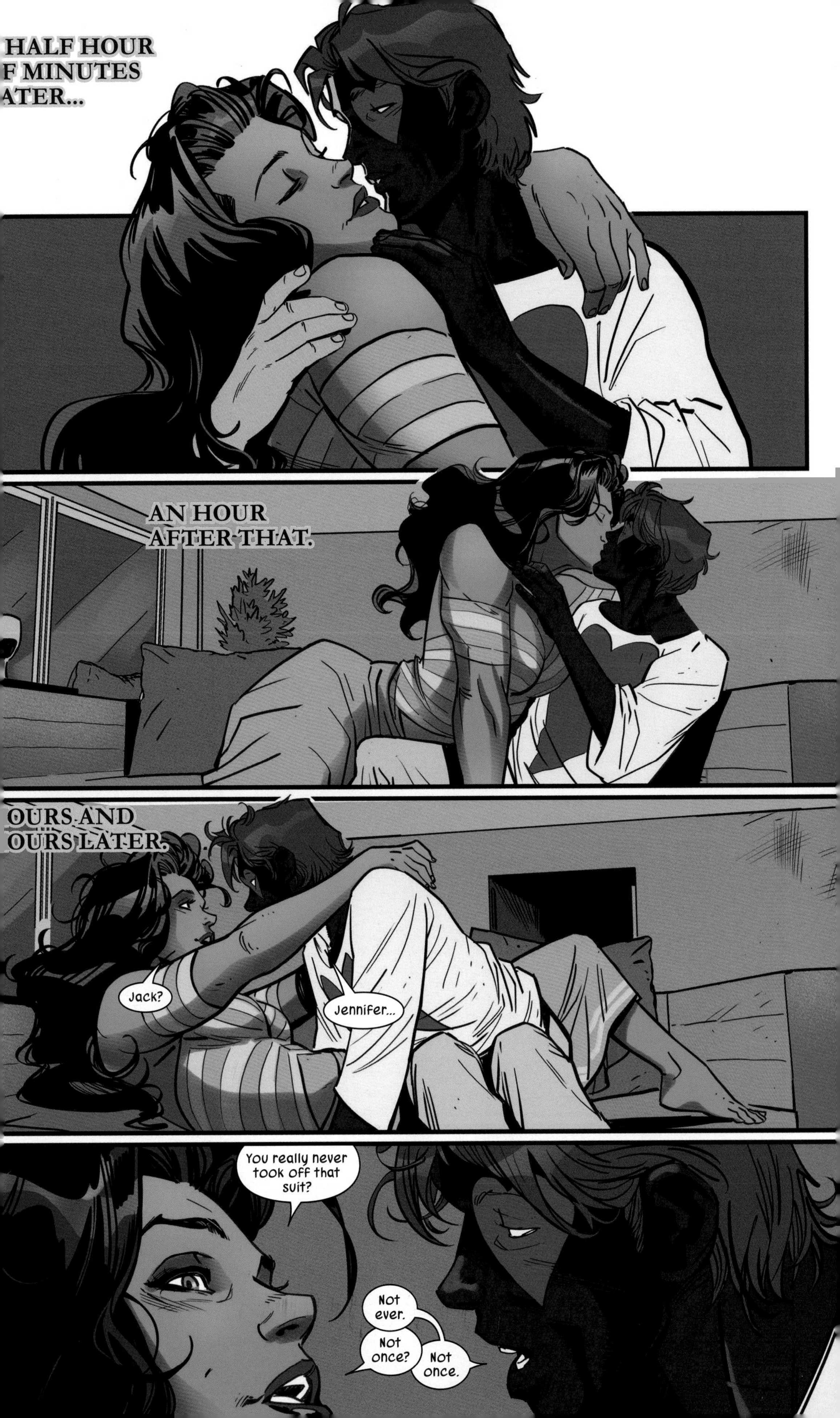
HALF HOUR
F MINUTES
ATER...
AN HOUR
AFTER THAT.
OURS AND
OURS LATER.
Jack?
Jennifer...
You really never took off that suit?
Not ever.
Not once?
Not once.

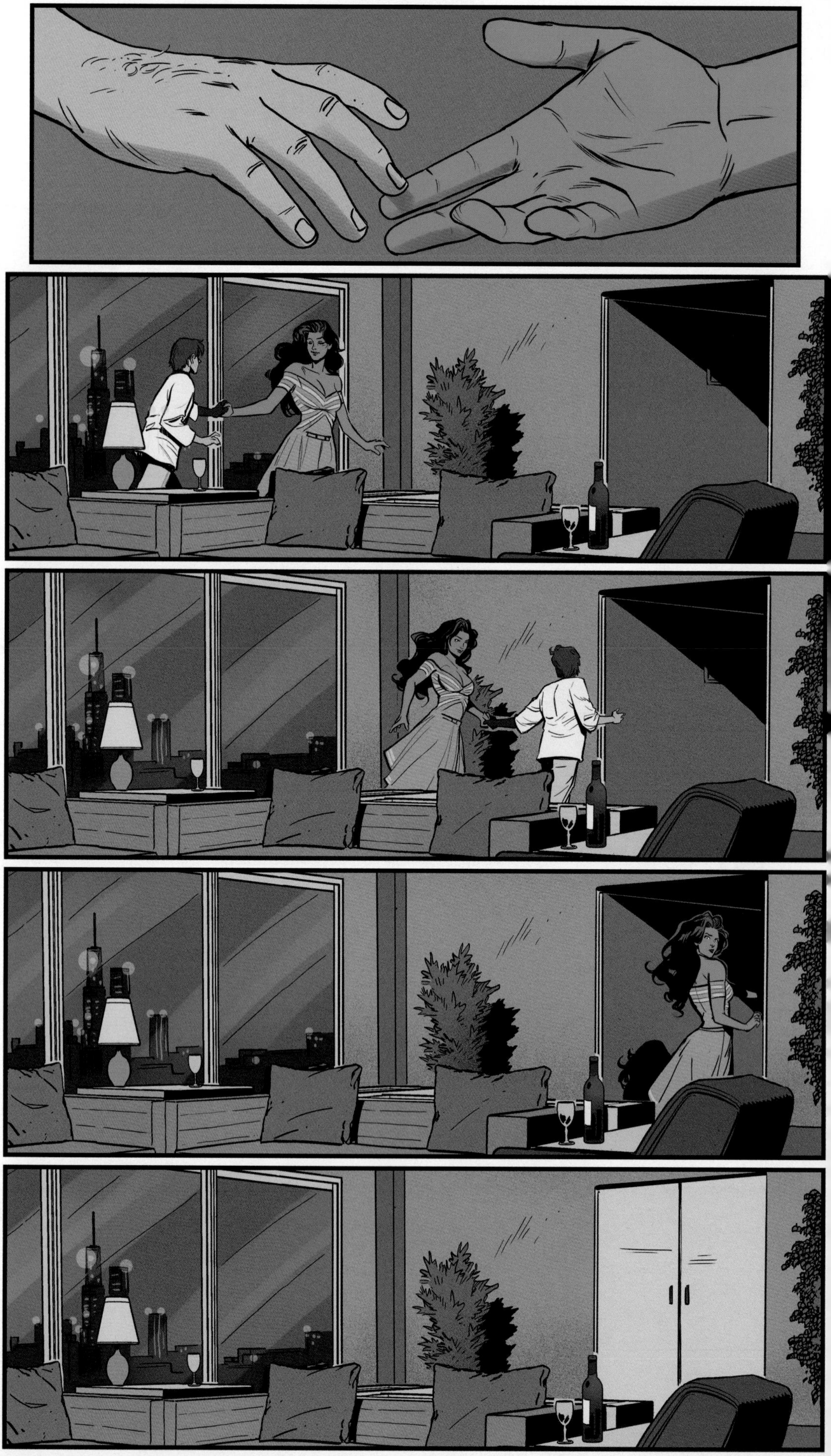

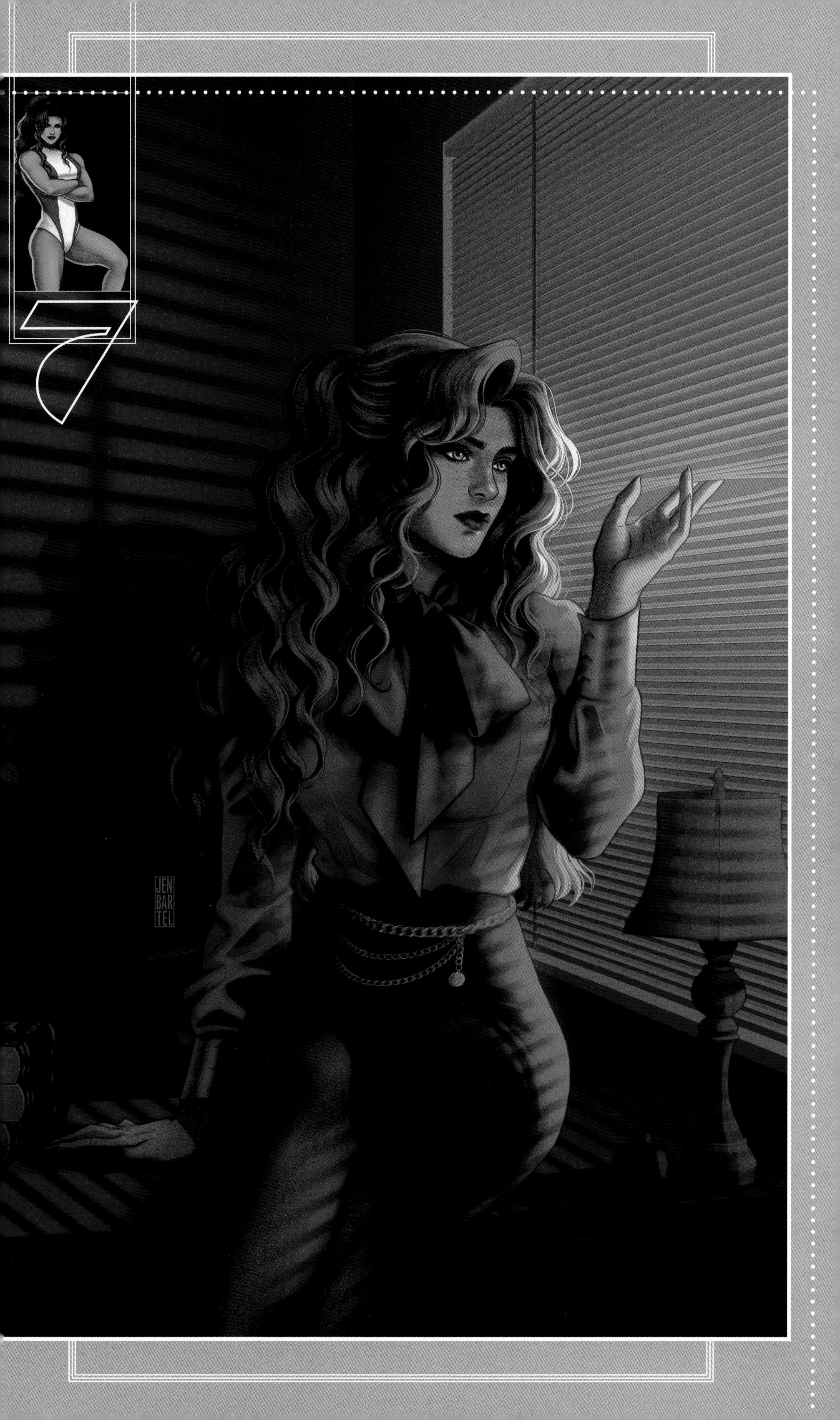
7
JEN BARTEL

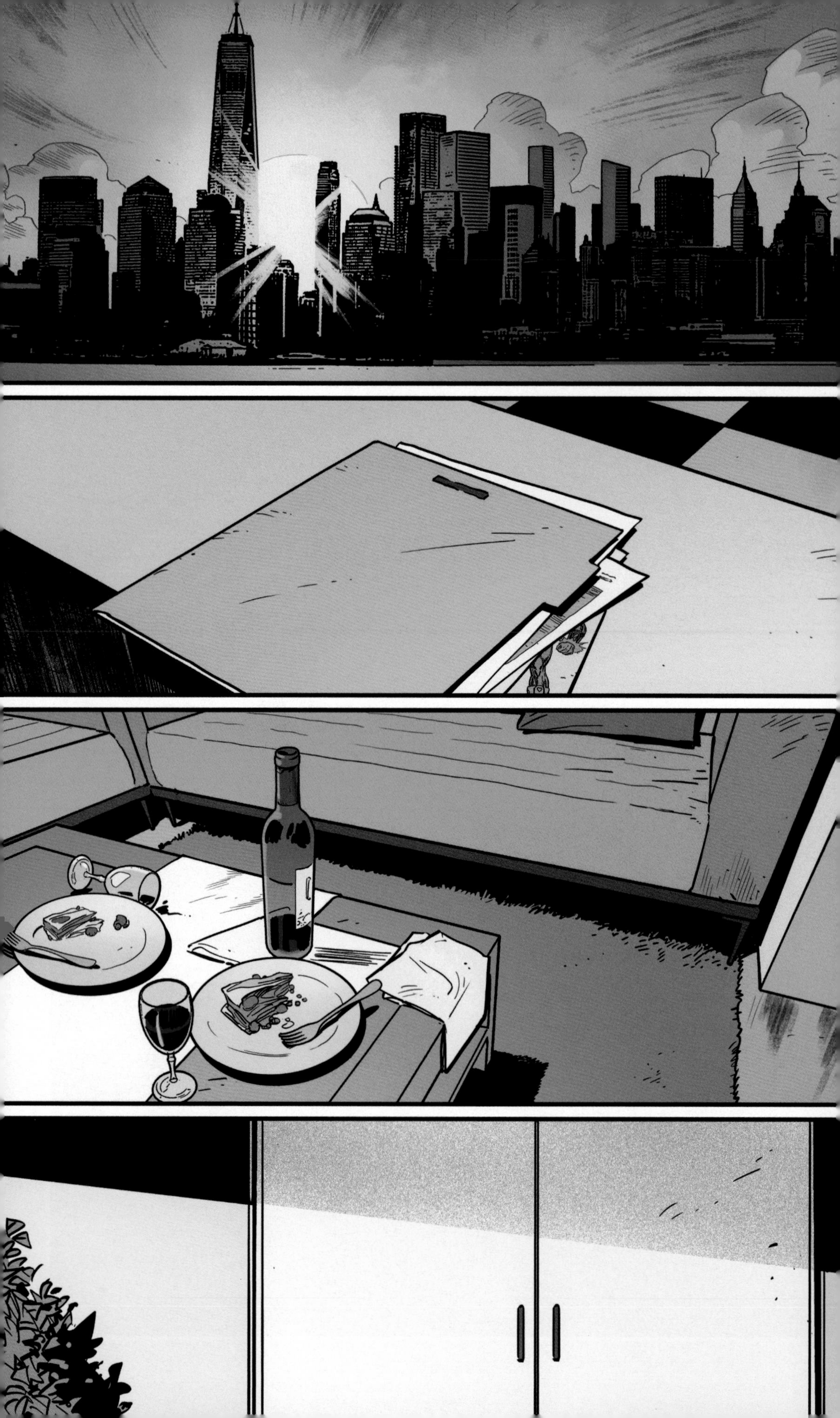

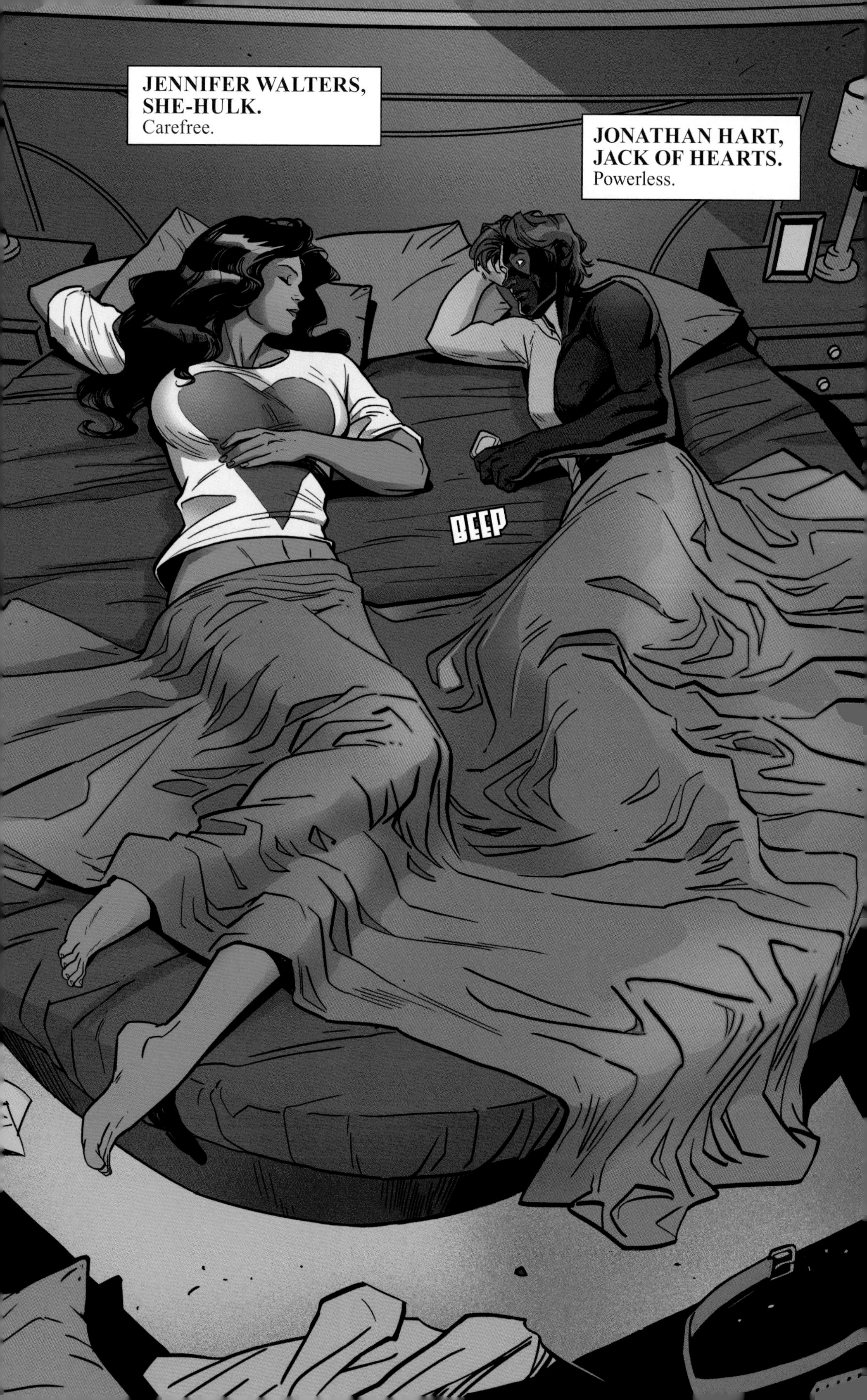
JENNIFER WALTERS,
SHE-HULK.
Carefree.
JONATHAN HART,
JACK OF HEARTS.
Powerless.
BEEP

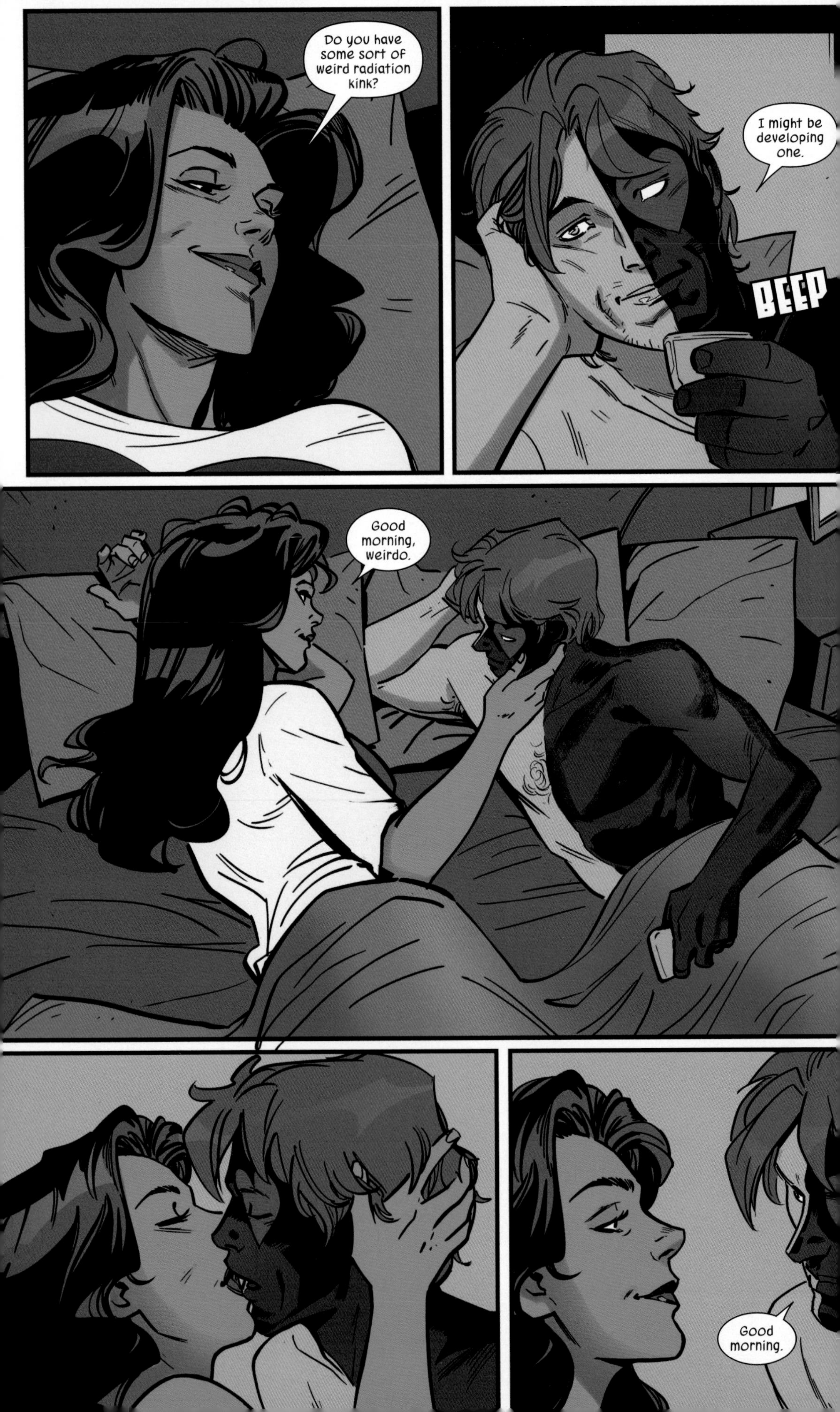

Do you have some sort of weird radiation kink?
I might be developing one.
BEEP
Good morning, weirdo.
Good morning.

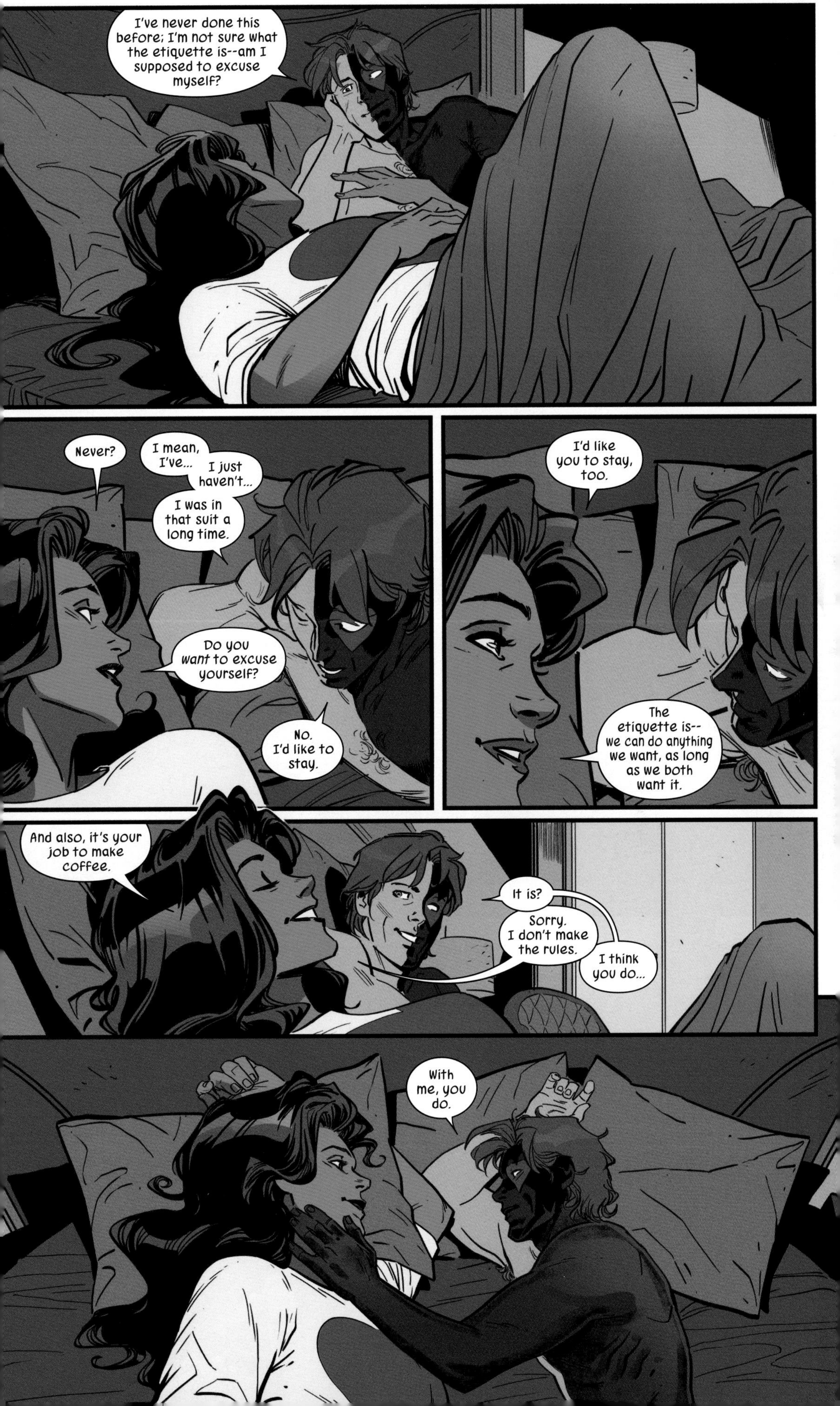

I've never done this before; I'm not sure what the etiquette is--am I supposed to excuse myself?
Never?
I mean, I've...
I just haven't...
I was in that suit a long time.
Do you want to excuse yourself?
No. I'd like to stay.
I'd like you to stay, too.
The etiquette is--we can do anything we want, as long as we both want it.
And also, it's your job to make coffee.
It is?
Sorry. I don't make the rules.
I think you do...
With me, you do.

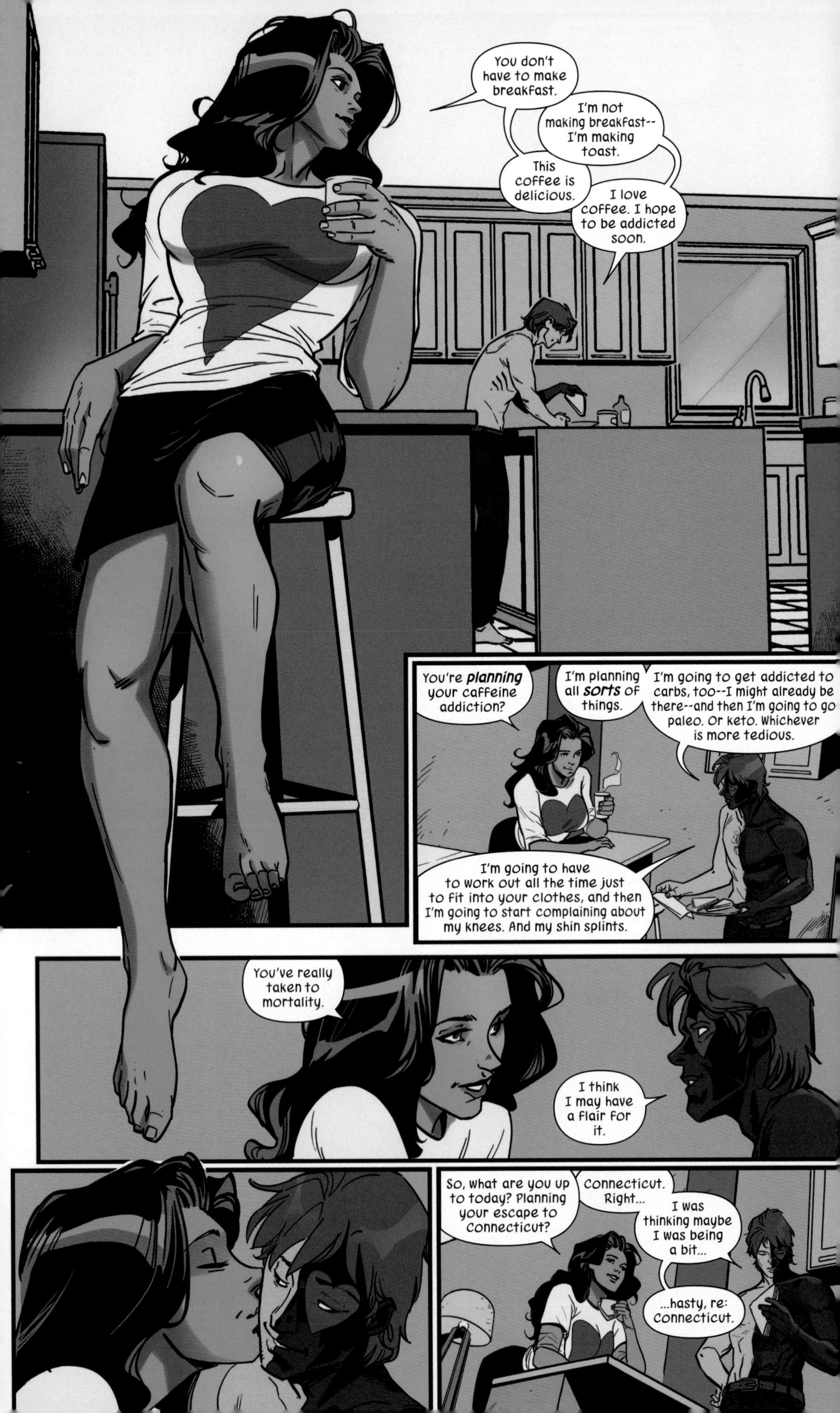

You don't have to make breakfast.
I'm not making breakfast-- I'm making toast.
This coffee is delicious.
I love coffee. I hope to be addicted soon.
You're ***planning*** your caffeine addiction?
I'm planning all ***sorts*** of things.
I'm going to get addicted to carbs, too--I might already be there--and then I'm going to go paleo. Or keto. Whichever is more tedious.
I'm going to have to work out all the time just to fit into your clothes, and then I'm going to start complaining about my knees. And my shin splints.
You've really taken to mortality.
I think I may have a flair for it.
So, what are you up to today? Planning your escape to Connecticut?
Connecticut. Right...
I was thinking maybe I was being a bit...
...hasty, re: Connecticut.

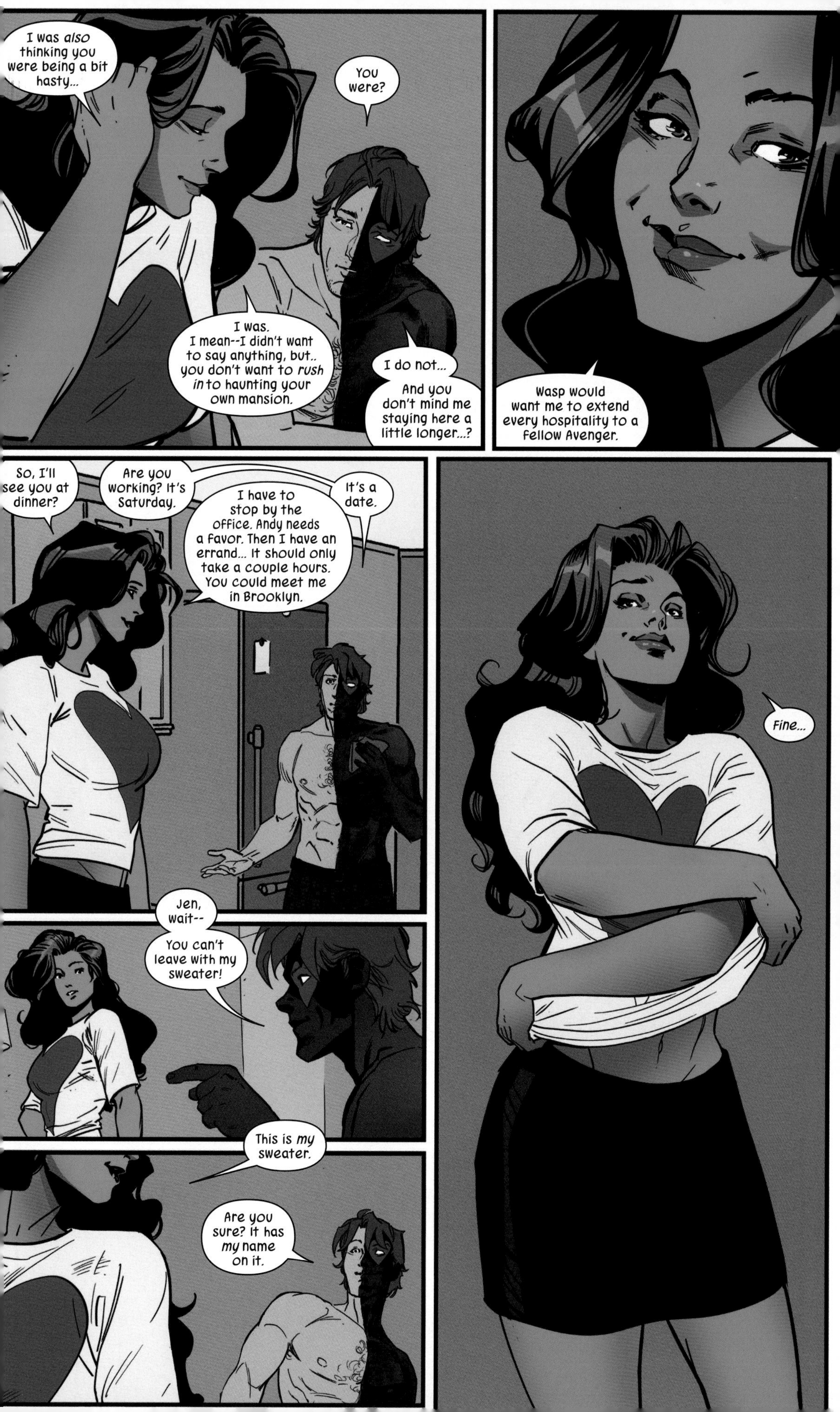
I was *also* thinking you were being a bit hasty...
You were?
I was. I mean--I didn't want to say anything, but.. you don't want to *rush in* to haunting your own mansion.
I do not...
And you don't mind me staying here a little longer...?
Wasp would want me to extend every hospitality to a fellow Avenger.
So, I'll see you at dinner?
Are you working? It's Saturday.
I have to stop by the office. Andy needs a favor. Then I have an errand... It should only take a couple hours. You could meet me in Brooklyn.
It's a date.
Jen, wait--
You can't leave with my sweater!
This is *my* sweater.
Are you sure? It has *my* name on it.
Fine...

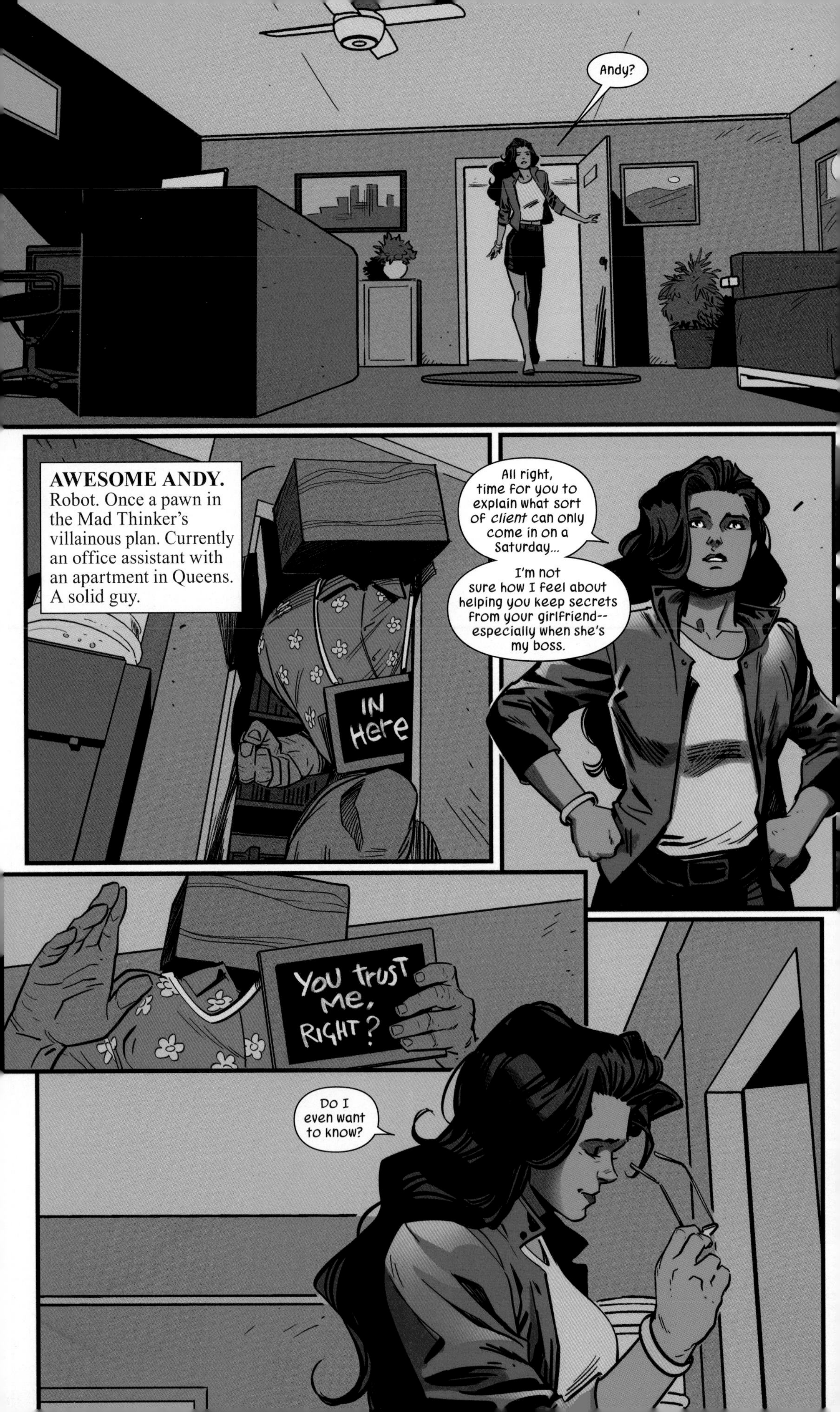
Andy?
AWESOME ANDY.
Robot. Once a pawn in the Mad Thinker's villainous plan. Currently an office assistant with an apartment in Queens. A solid guy.
IN Here
All right, time for you to explain what sort of *client* can only come in on a Saturday...
I'm not sure how I feel about helping you keep secrets from your girlfriend--especially when she's my boss.
YOU TRUST ME, RIGHT?
Do I even want to know?

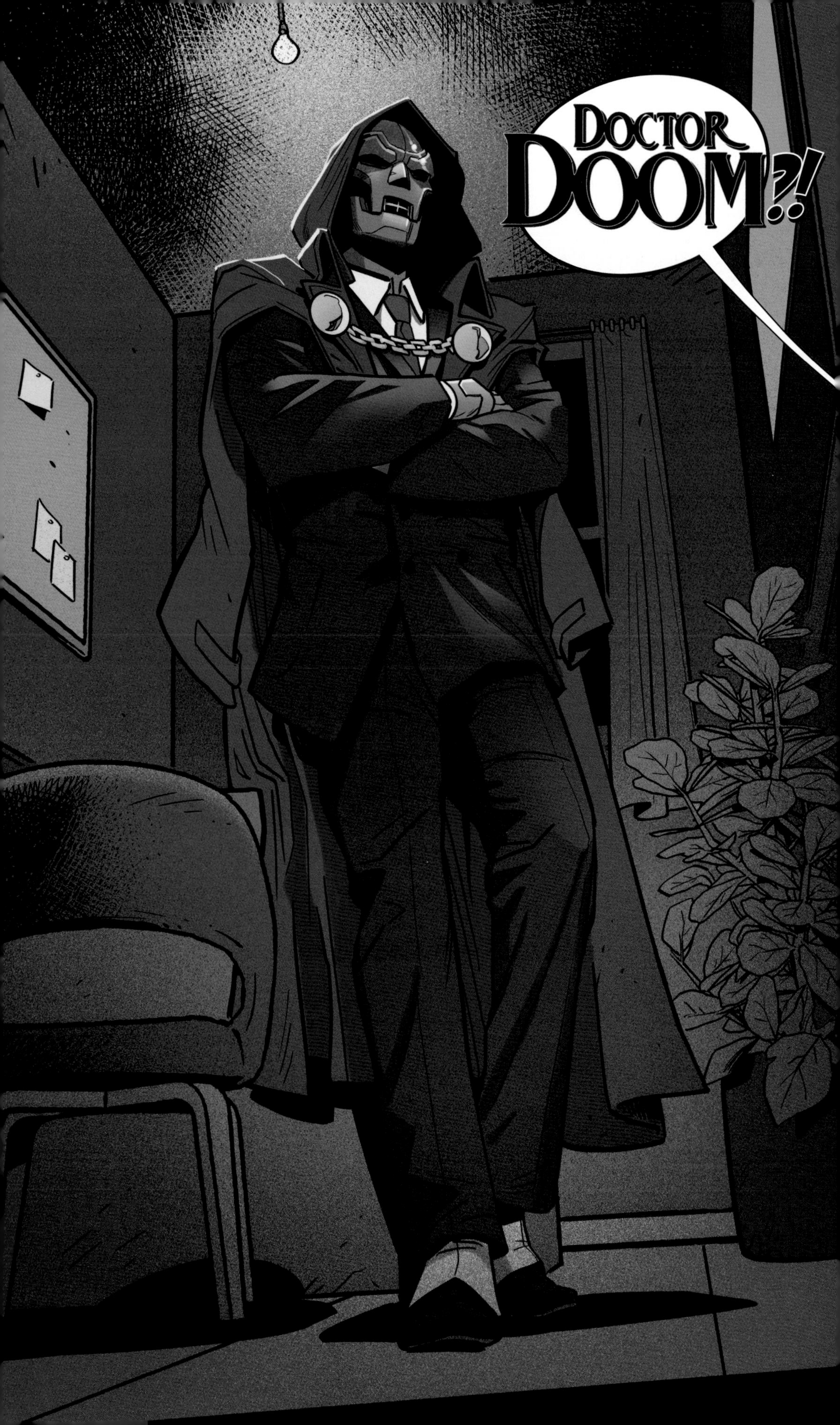
DOCTOR DOOM?!

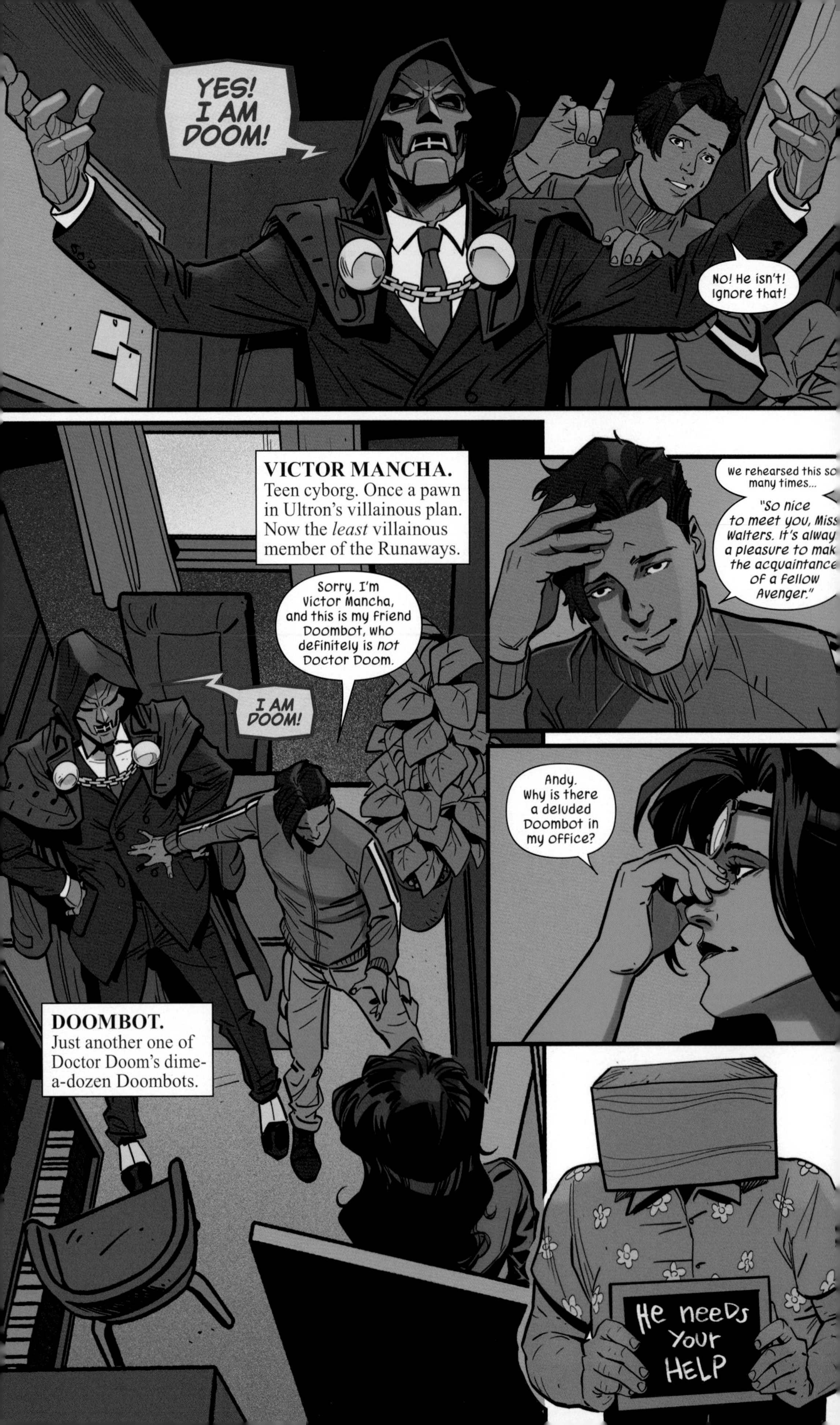

YES! I AM DOOM!
No! He isn't! Ignore that!
VICTOR MANCHA. Teen cyborg. Once a pawn in Ultron's villainous plan. Now the *least* villainous member of the Runaways.
Sorry. I'm Victor Mancha, and this is my friend Doombot, who definitely is *not* Doctor Doom.
I AM DOOM!
DOOMBOT. Just another one of Doctor Doom's dime-a-dozen Doombots.
We rehearsed this so many times...
"So nice to meet you, Miss Walters. It's alway a pleasure to mak the acquaintance of a fellow Avenger."
Andy. Why is there a deluded Doombot in my office?
He needs your HELP

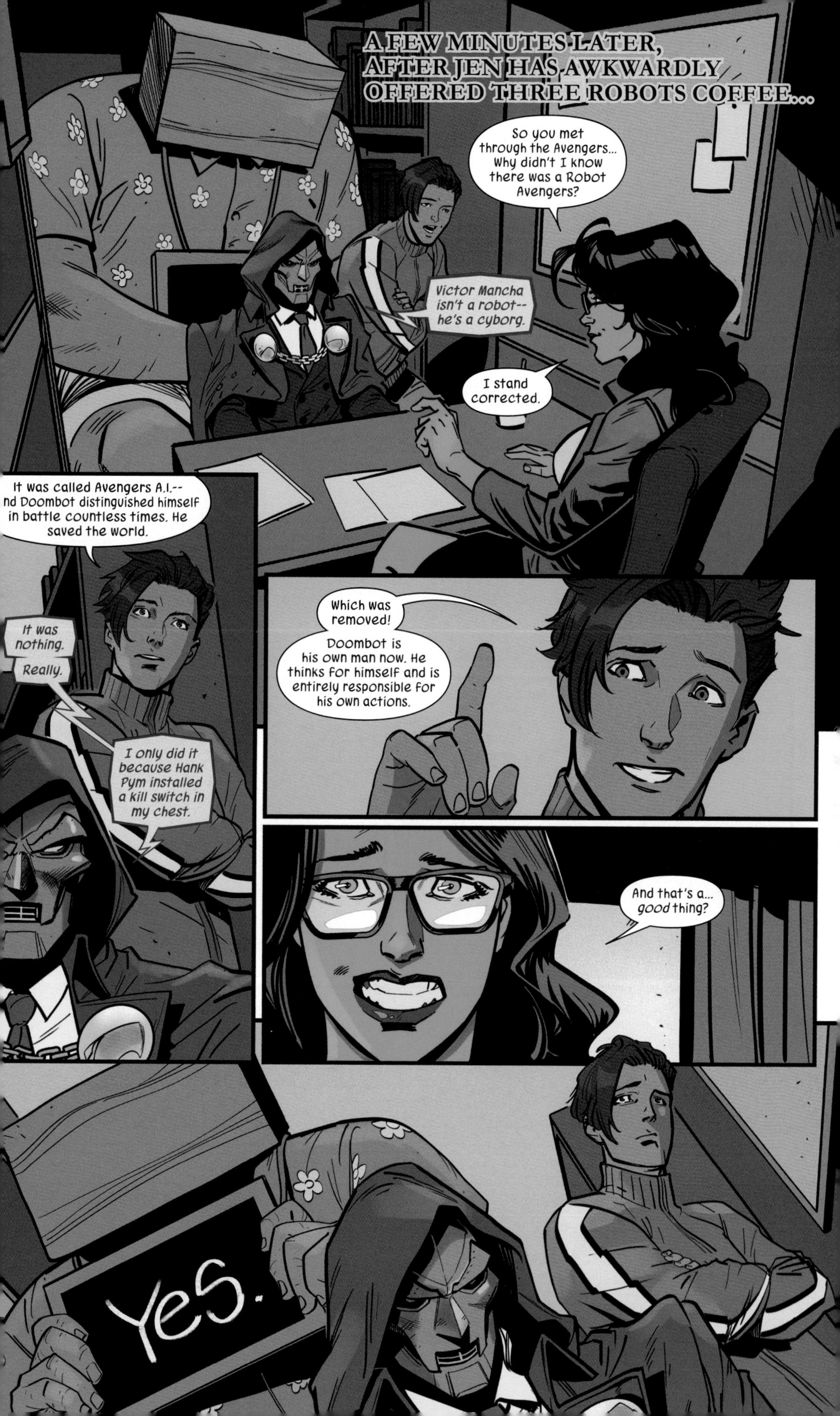
A FEW MINUTES LATER, AFTER JEN HAS AWKWARDLY OFFERED THREE ROBOTS COFFEE...
So you met through the Avengers... Why didn't I know there was a Robot Avengers?
Victor Mancha isn't a robot-- he's a cyborg.
I stand corrected.
It was called Avengers A.I.-- nd Doombot distinguished himself in battle countless times. He saved the world.
It was nothing.
Really.
I only did it because Hank Pym installed a kill switch in my chest.
Which was removed!
Doombot is his own man now. He thinks for himself and is entirely responsible for his own actions.
And that's a... good thing?
YES.

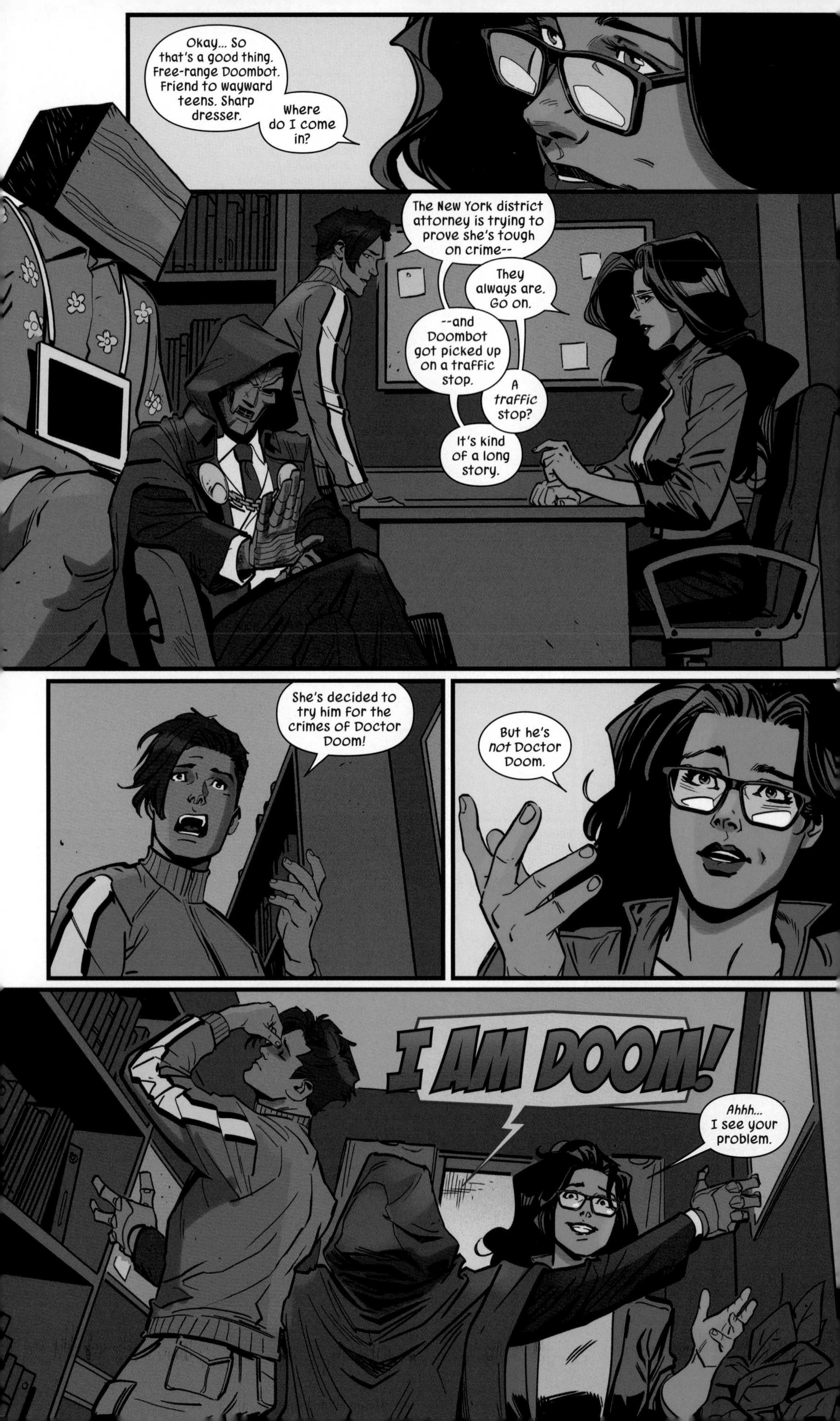

Okay... So that's a good thing. Free-range Doombot. Friend to wayward teens. Sharp dresser.
Where do I come in?
The New York district attorney is trying to prove she's tough on crime--
They always are. Go on.
--and Doombot got picked up on a traffic stop.
A *traffic* stop?
It's kind of a long story.
She's decided to try him for the crimes of Doctor Doom!
But he's *not* Doctor Doom.
I AM DOOM!
Ahhh... I see your problem.

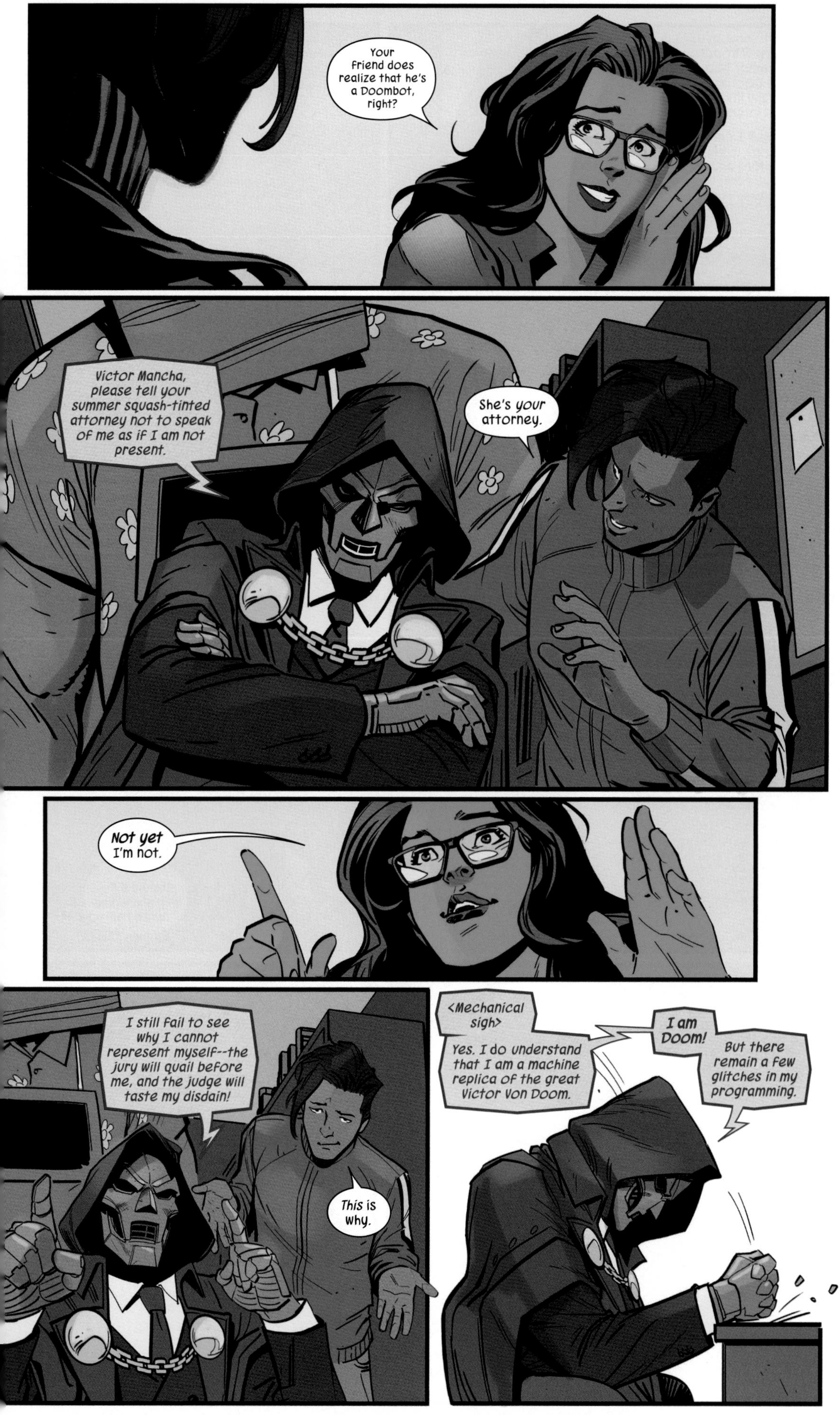
Your friend does realize that he's a Doombot, right?
Victor Mancha, please tell your summer squash-tinted attorney not to speak of me as if I am not present.
She's your attorney.
Not yet I'm not.
I still fail to see why I cannot represent myself--the jury will quail before me, and the judge will taste my disdain!
This is why.
<Mechanical sigh>
Yes. I do understand that I am a machine replica of the great Victor Von Doom.
I am Doom!
But there remain a few glitches in my programming.

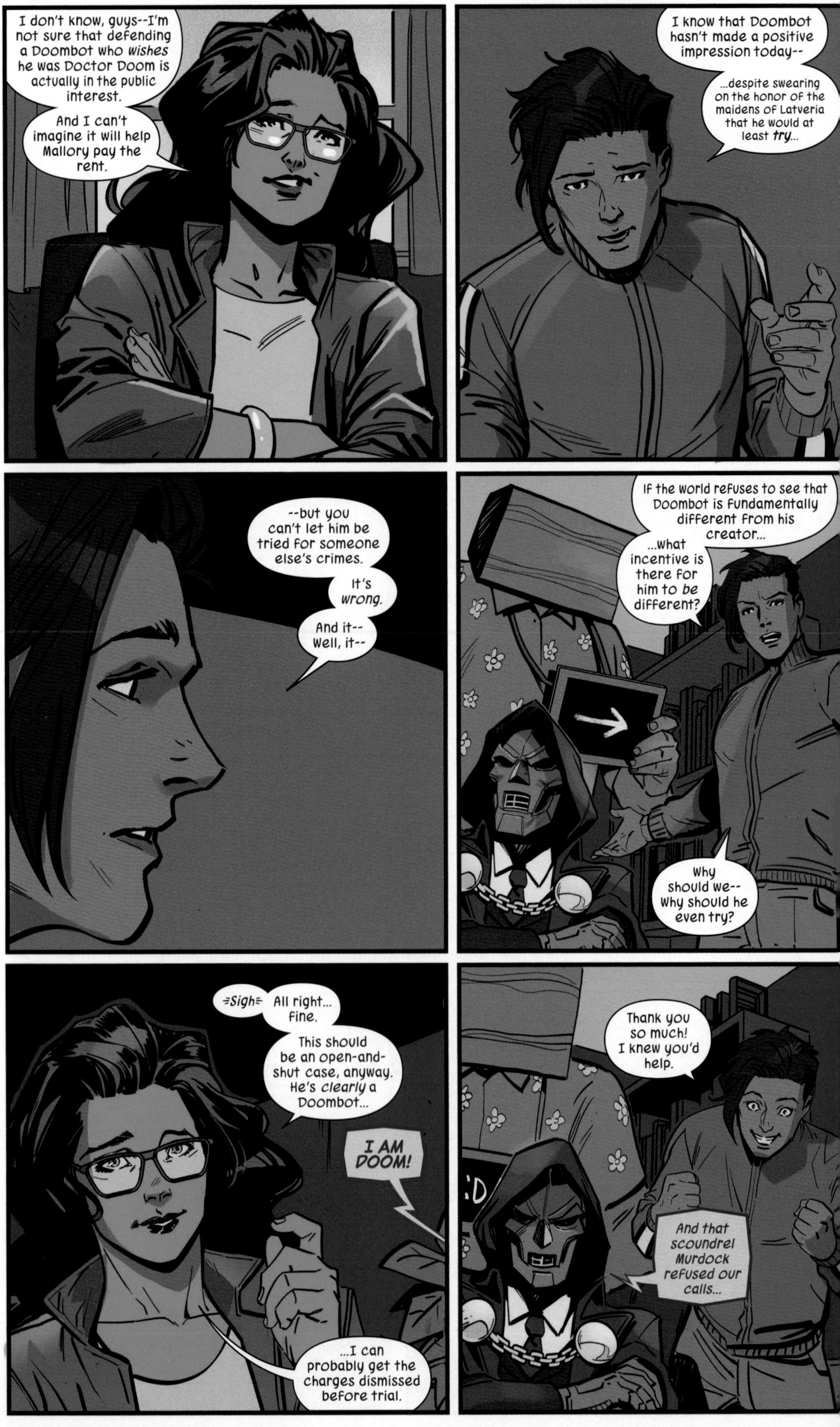
I don't know, guys--I'm not sure that defending a Doombot who *wishes* he was Doctor Doom is actually in the public interest.
And I can't imagine it will help Mallory pay the rent.
I know that Doombot hasn't made a positive impression today--
...despite swearing on the honor of the maidens of Latveria that he would at least *try*...
--but you can't let him be tried for someone else's crimes.
It's *wrong.*
And it-- Well, it--
If the world refuses to see that Doombot is fundamentally different from his creator...
...what incentive is there for him to *be* different?
Why should we-- Why should he even try?
=Sigh= All right... Fine.
This should be an open-and-shut case, anyway. He's *clearly* a Doombot...
I AM DOOM!
...I can probably get the charges dismissed before trial.
Thank you so much! I knew you'd help.
And that scoundrel Murdock refused our calls...

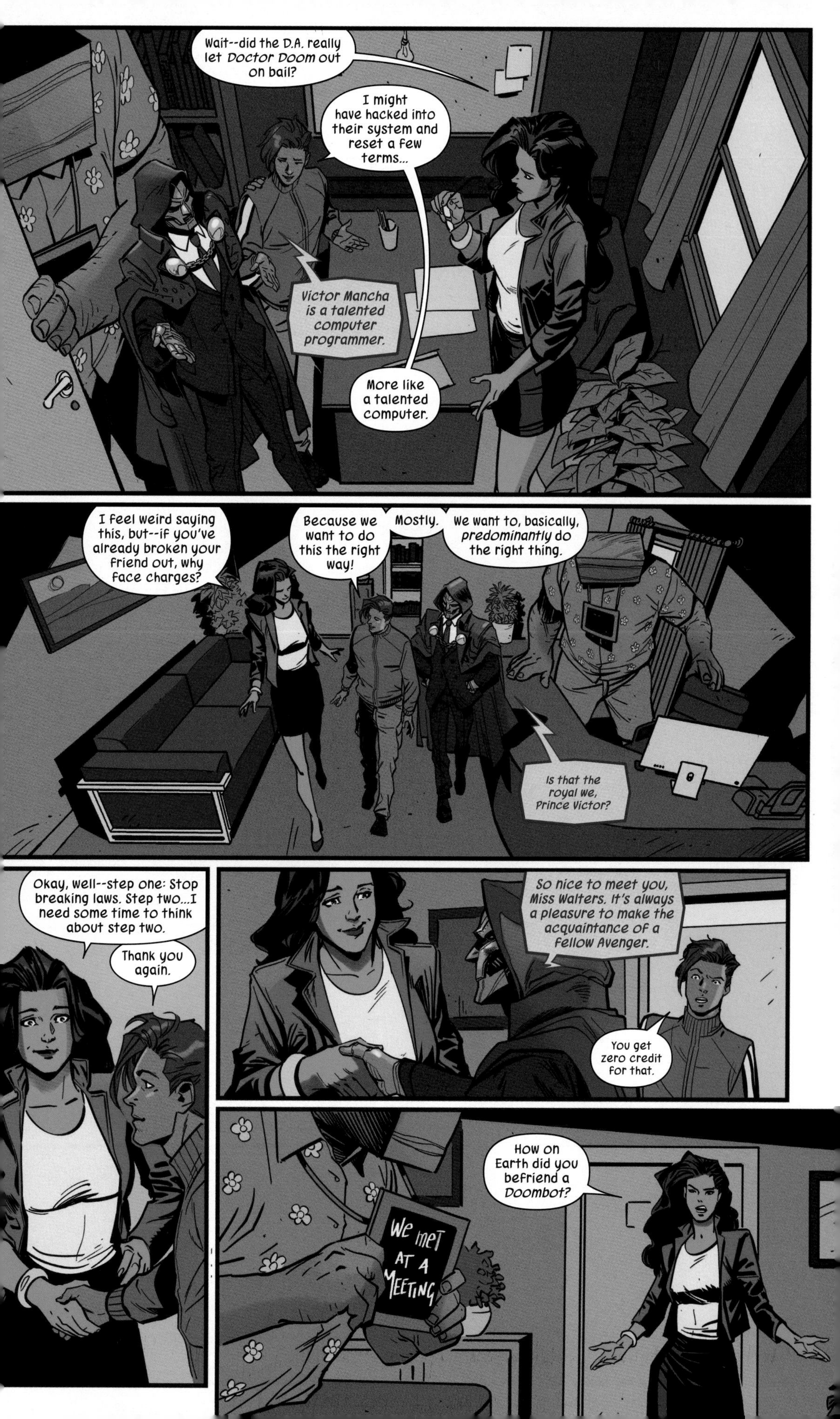
Wait--did the D.A. really let *Doctor Doom* out on bail?
I might have hacked into their system and reset a few terms...
Victor Mancha is a talented computer programmer.
More like a talented computer.
I feel weird saying this, but--if you've already broken your friend out, why face charges?
Because we want to do this the right way!
Mostly.
We want to, basically, *predominantly* do the right thing.
Is that the royal we, Prince Victor?
Okay, well--step one: Stop breaking laws. Step two...I need some time to think about step two.
Thank you again.
So nice to meet you, Miss Walters. It's always a pleasure to make the acquaintance of a fellow Avenger.
You get zero credit for that.
How on Earth did you befriend a *Doombot*?
WE MET AT A MEETING

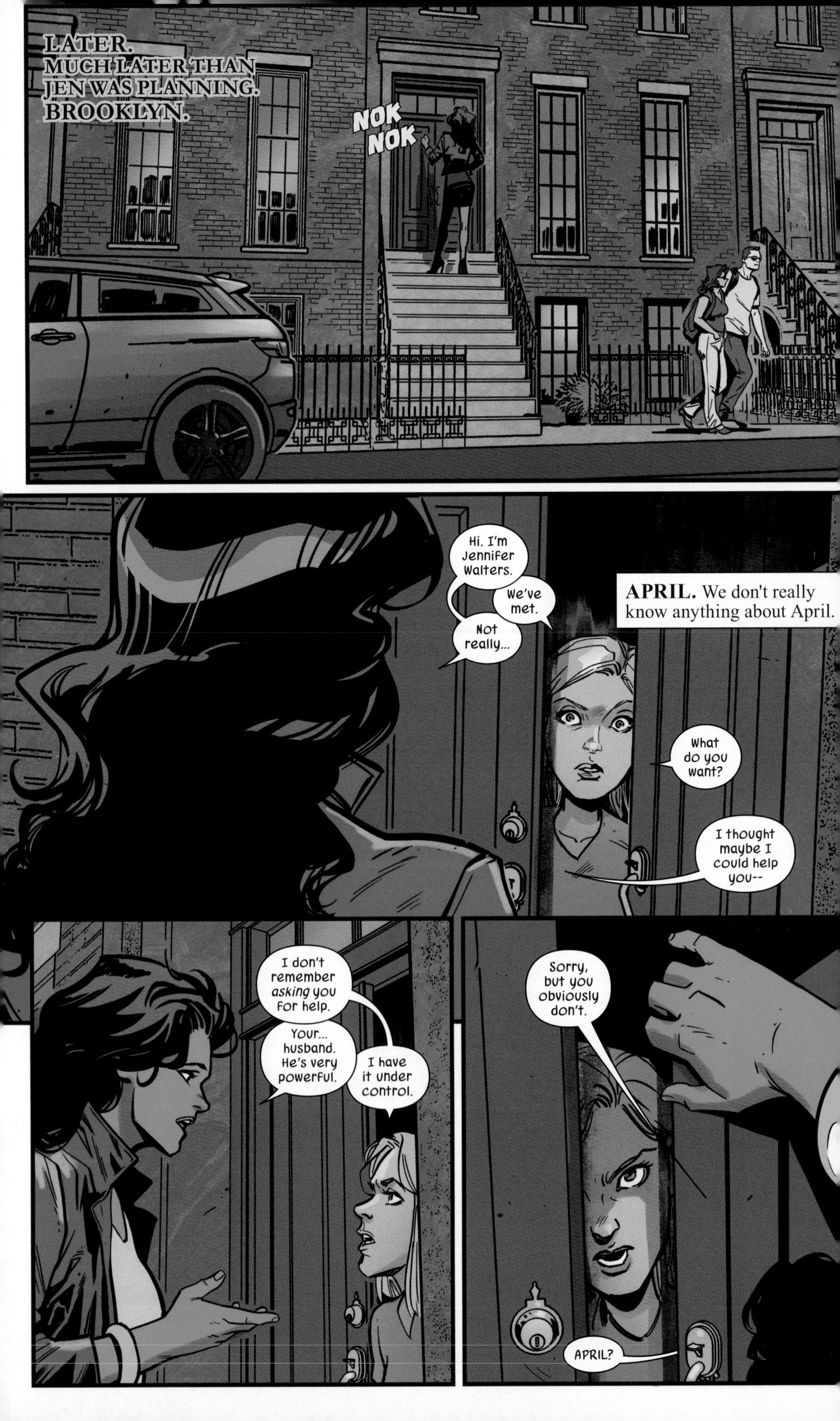
LATER.
MUCH LATER THAN JEN WAS PLANNING.
BROOKLYN.
NOK NOK
Hi. I'm Jennifer Walters.
We've met.
Not really...
APRIL. We don't really know anything about April.
What do you want?
I thought maybe I could help you--
I don't remember *asking* you for help.
Your... husband. He's very powerful.
I have it under control.
Sorry, but you obviously don't.
APRIL?

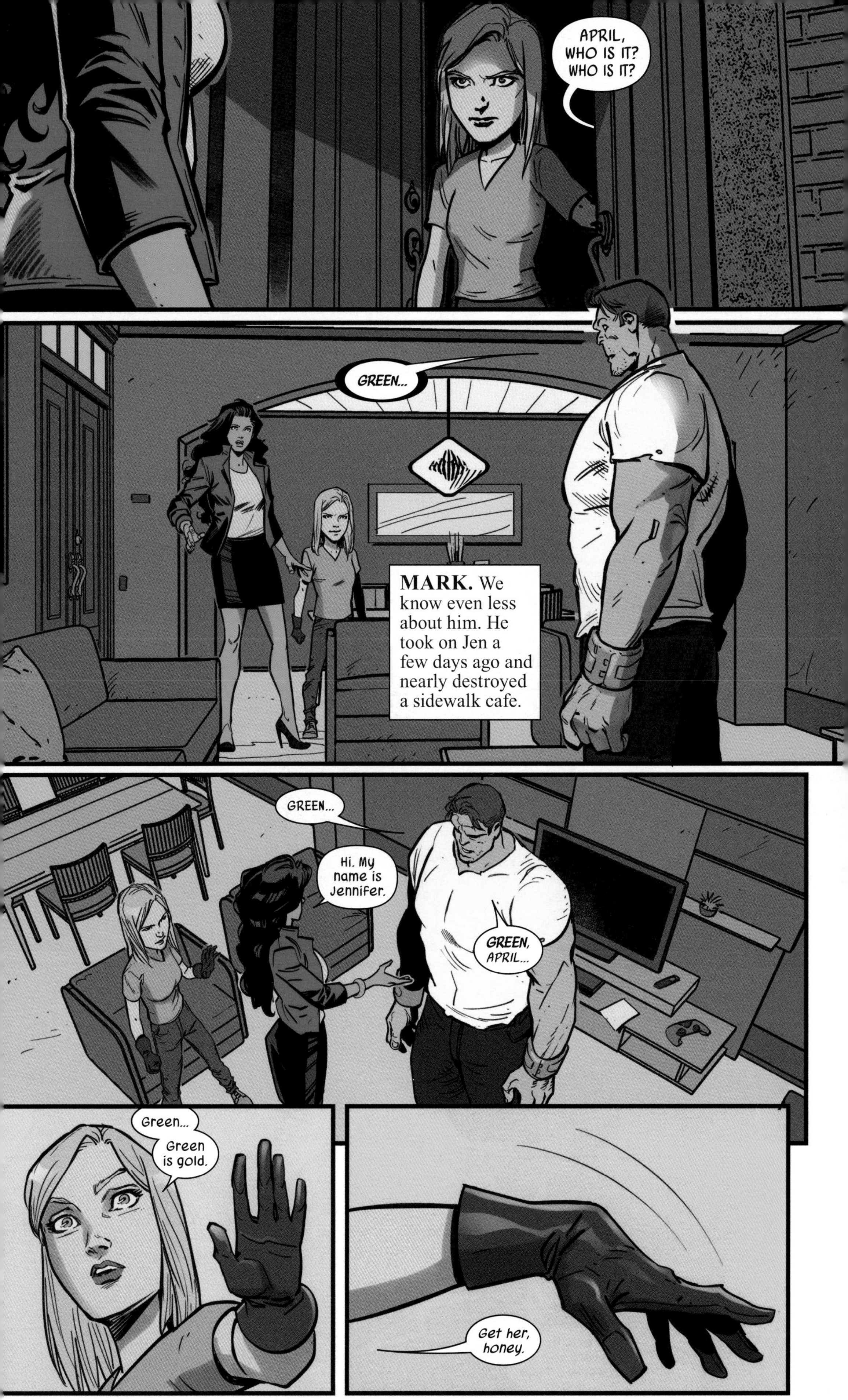

APRIL, WHO IS IT? WHO IS IT?
GREEN...
MARK. We know even less about him. He took on Jen a few days ago and nearly destroyed a sidewalk cafe.
GREEN...
Hi. My name is Jennifer.
GREEN, APRIL...
Green...
Green is gold.
Get her, honey.

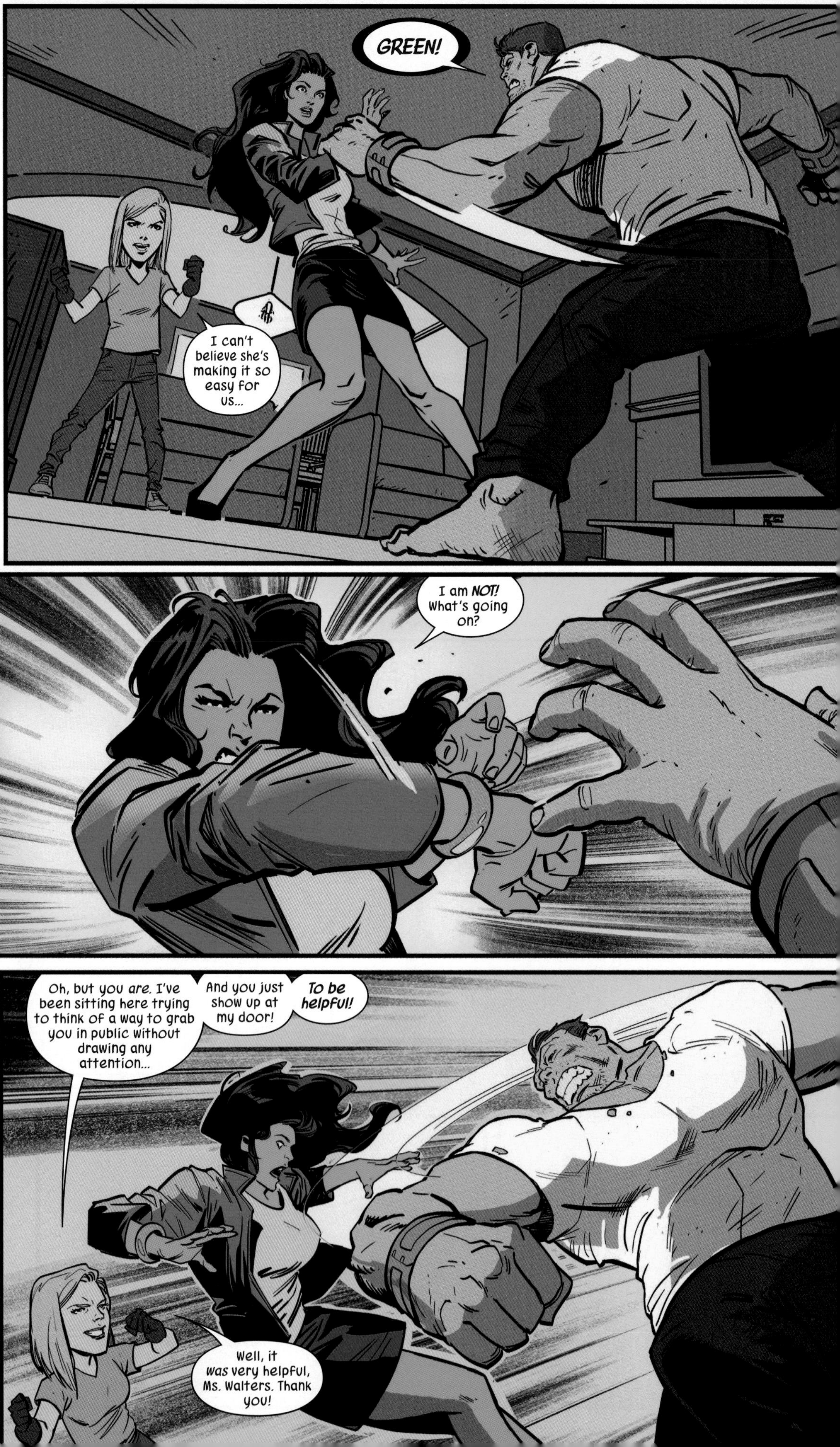
GREEN!
I can't believe she's making it so easy for us...
I am NOT! What's going on?
Oh, but you are. I've been sitting here trying to think of a way to grab you in public without drawing any attention...
And you just show up at my door!
To be helpful!
Well, it was very helpful, Ms. Walters. Thank you!

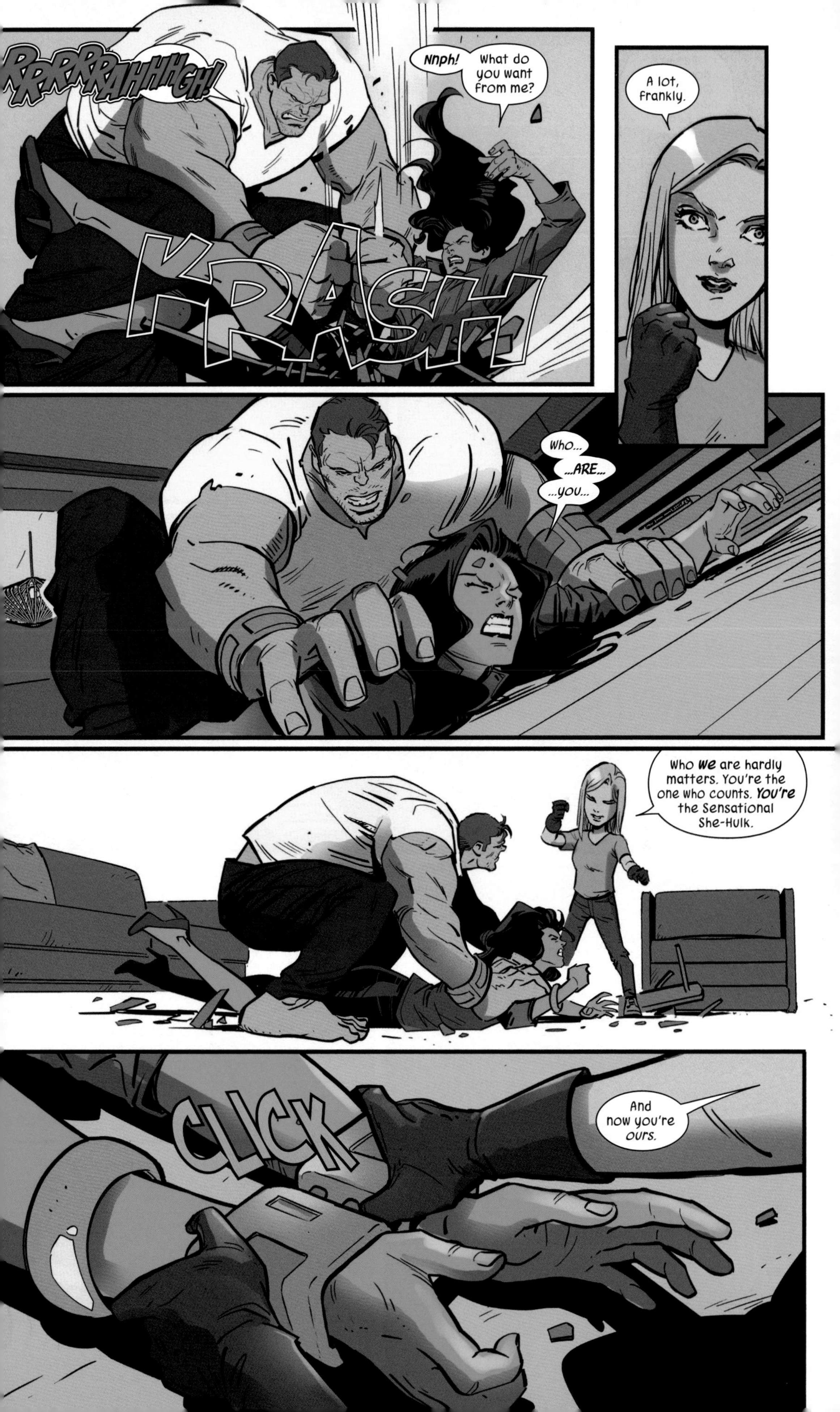
RRRRRAHHHGH!
Nnph! What do you want from me?
KRASH
A lot, frankly.
Who... ...ARE... ...you...
Who WE are hardly matters. You're the one who counts. YOU'RE the Sensational She-Hulk.
CLICK
And now you're ours.

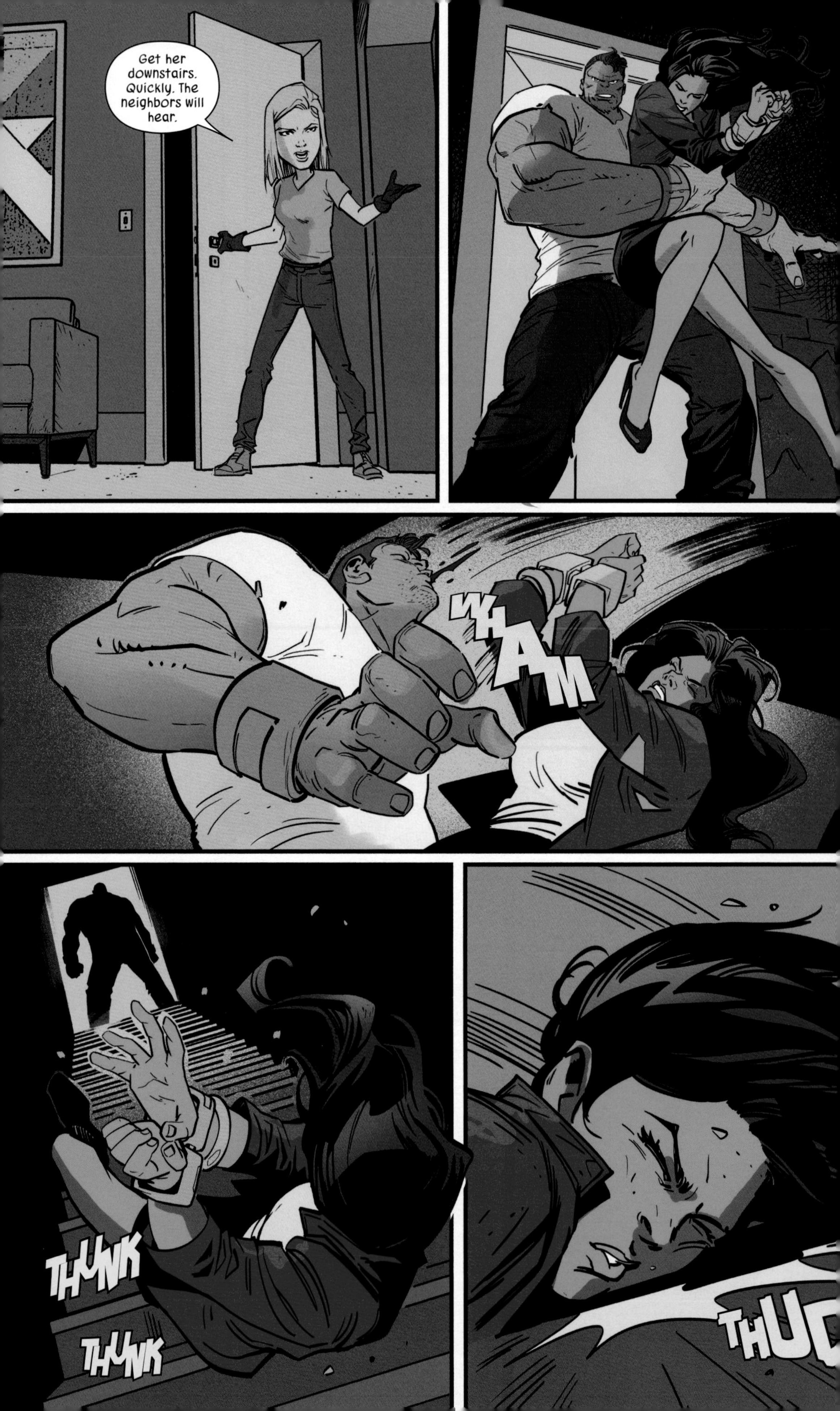
Get her downstairs. Quickly. The neighbors will hear.
WHAM
THUNK
THUNK
THUD

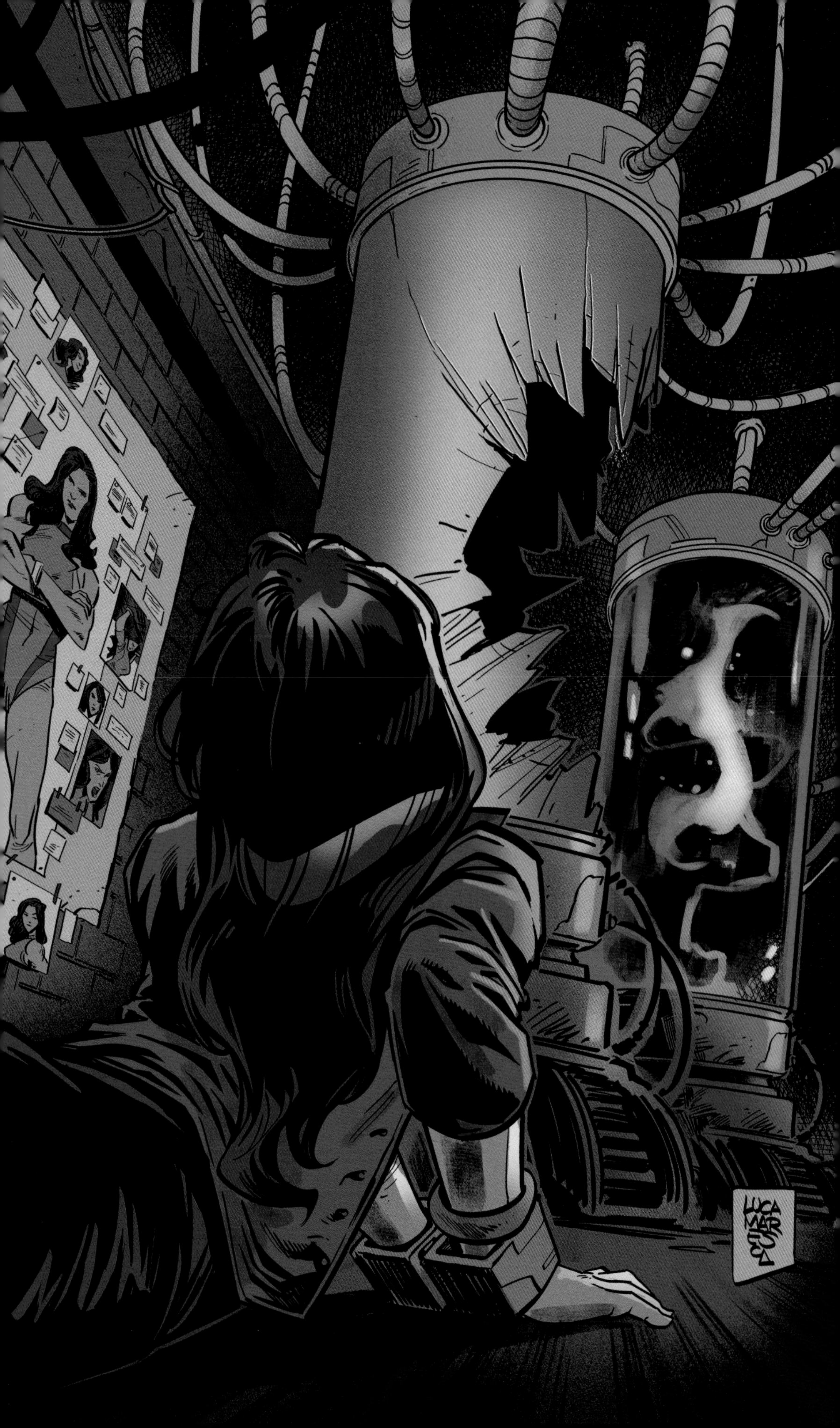

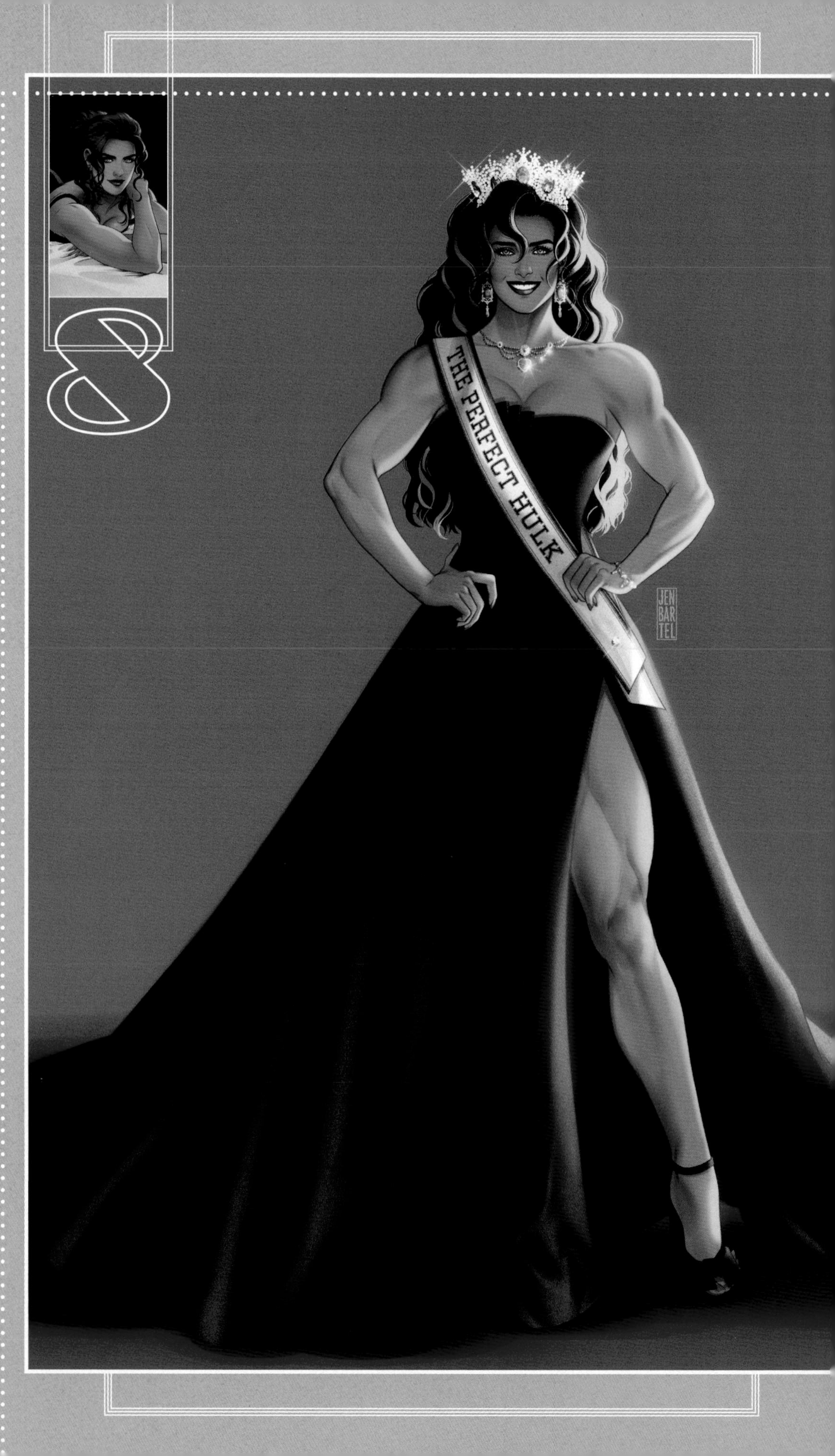
8
THE PERFECT HULK
JEN BARTEL

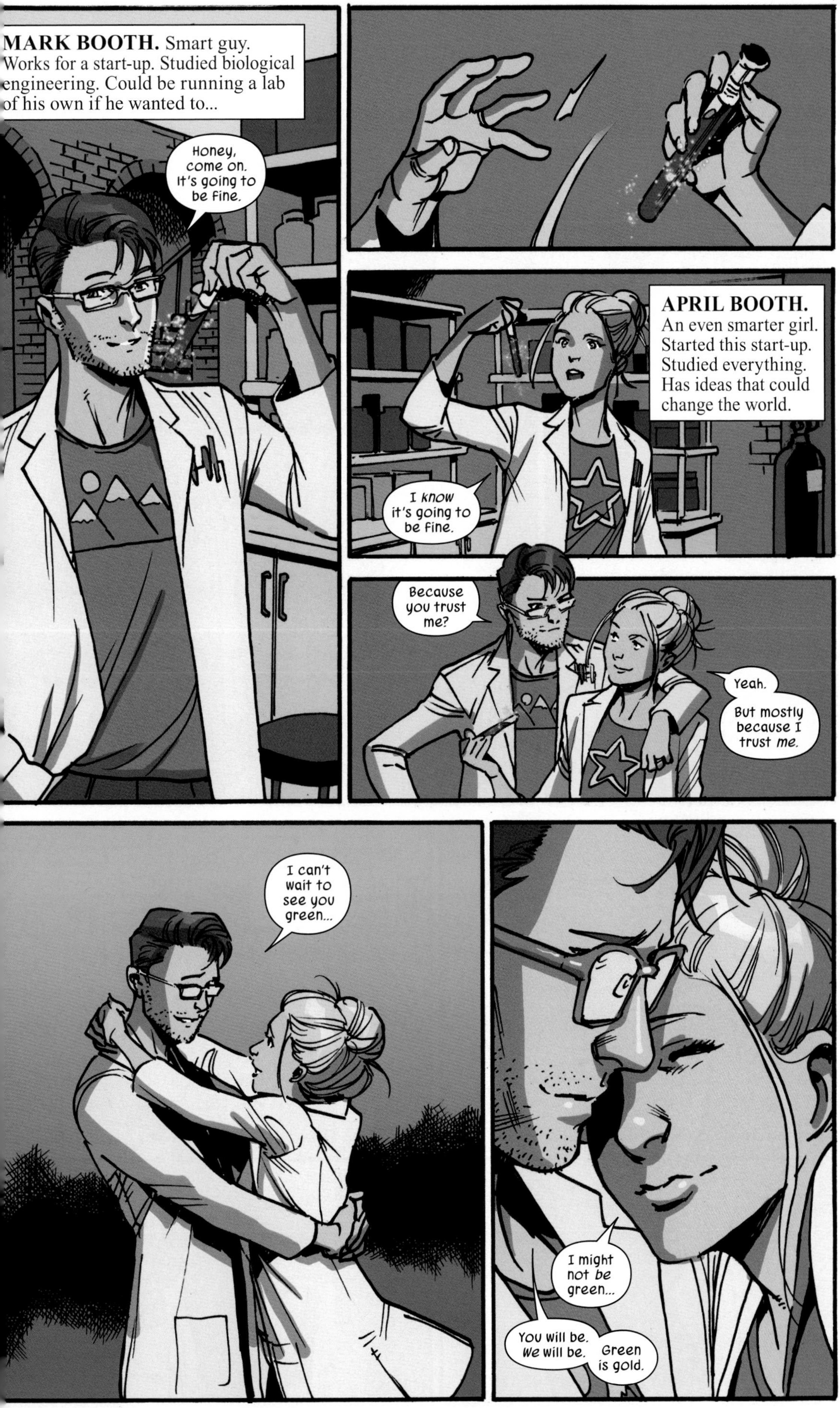

MARK BOOTH. Smart guy. Works for a start-up. Studied biological engineering. Could be running a lab of his own if he wanted to...
Honey, come on. It's going to be fine.
APRIL BOOTH. An even smarter girl. Started this start-up. Studied everything. Has ideas that could change the world.
I know it's going to be fine.
Because you trust me?
Yeah.
But mostly because I trust me.
I can't wait to see you green...
I might not be green...
You will be. We will be.
Green is gold.

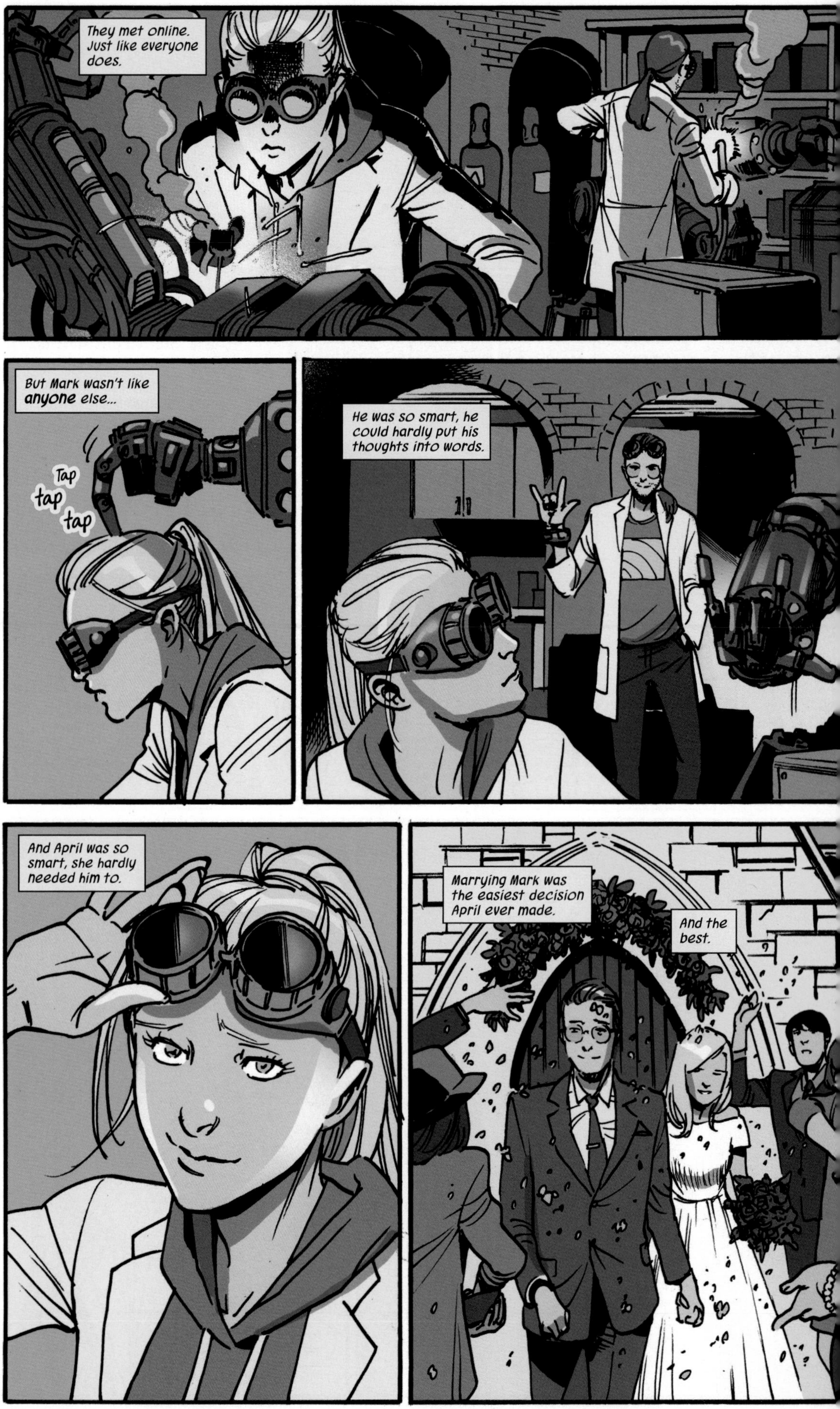
They met online. Just like everyone does.
But Mark wasn't like anyone else...
Tap tap tap
He was so smart, he could hardly put his thoughts into words.
And April was so smart, she hardly needed him to.
Marrying Mark was the easiest decision April ever made.
And the best.

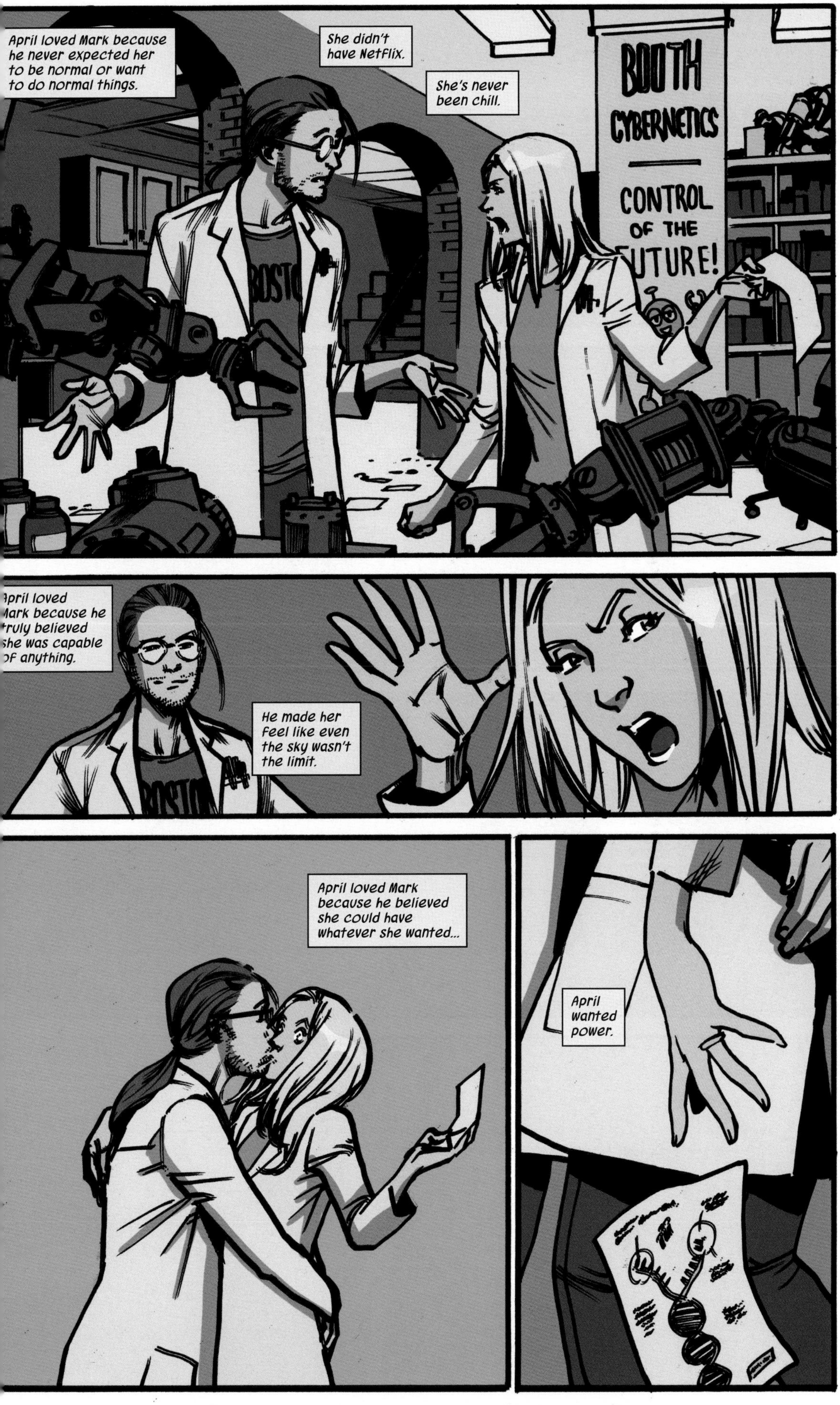
April loved Mark because he never expected her to be normal or want to do normal things.
She didn't have Netflix.
She's never been chill.
BOOTH CYBERNETICS
CONTROL OF THE FUTURE!
April loved Mark because he truly believed she was capable of anything.
He made her feel like even the sky wasn't the limit.
April loved Mark because he believed she could have whatever she wanted...
April wanted power.

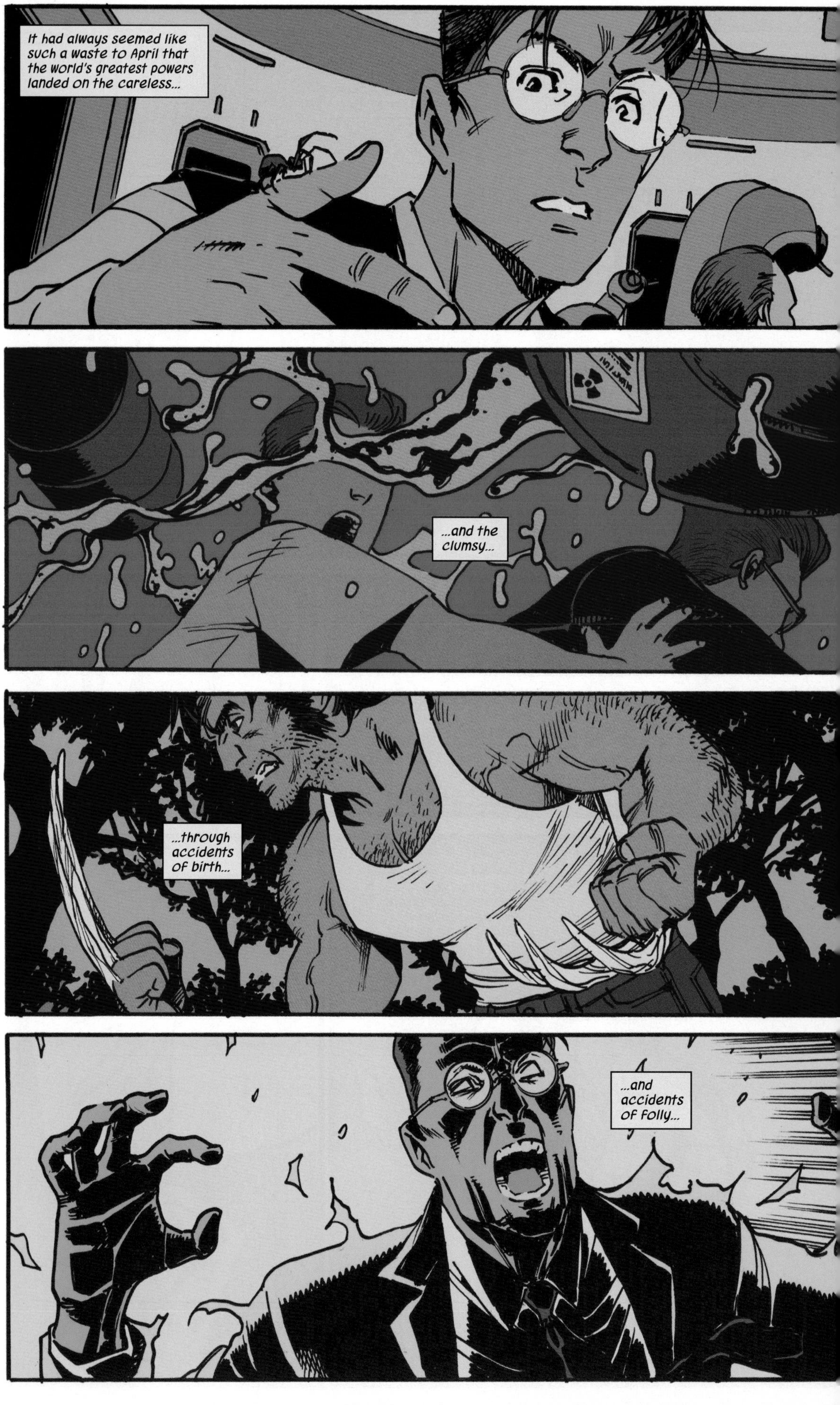
It had always seemed like such a waste to April that the world's greatest powers landed on the careless...
...and the clumsy...
...through accidents of birth...
...and accidents of folly...

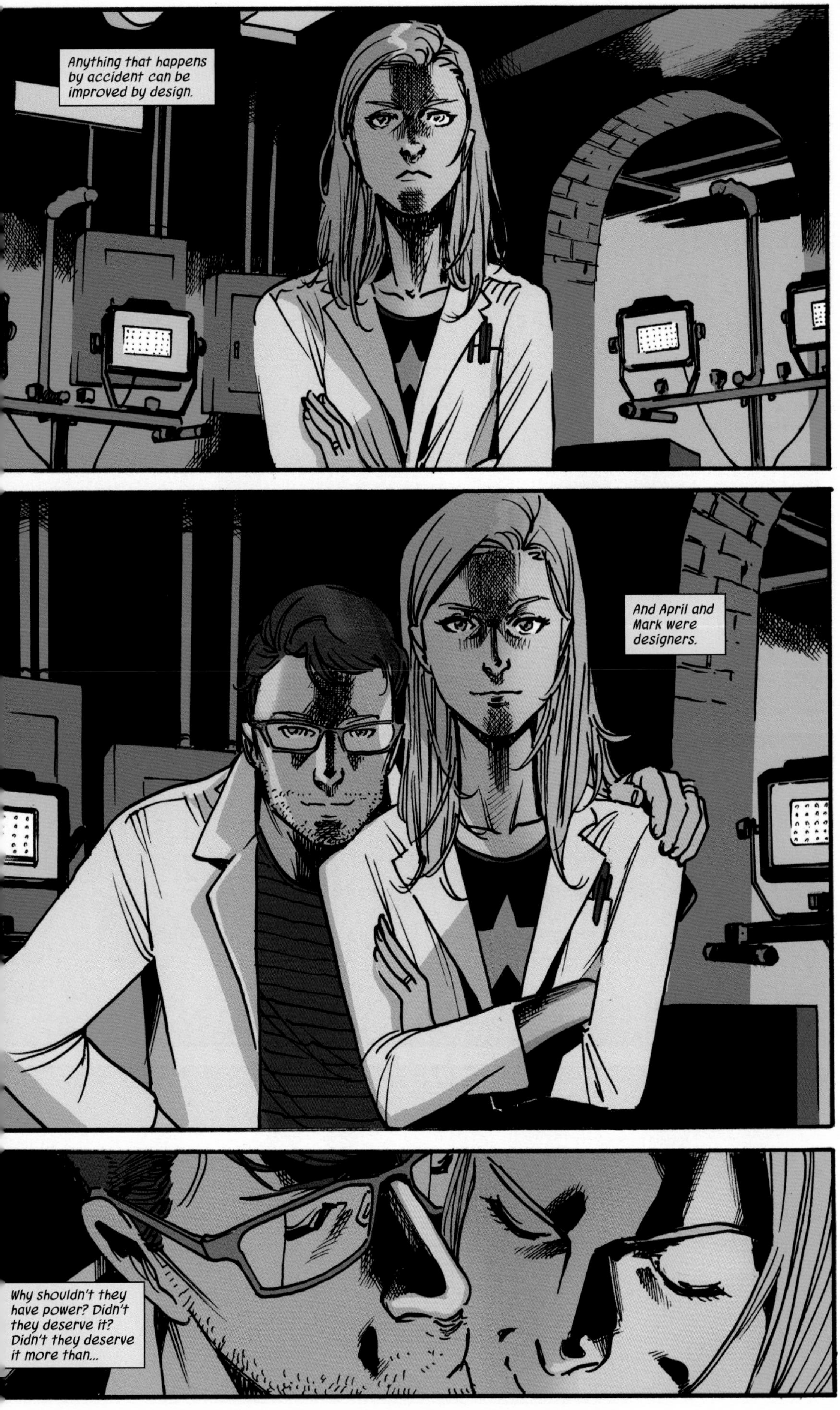
Anything that happens by accident can be improved by design.
And April and Mark were designers.
Why shouldn't they have power? Didn't they deserve it? Didn't they deserve it more than...

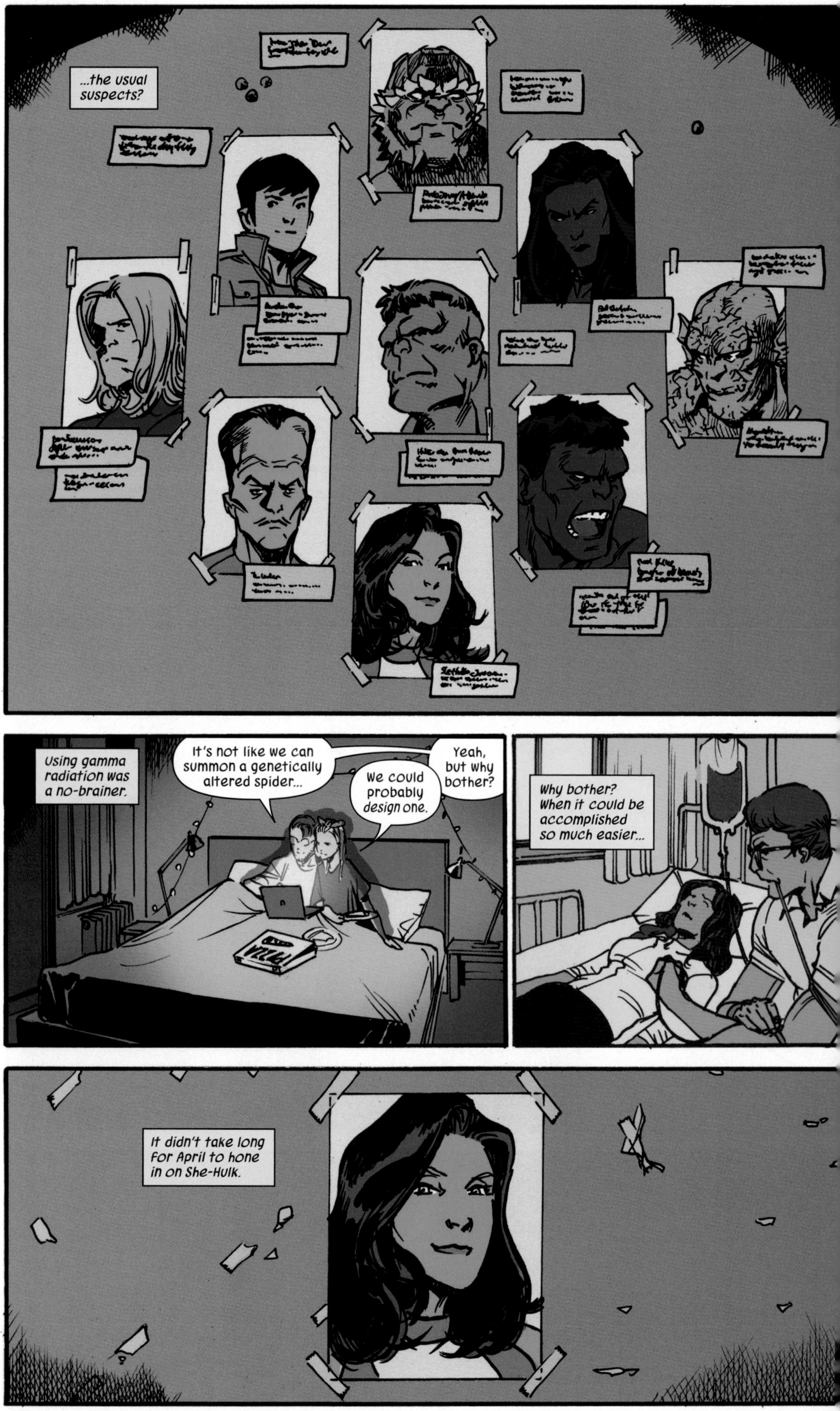
...the usual suspects?
Using gamma radiation was a no-brainer.
It's not like we can summon a genetically altered spider...
We could probably design one.
Yeah, but why bother?
Why bother? When it could be accomplished so much easier...
It didn't take long for April to hone in on She-Hulk.

She's obviously the best Hulk.

She-Hulk has everything... Power and control. Strength and intelligence.

Invulnerability.

You sure you won't mind being green?

Why--will *you* mind me being green?

Nope. I'm here for all of it. Sickness, health, gammafication.

I hope I'm super jacked. Like, so jacked I can't shop at normal stores.

We could end up like the Hulk... It is *his* blood. Ultimately.

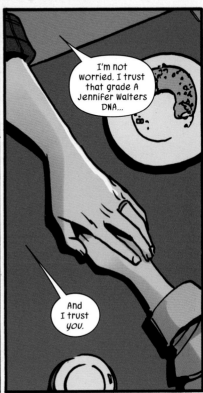

I'm not worried. I trust that grade A Jennifer Walters DNA...

And I trust *you*.

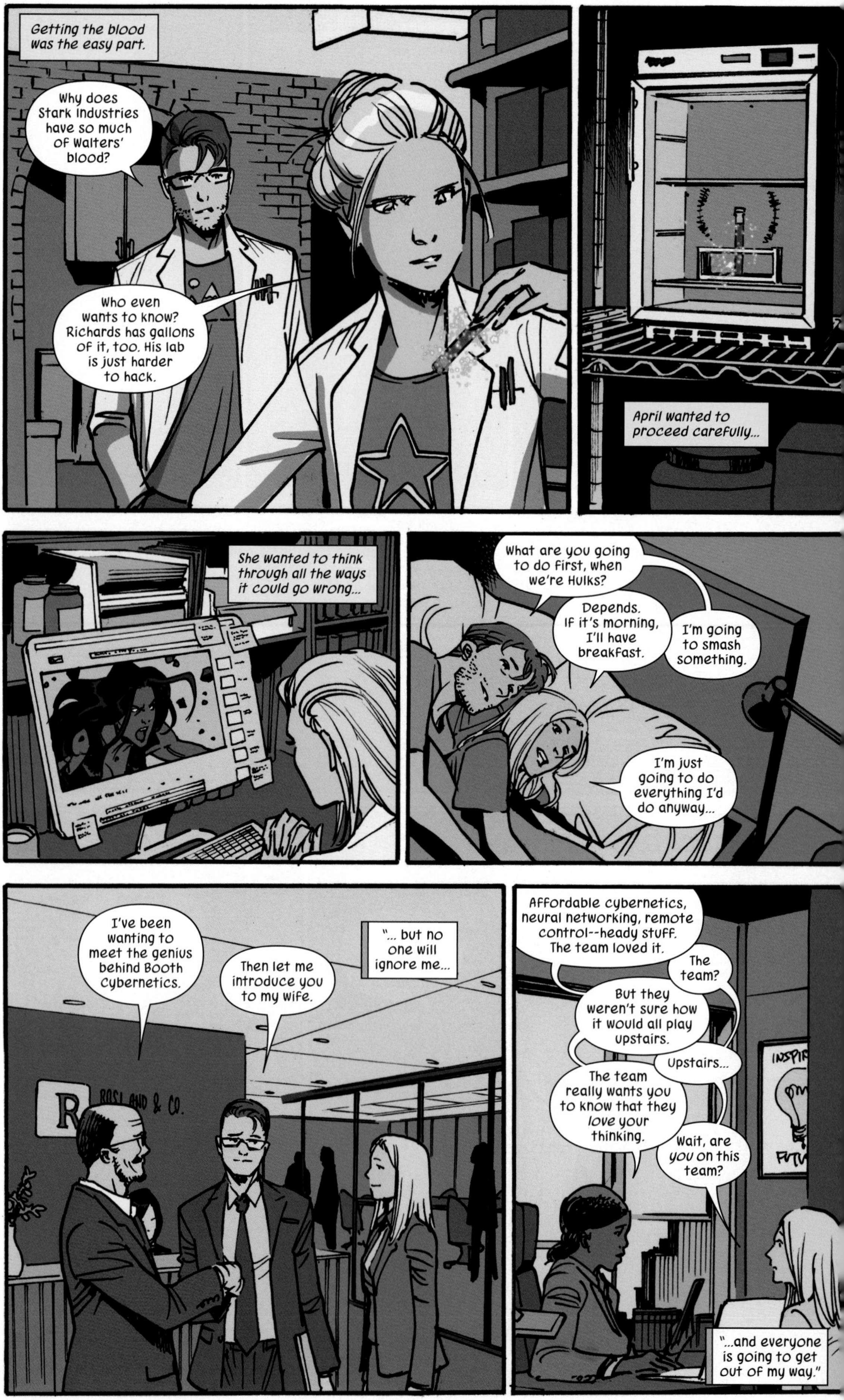
Getting the blood was the easy part.
Why does Stark Industries have so much of Walters' blood?
Who even wants to know? Richards has gallons of it, too. His lab is just harder to hack.
April wanted to proceed carefully...
She wanted to think through all the ways it could go wrong...
What are you going to do first, when we're Hulks?
Depends. If it's morning, I'll have breakfast.
I'm going to smash something.
I'm just going to do everything I'd do anyway...
I've been wanting to meet the genius behind Booth Cybernetics.
Then let me introduce you to my wife.
"... but no one will ignore me...
ROSLAND & CO.
Affordable cybernetics, neural networking, remote control--heady stuff. The team loved it.
The team?
But they weren't sure how it would all play upstairs.
Upstairs...
The team really wants you to know that they *love* your thinking.
Wait, are *you* on this team?
"...and everyone is going to get out of my way."

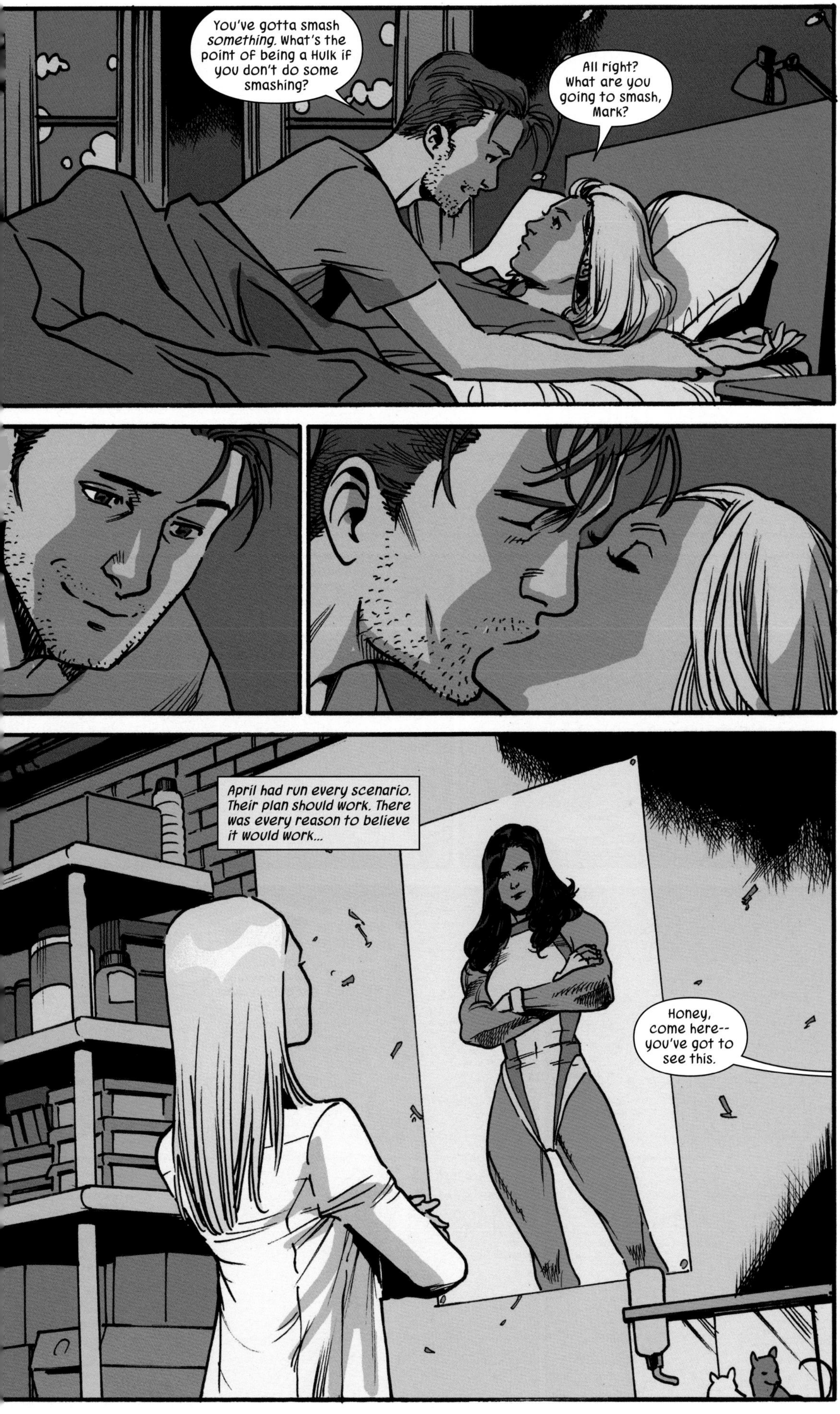
You've gotta smash *something.* What's the point of being a Hulk if you don't do some smashing?
All right? What are you going to smash, Mark?
April had run every scenario. Their plan should work. There was every reason to believe it would work...
Honey, come here-- you've got to see this.

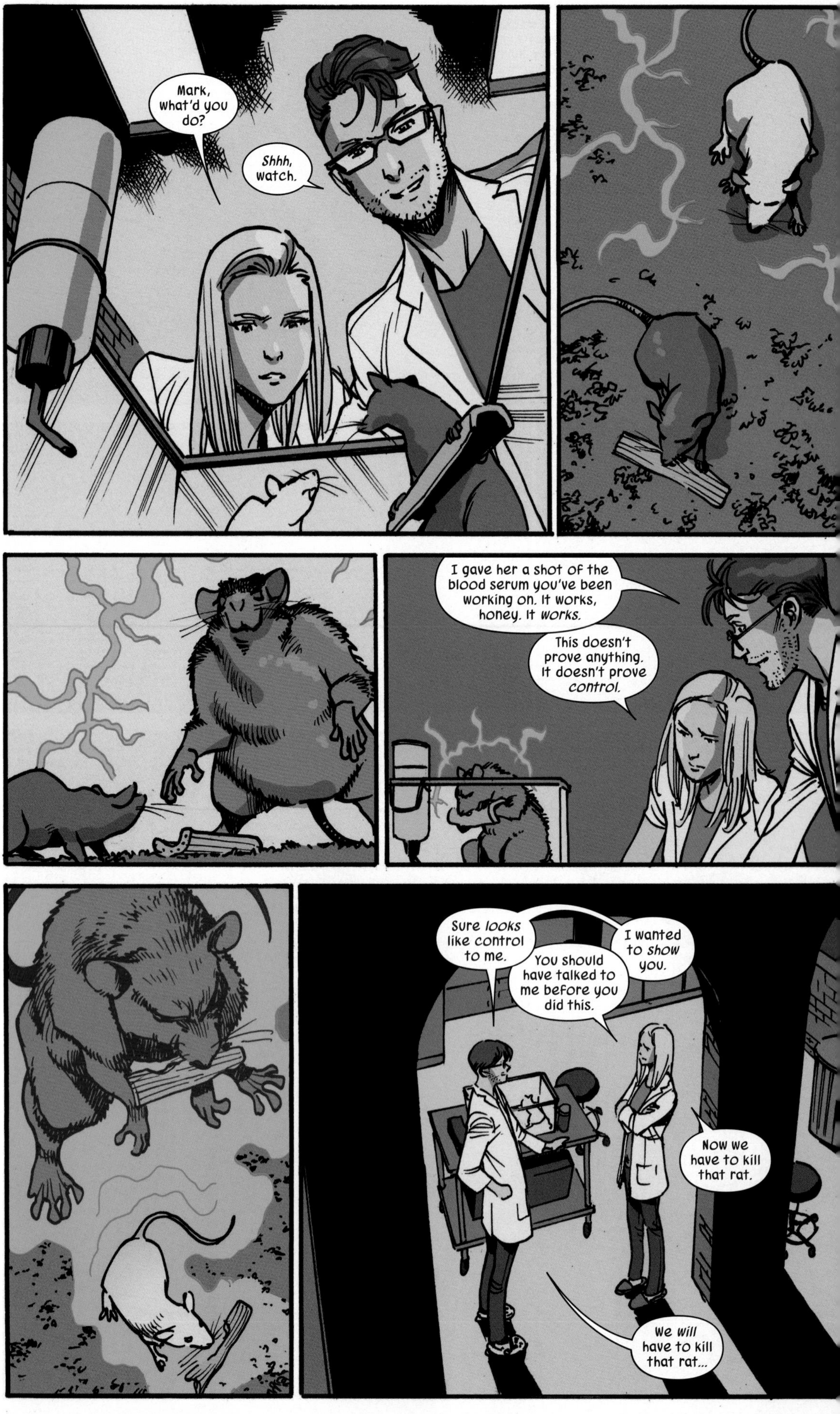
Mark, what'd you do?
Shhh, watch.
I gave her a shot of the blood serum you've been working on. It works, honey. It works.
This doesn't prove anything. It doesn't prove control.
Sure looks like control to me.
I wanted to show you.
You should have talked to me before you did this.
Now we have to kill that rat.
We will have to kill that rat...

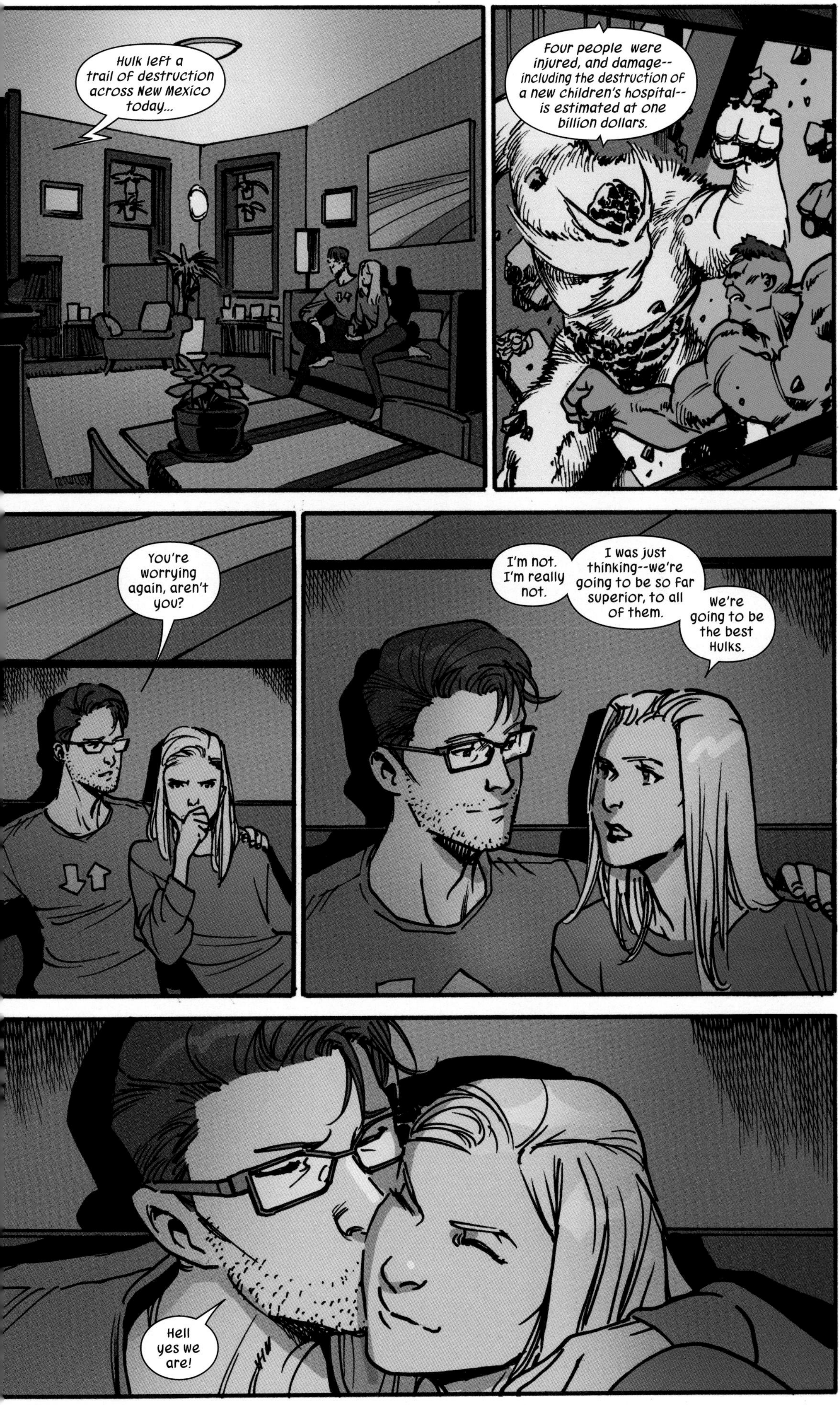

Hulk left a trail of destruction across New Mexico today...
Four people were injured, and damage--including the destruction of a new children's hospital--is estimated at one billion dollars.
You're worrying again, aren't you?
I'm not. I'm really not.
I was just thinking--we're going to be so far superior, to all of them.
We're going to be the best Hulks.
Hell yes we are!

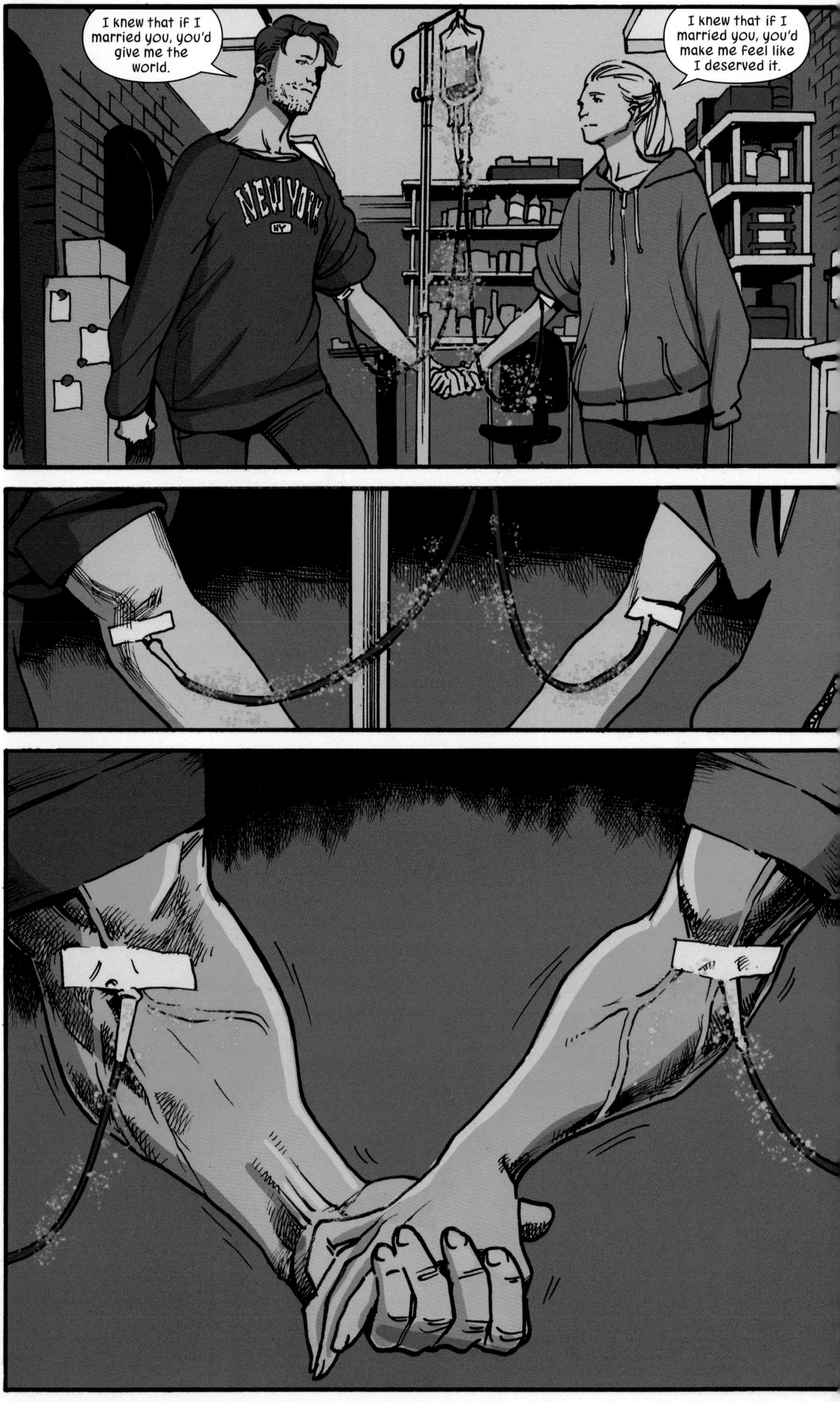
I knew that if I married you, you'd give me the world.
I knew that if I married you, you'd make me feel like I deserved it.
NEW YORK
NY

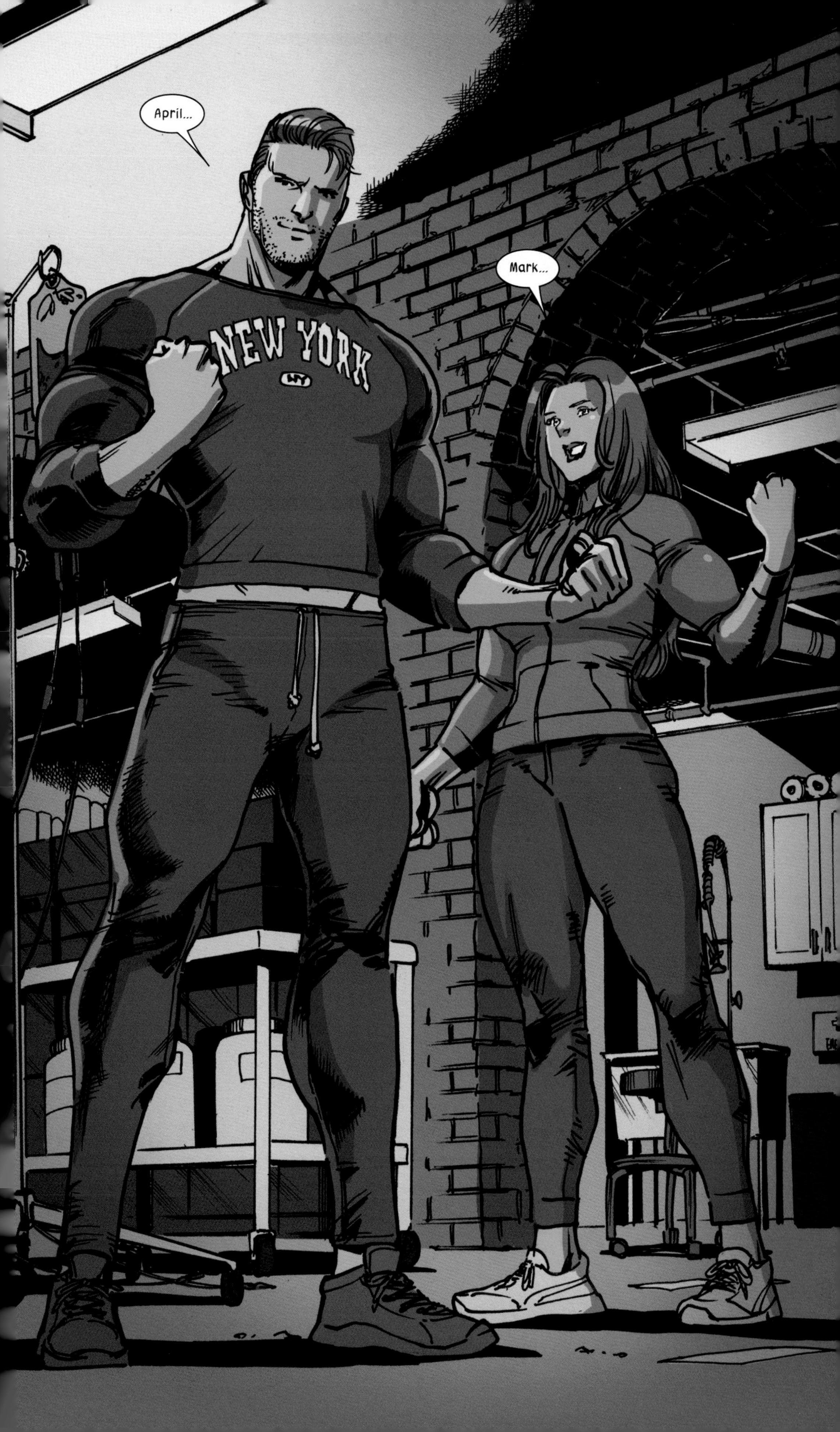

April...
Mark...
NEW YORK

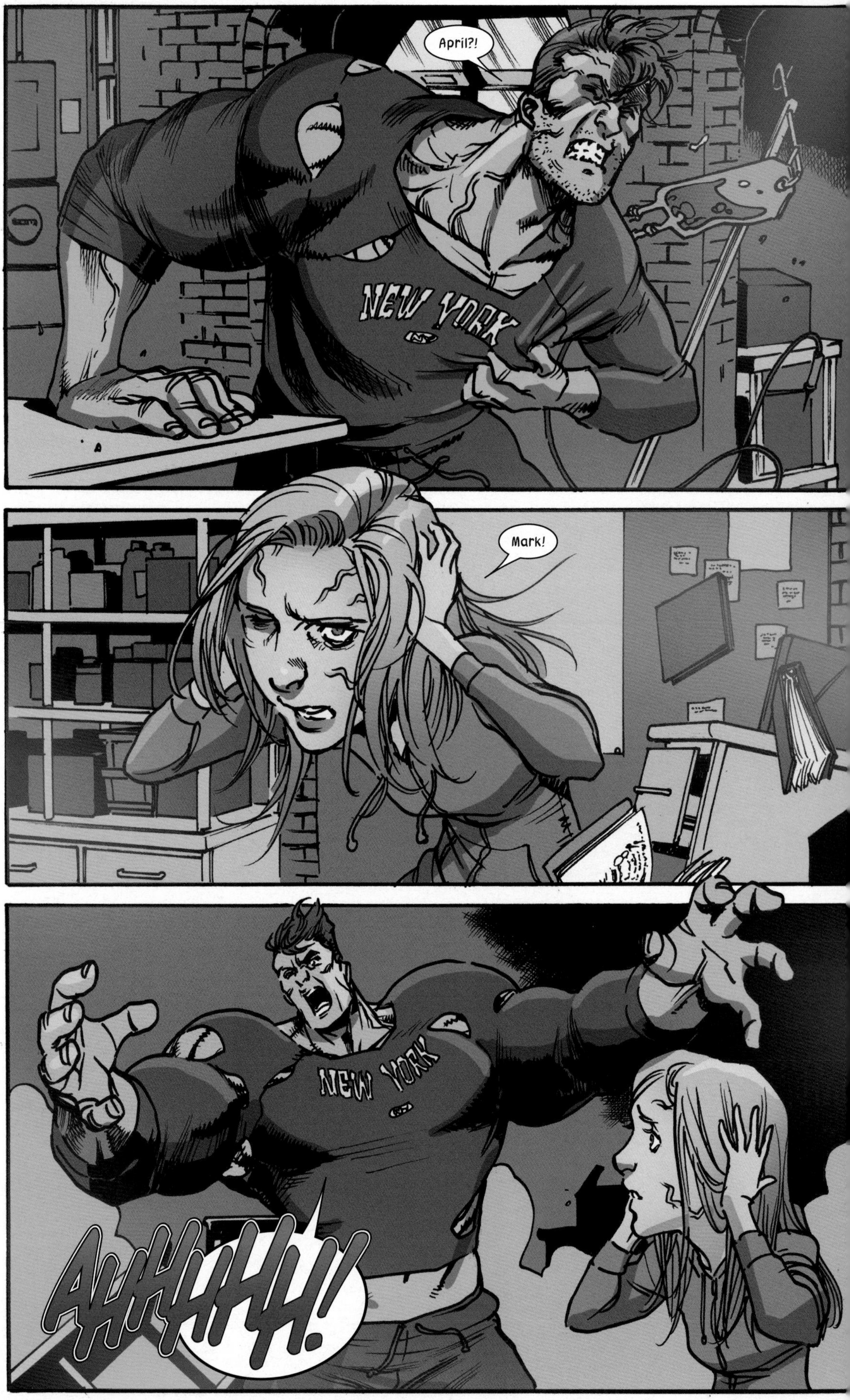
April?!
NEW YORK
Mark!
NEW YORK
AHHHHH!

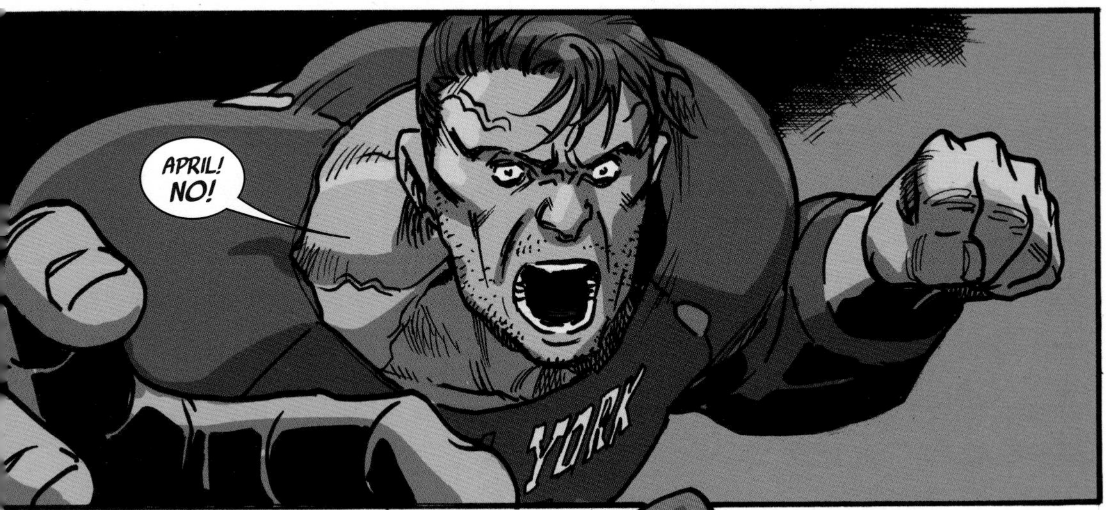
APRIL! NO!

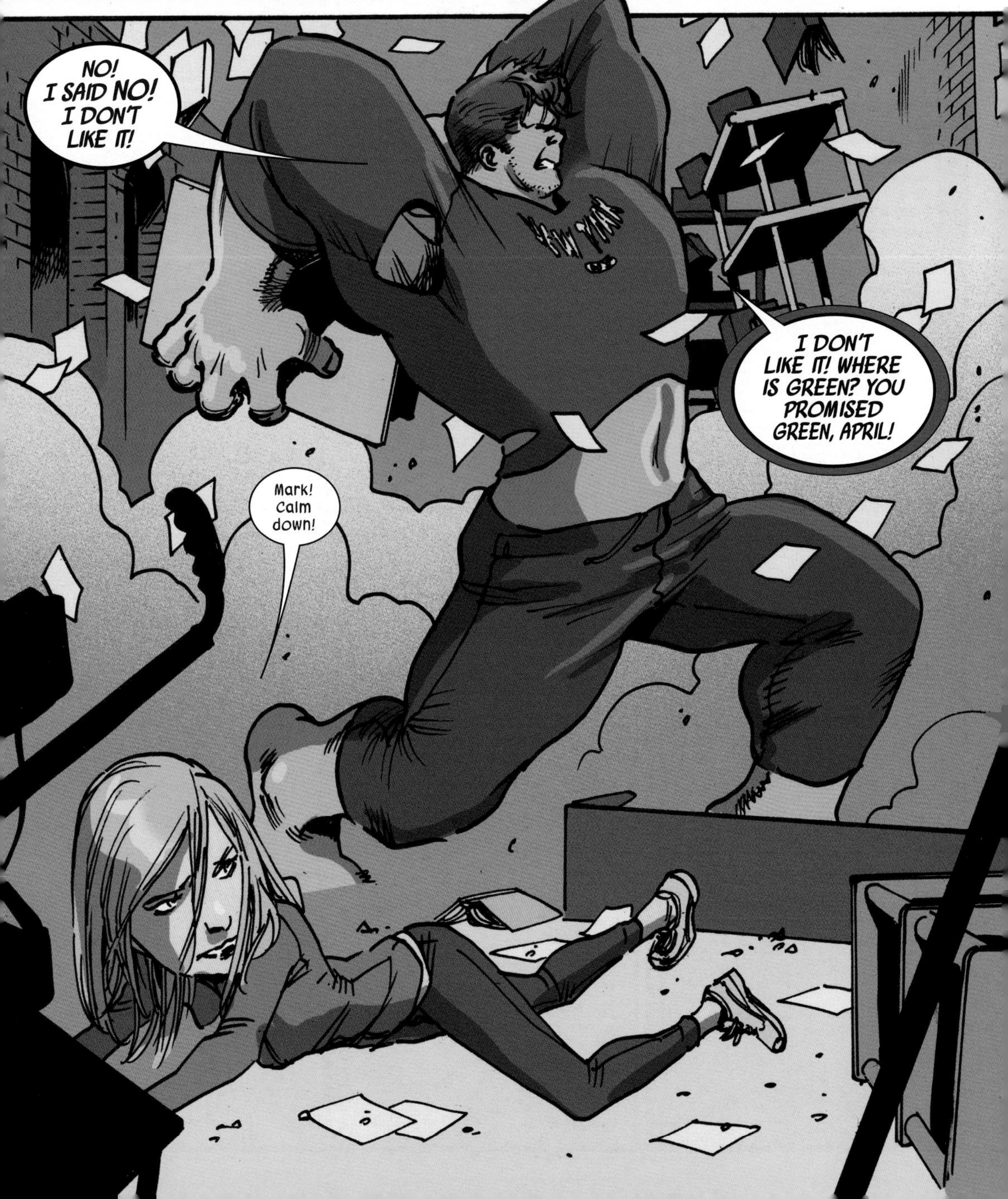
NO! I SAID NO! I DON'T LIKE IT!
I DON'T LIKE IT! WHERE IS GREEN? YOU PROMISED GREEN, APRIL!
Mark! Calm down!

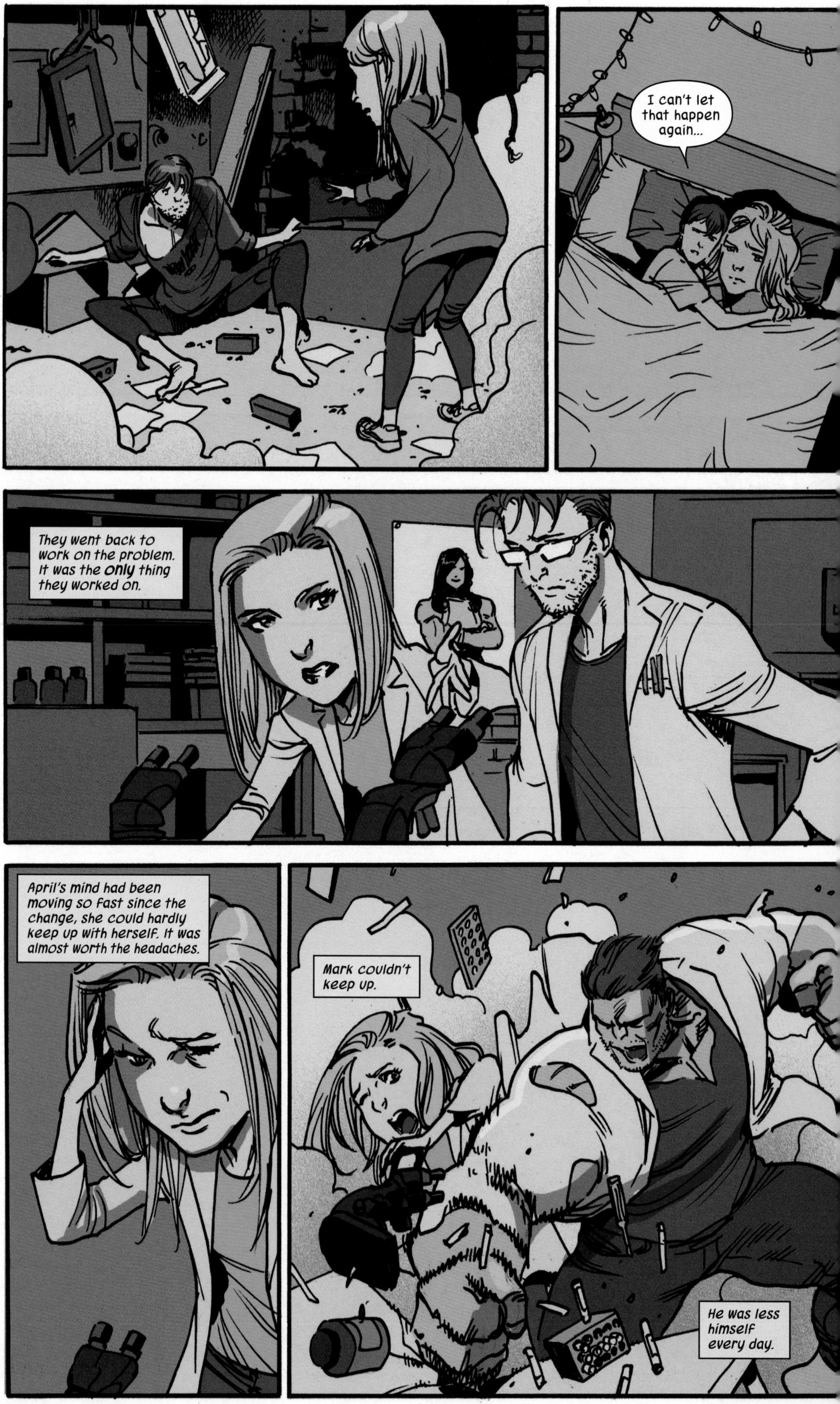
I can't let that happen again...
They went back to work on the problem. It was the only thing they worked on.
April's mind had been moving so fast since the change, she could hardly keep up with herself. It was almost worth the headaches.
Mark couldn't keep up.
He was less himself every day.

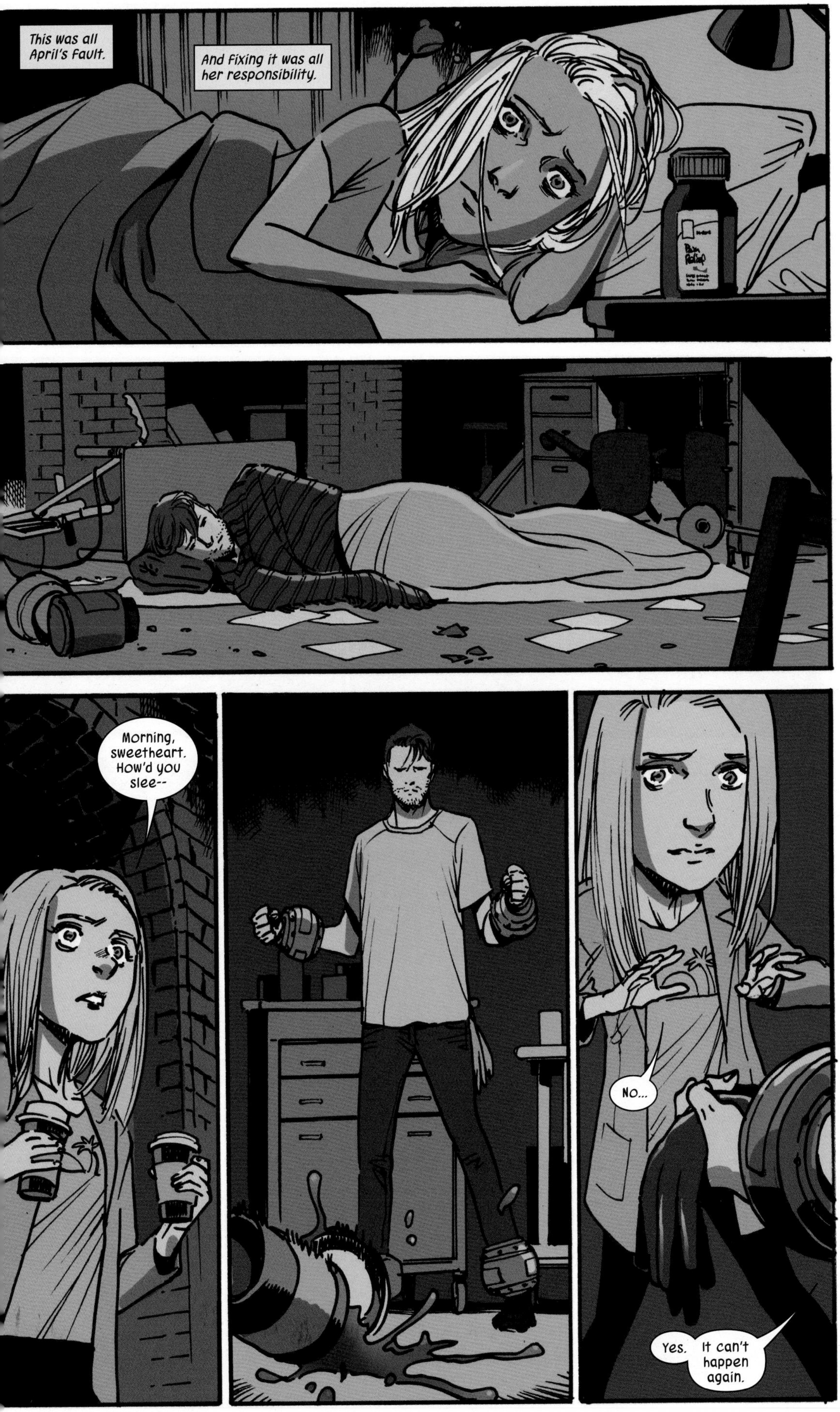
This was all April's Fault.
And fixing it was all her responsibility.
Morning, sweetheart. How'd you slee--
NO...
Yes.
It can't happen again.

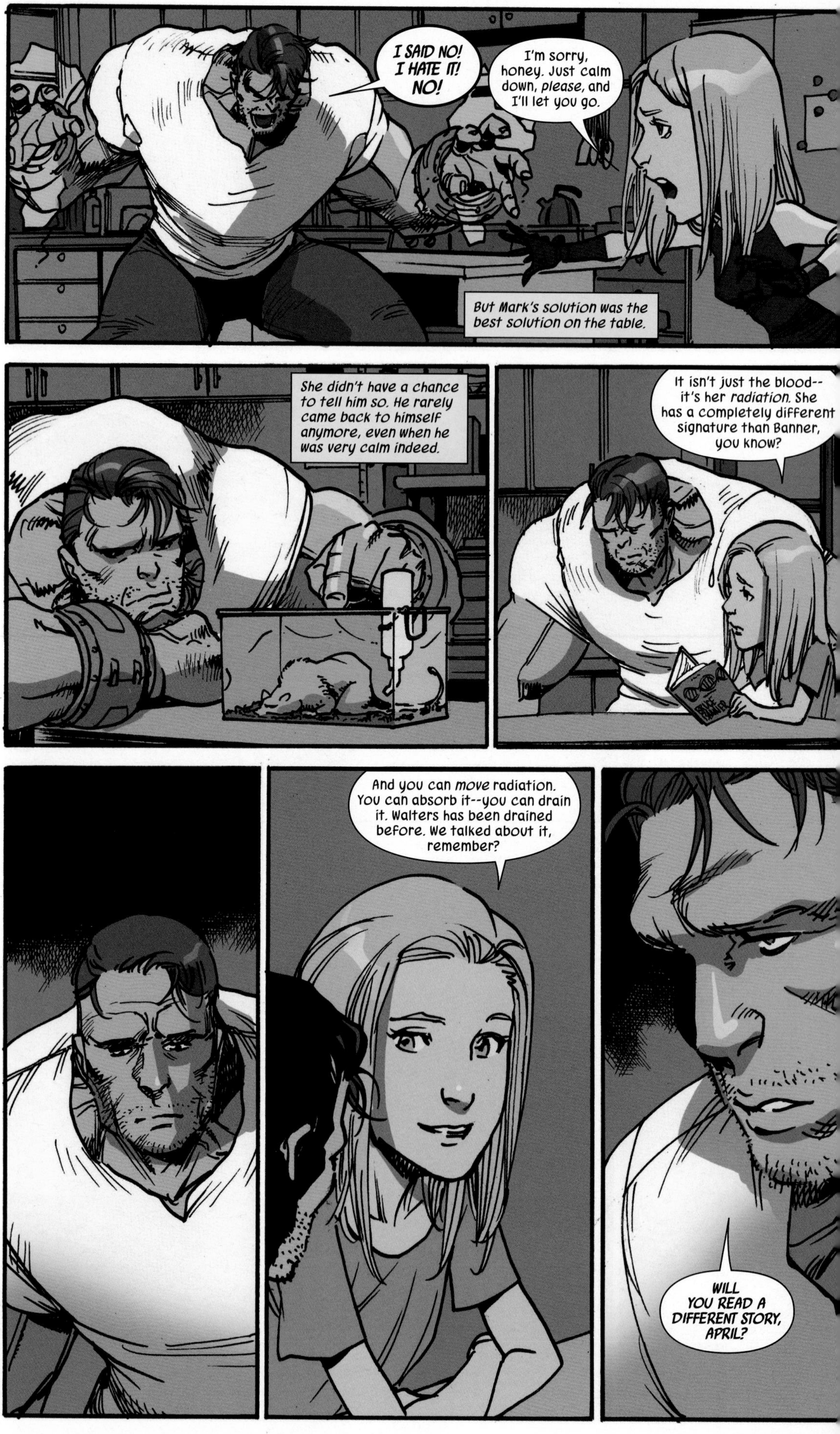
I SAID NO! I HATE IT! NO!
I'm sorry, honey. Just calm down, *please*, and I'll let you go.
But Mark's solution was the best solution on the table.
She didn't have a chance to tell him so. He rarely came back to himself anymore, even when he was very calm indeed.
It isn't just the blood-- it's her *radiation*. She has a completely different signature than Banner, you know?
And you can *move* radiation. You can absorb it--you can drain it. Walters has been drained before. We talked about it, remember?
WILL YOU READ A DIFFERENT STORY, APRIL?

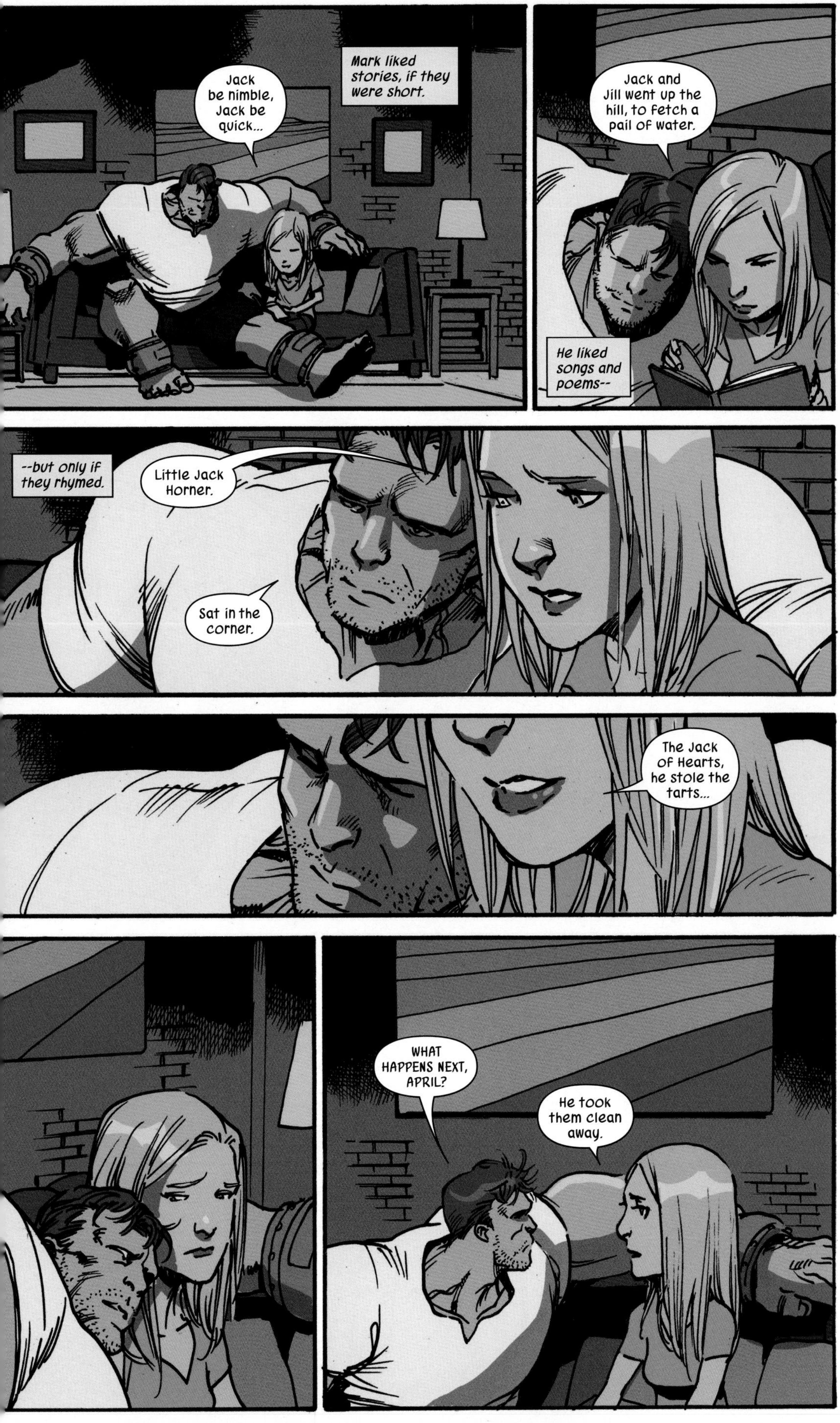
Jack be nimble, Jack be quick...
Mark liked stories, if they were short.
Jack and Jill went up the hill, to fetch a pail of water.
He liked songs and poems--
--but only if they rhymed.
Little Jack Horner.
Sat in the corner.
The Jack of Hearts, he stole the tarts...
WHAT HAPPENS NEXT, APRIL?
He took them clean away.

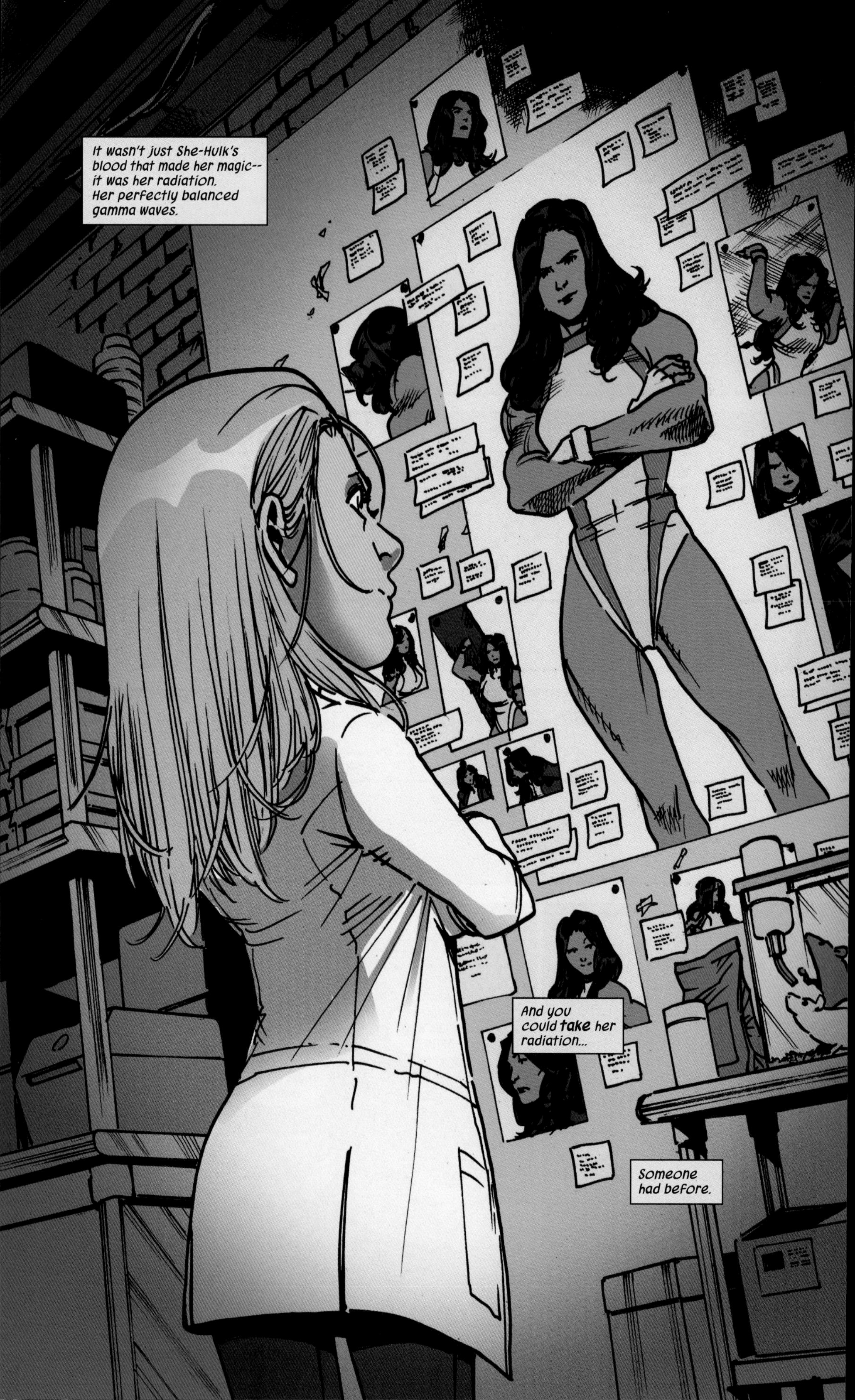
It wasn't just She-Hulk's blood that made her magic-- it was her radiation. Her perfectly balanced gamma waves.
And you could take her radiation...
Someone had before.

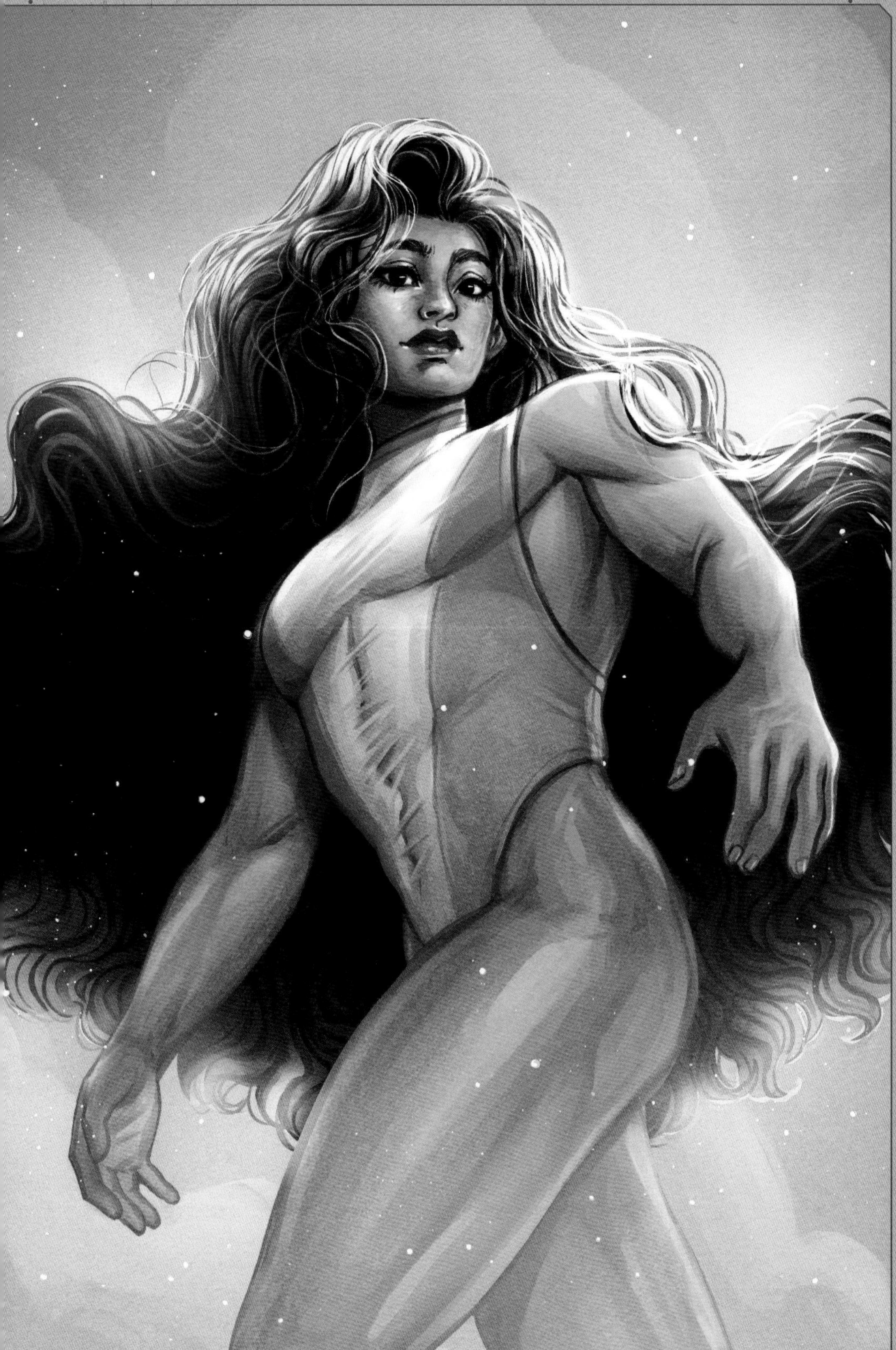

#6 VARIANT BY **EJIWA "EDGE" EBENEBE**

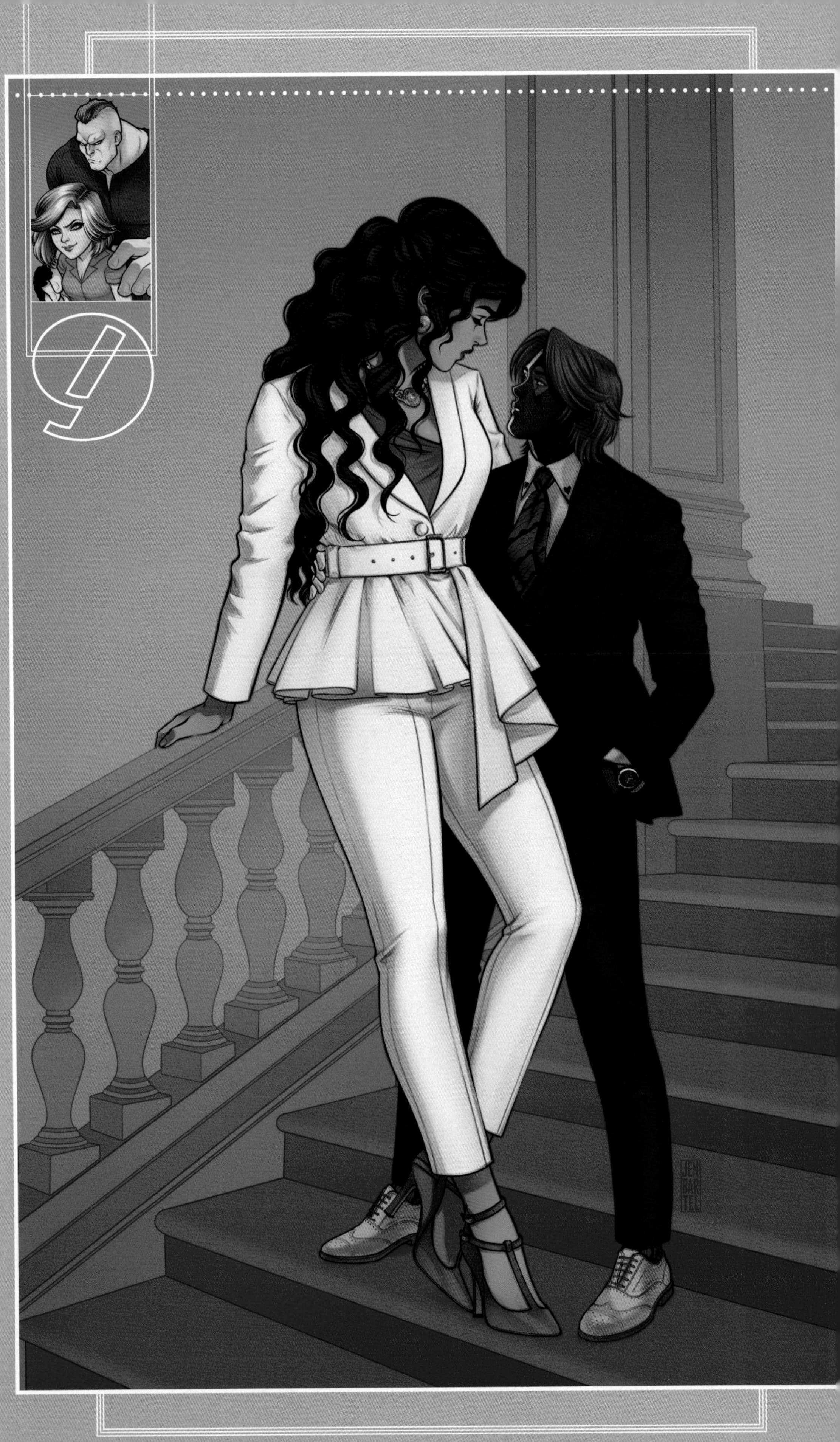
9
JEN
BAR
TEL

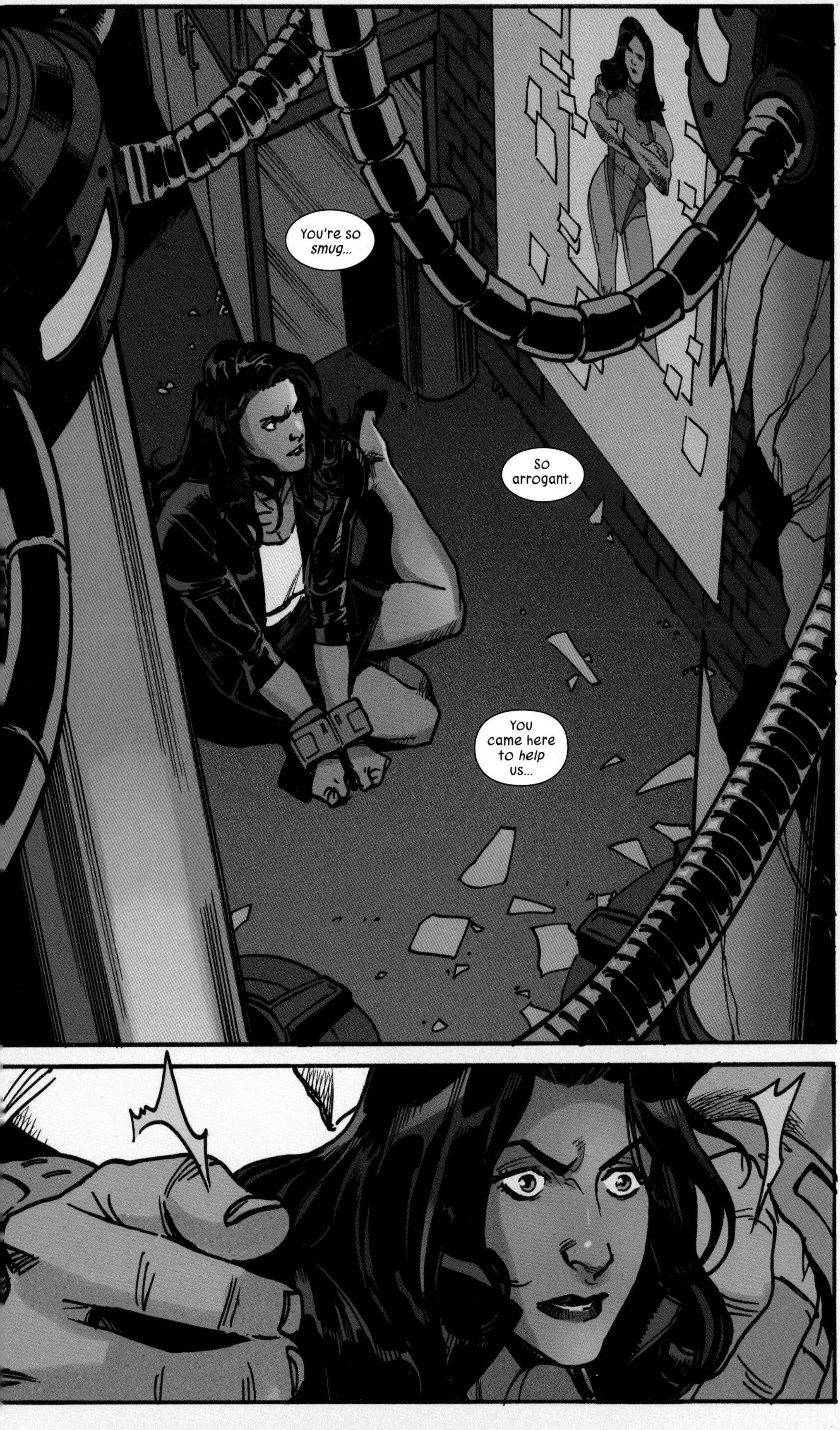
You're so smug...
So arrogant.
You came here to help us...

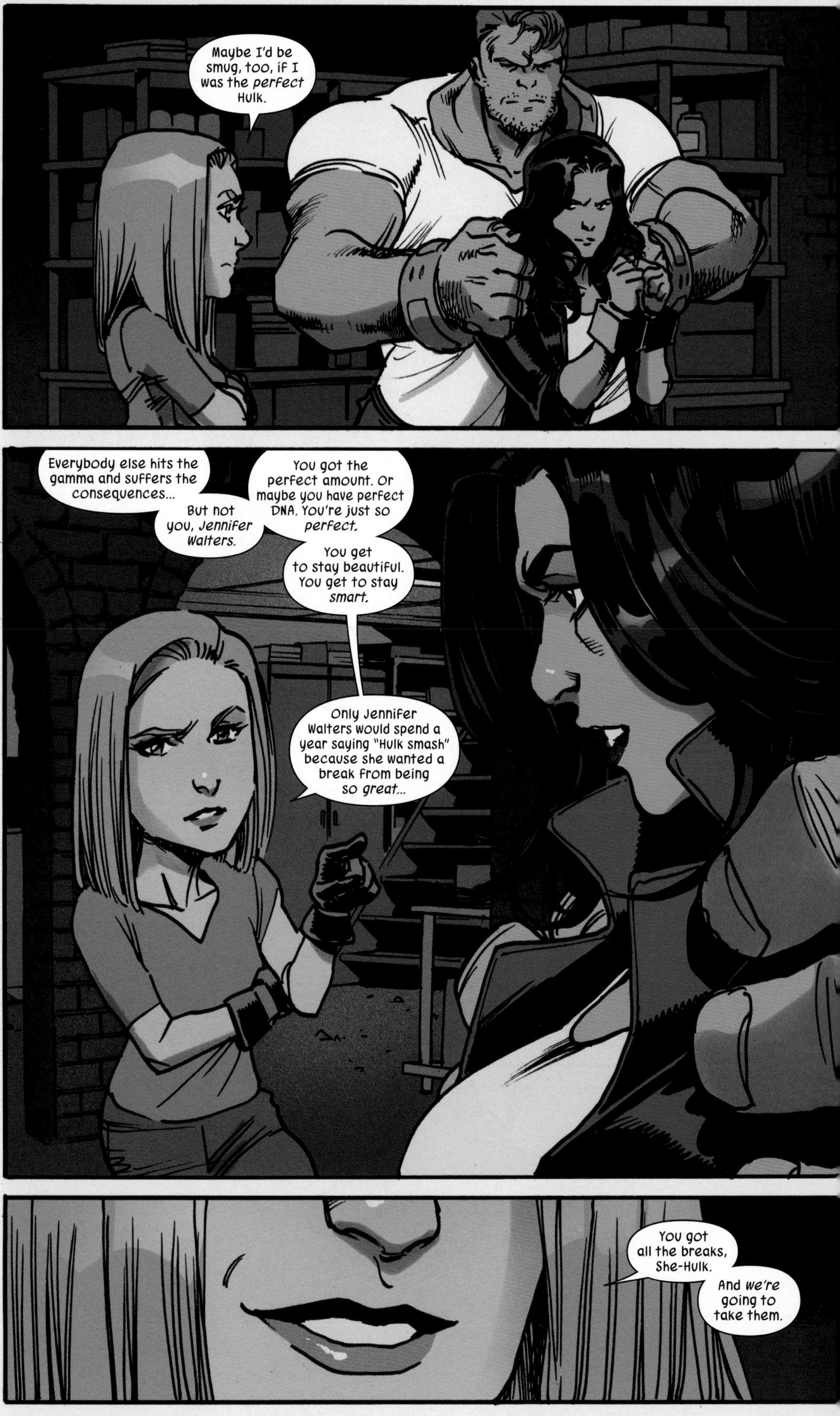

Maybe I'd be smug, too, if I was the *perfect* Hulk.
Everybody else hits the gamma and suffers the consequences...
But not you, Jennifer Walters.
You got the perfect amount. Or maybe you have perfect DNA. You're just so *perfect*.
You get to stay beautiful. You get to stay *smart*.
Only Jennifer Walters would spend a year saying "Hulk smash" because she wanted a break from being so *great*...
You got all the breaks, She-Hulk.
And *we're* going to take them.

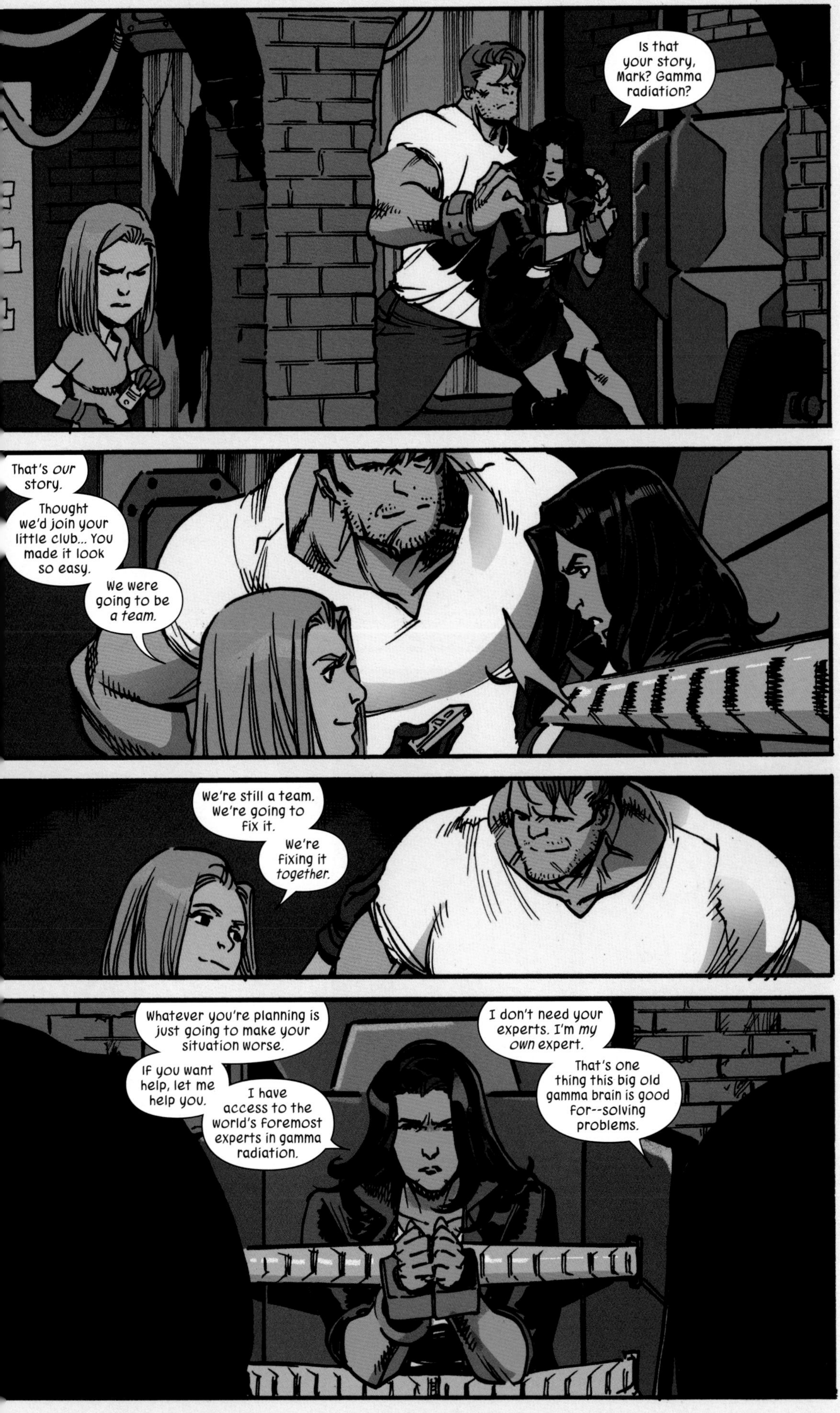

Is that your story, Mark? Gamma radiation?
That's *our* story.
Thought we'd join your little club... You made it look so easy.
We were going to be a *team.*
We're still a team. We're going to fix it.
We're fixing it *together.*
Whatever you're planning is just going to make your situation worse.
If you want help, let me help you.
I have access to the world's foremost experts in gamma radiation.
I don't need your experts. I'm *my own* expert.
That's one thing this big old gamma brain is good for--solving problems.

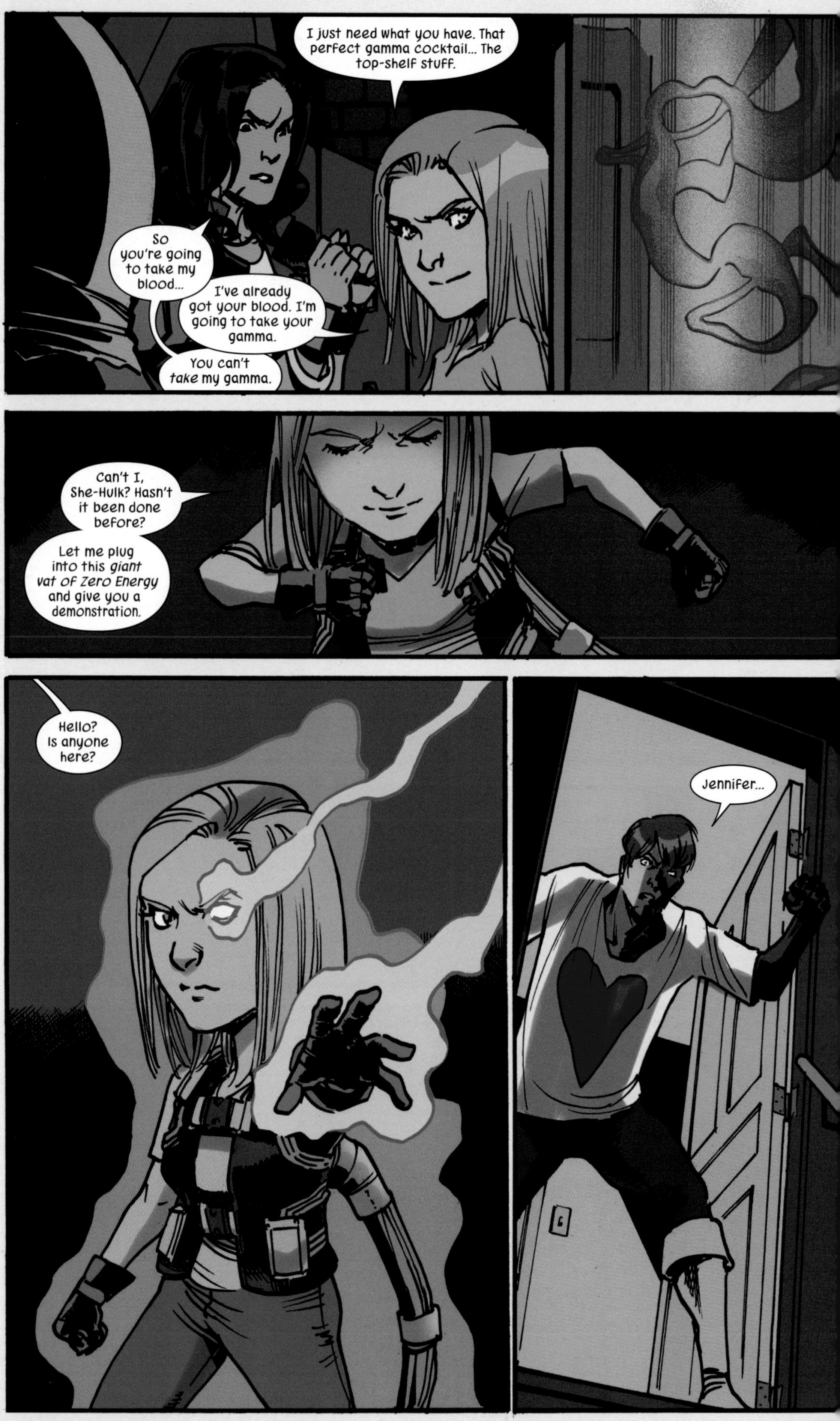
I just need what you have. That perfect gamma cocktail... The top-shelf stuff.
So you're going to take my blood...
I've already got your blood. I'm going to take your gamma.
You can't take my gamma.
Can't I, She-Hulk? Hasn't it been done before?
Let me plug into this giant vat of Zero Energy and give you a demonstration.
Hello? Is anyone here?
Jennifer...

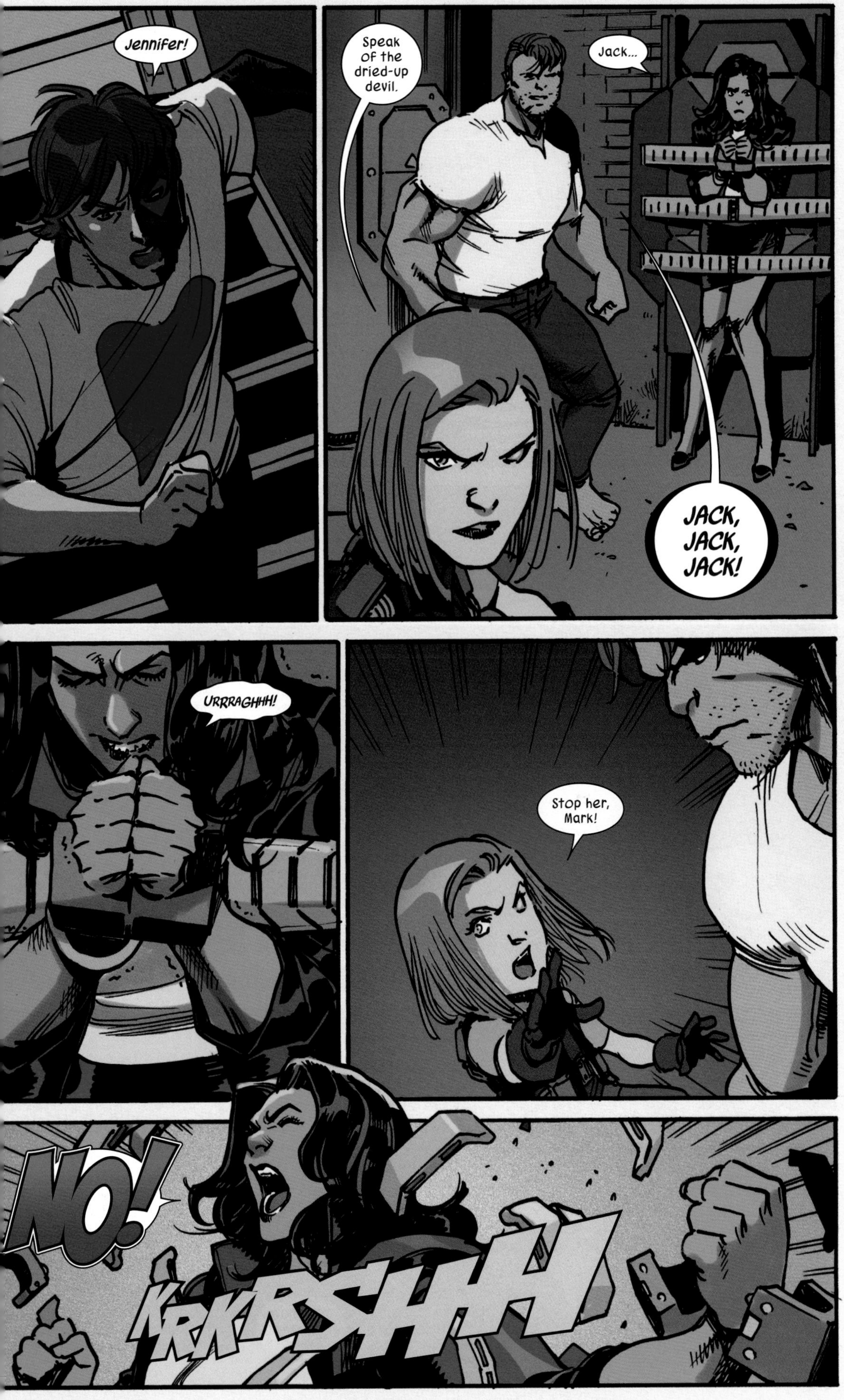
Jennifer!
Speak of the dried-up devil.
Jack...
JACK, JACK, JACK!
URRRAGHHH!
Stop her, Mark!
NO!
KRKRSHH

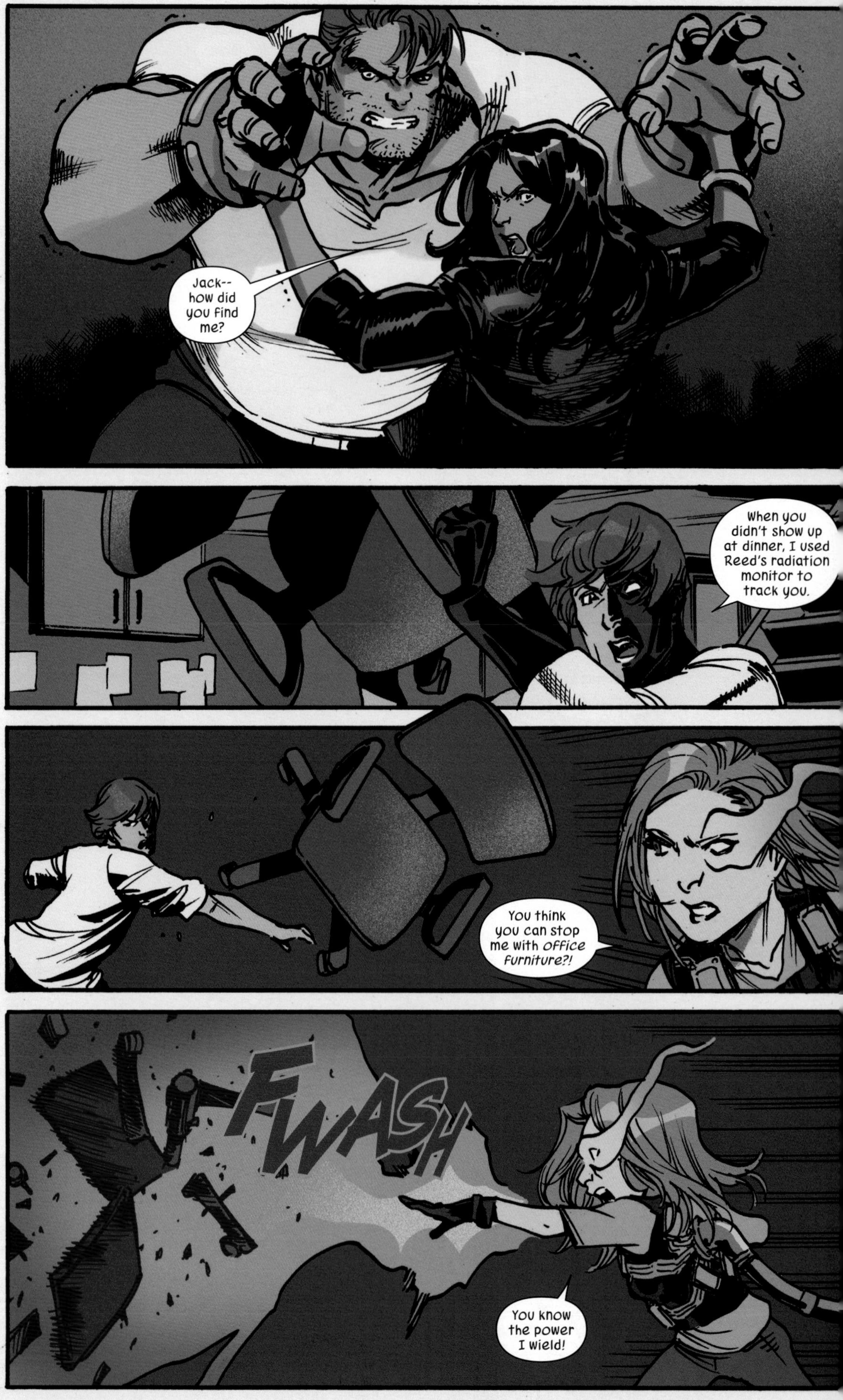
Jack-- how did you find me?
When you didn't show up at dinner, I used Reed's radiation monitor to track you.
You think you can stop me with *office furniture?!*
FWASH
You know the power I wield!

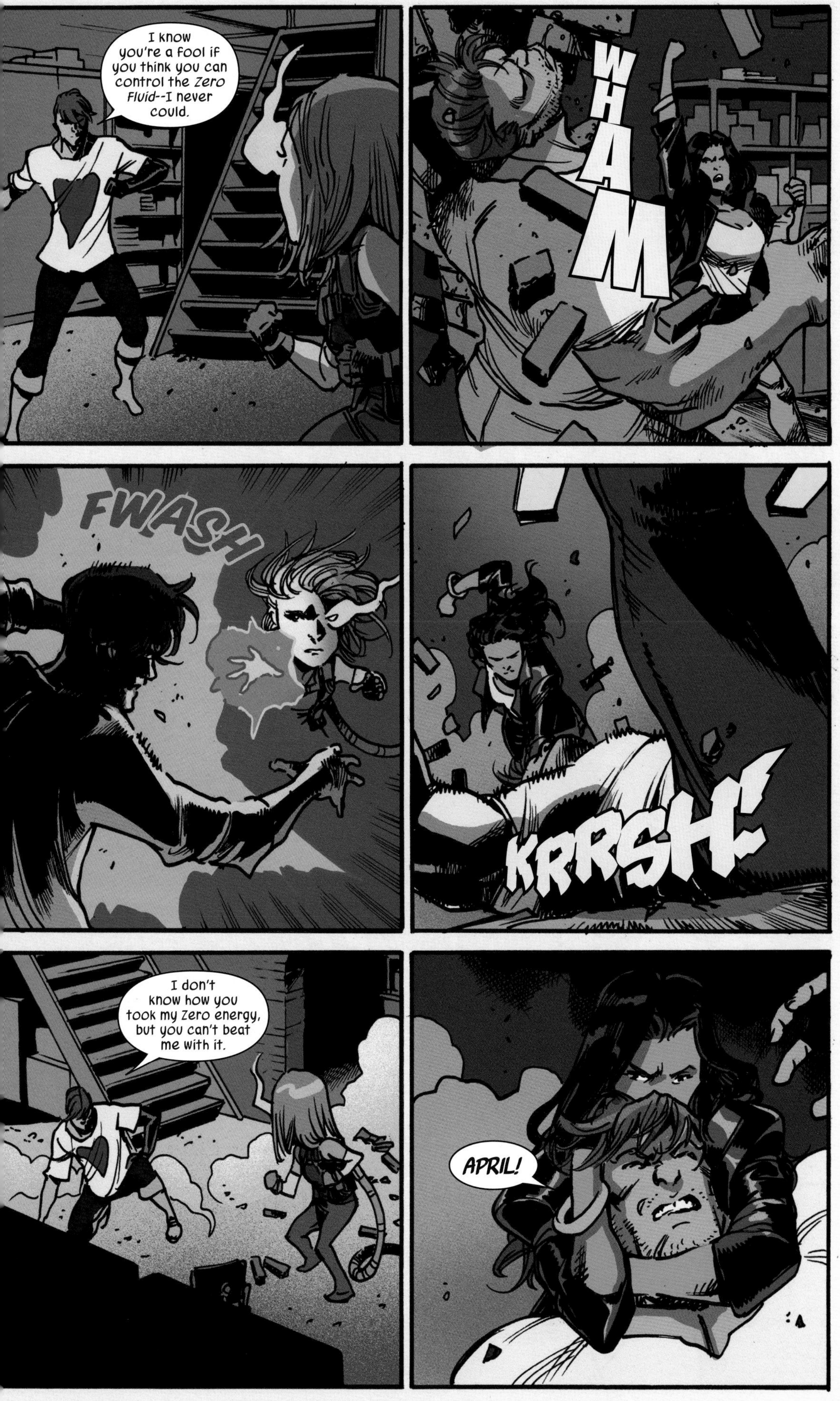
I know you're a fool if you think you can control the Zero Fluid--I never could.
WHAM
FWASH
KRRSH!
I don't know how you took my Zero energy, but you can't beat me with it.
APRIL!

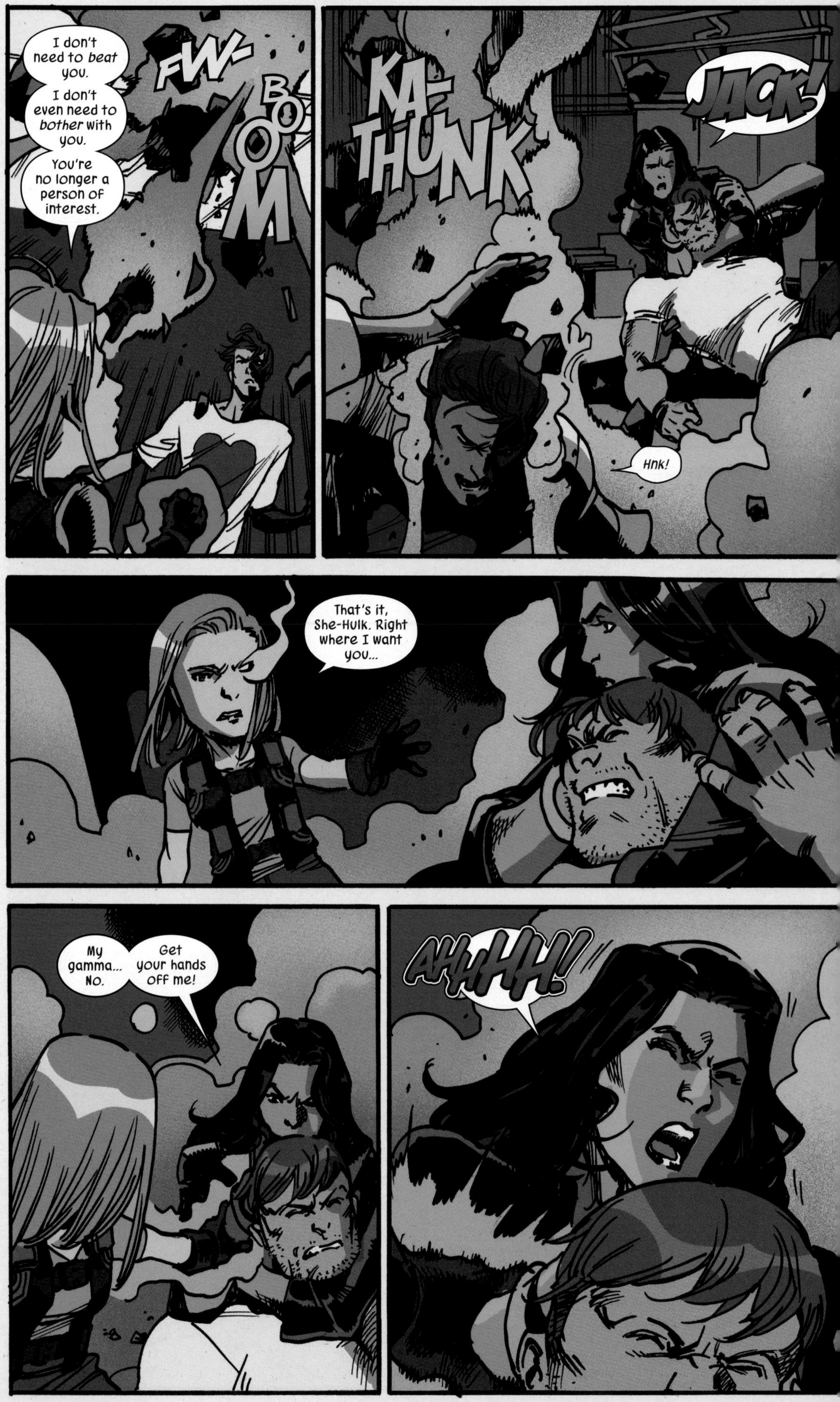
I don't need to beat you.
I don't even need to bother with you.
You're no longer a person of interest.
FW-BOOOM
KA-THUNK
JACK!
HNK!
That's it, She-Hulk. Right where I want you...
My gamma... No.
Get your hands off me!
AHHHH!

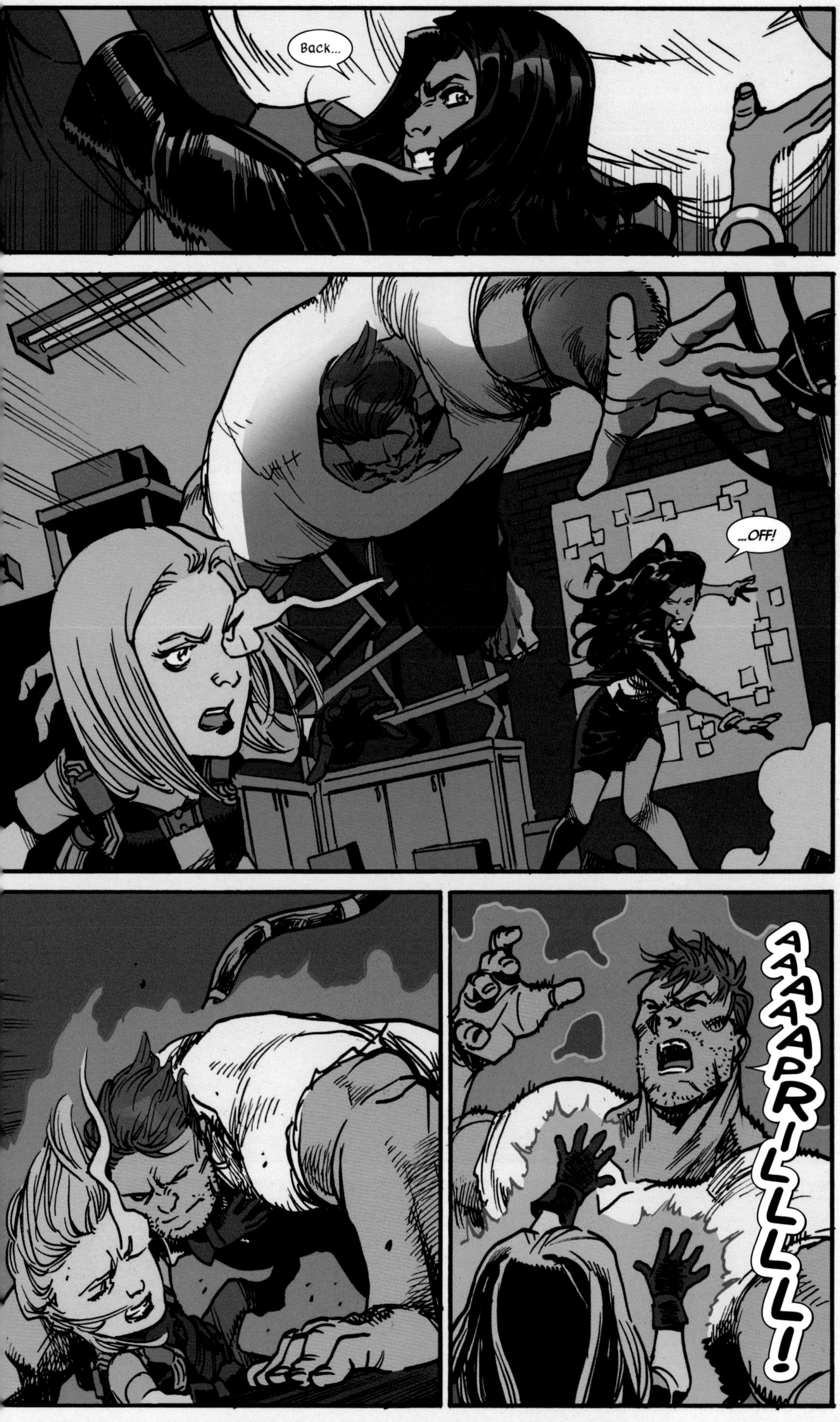
Back...
...OFF!
AAAAPRILLL!

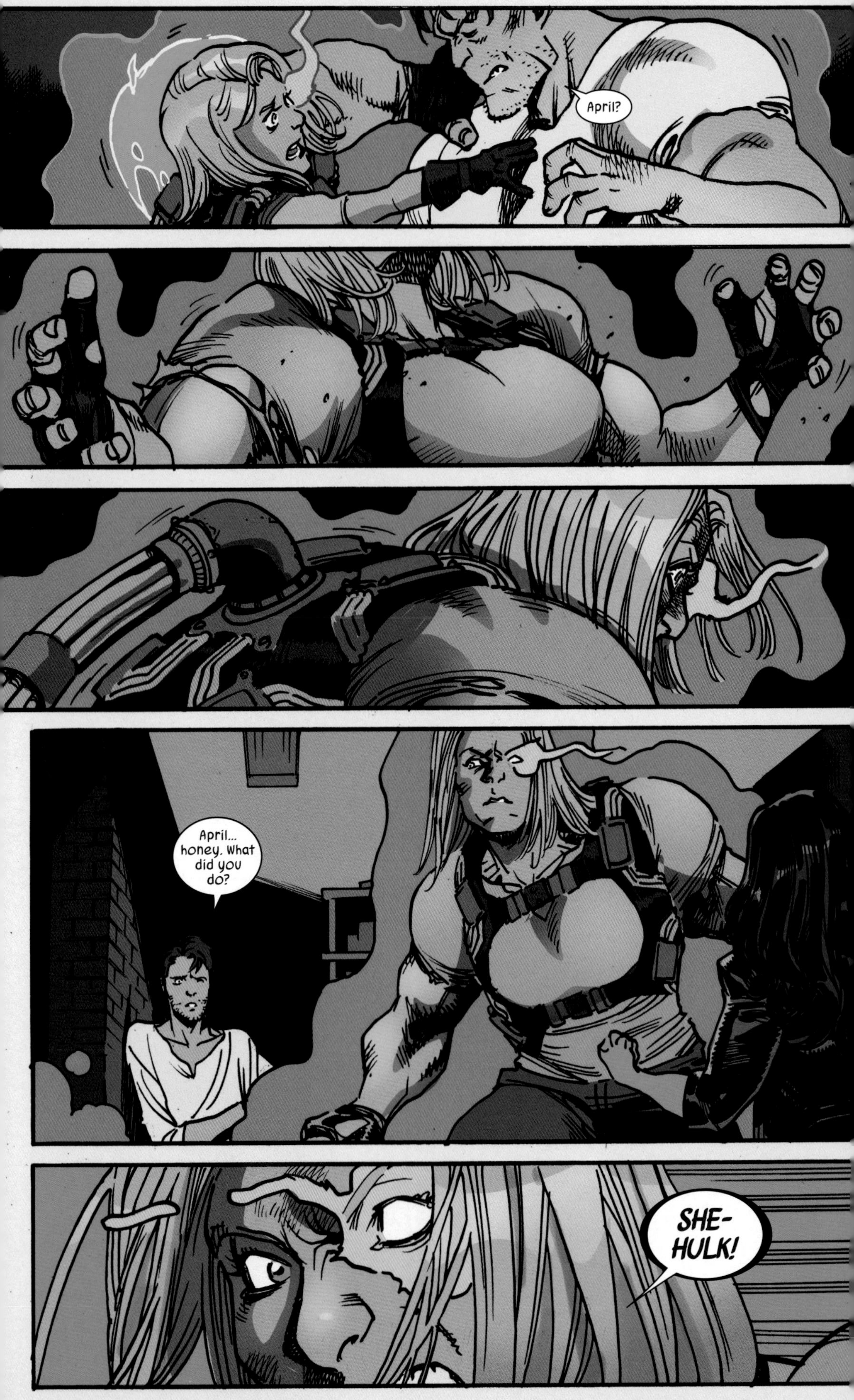
April?
April...
honey. What
did you
do?
SHE-
HULK!

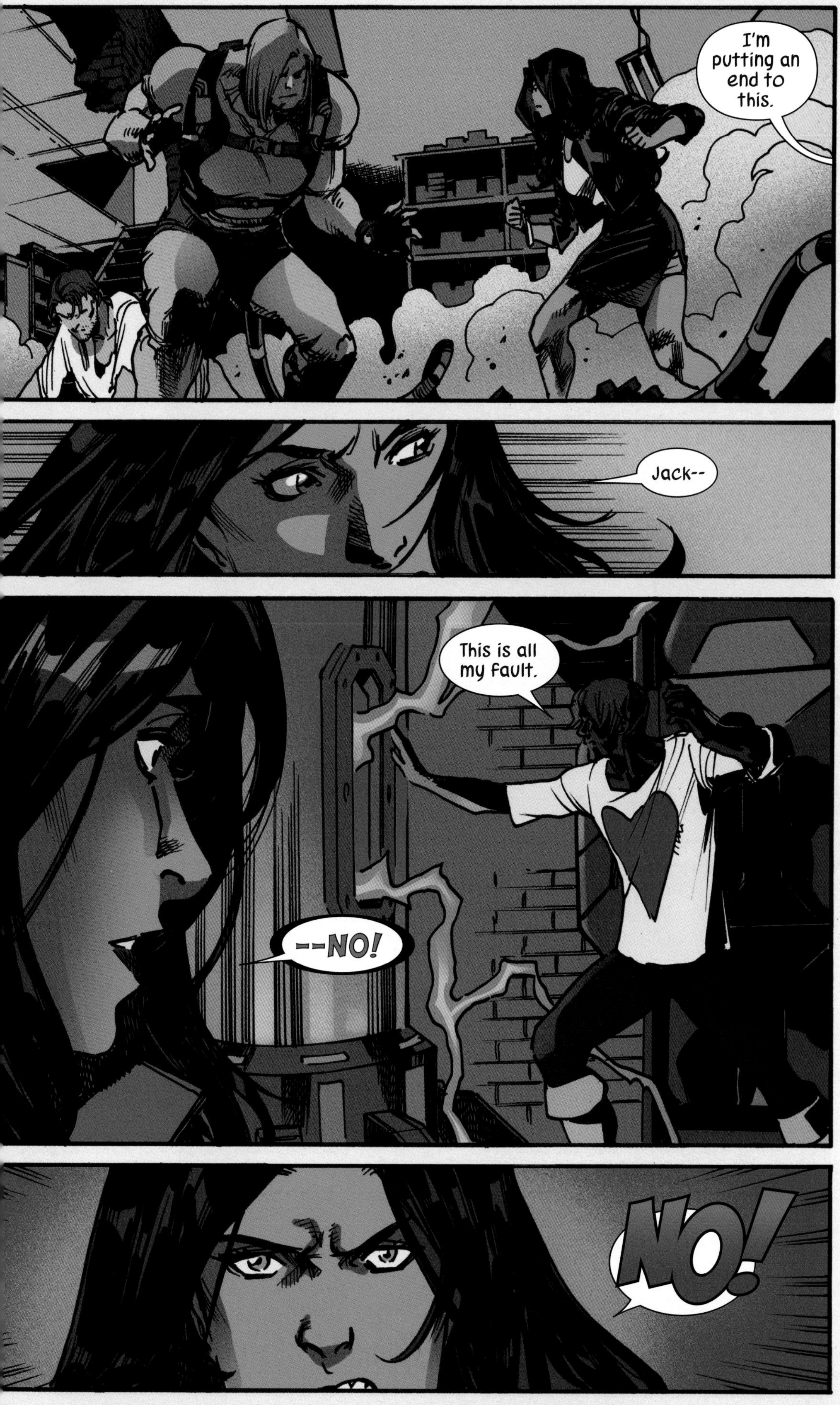
I'm putting an end to this.
Jack--
This is all my fault.
--NO!
NO!

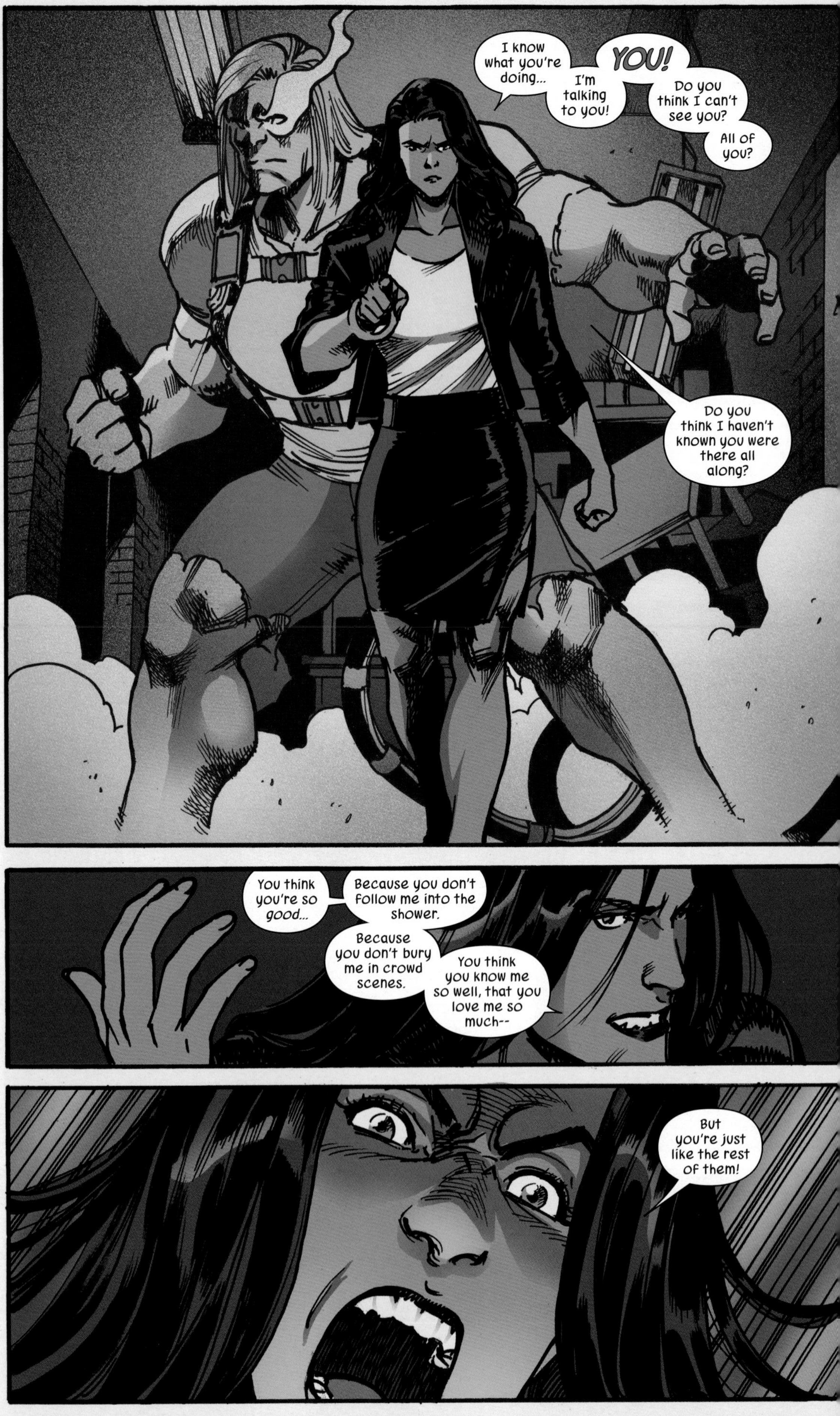
I know what you're doing...
YOU!
I'm talking to you!
Do you think I can't see you?
All of you?
Do you think I haven't known you were there all along?
You think you're so good...
Because you don't follow me into the shower.
Because you don't bury me in crowd scenes.
You think you know me so well, that you love me so much--
But you're just like the rest of them!

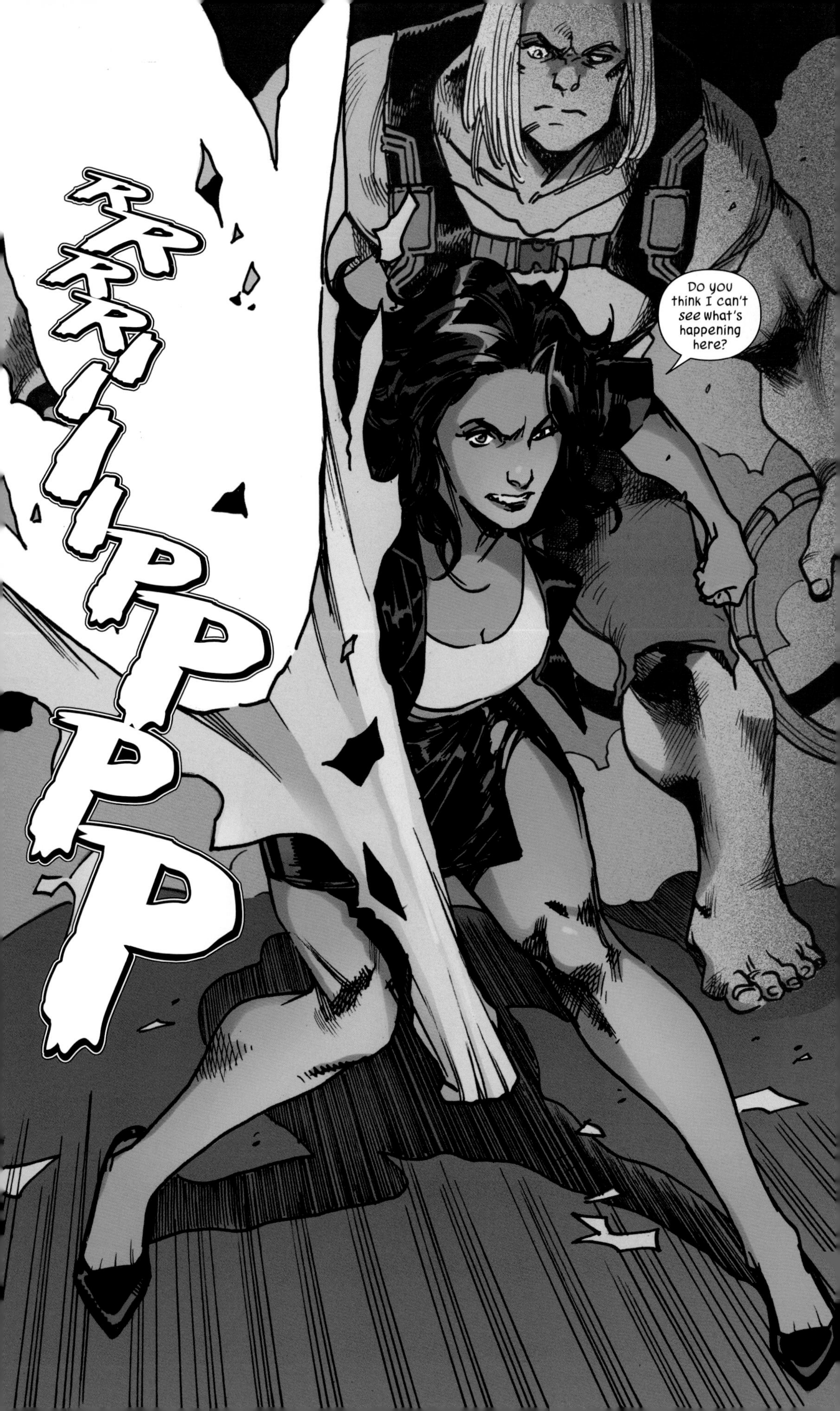
RRRRIIPPPP
Do you think I can't *see* what's happening here?

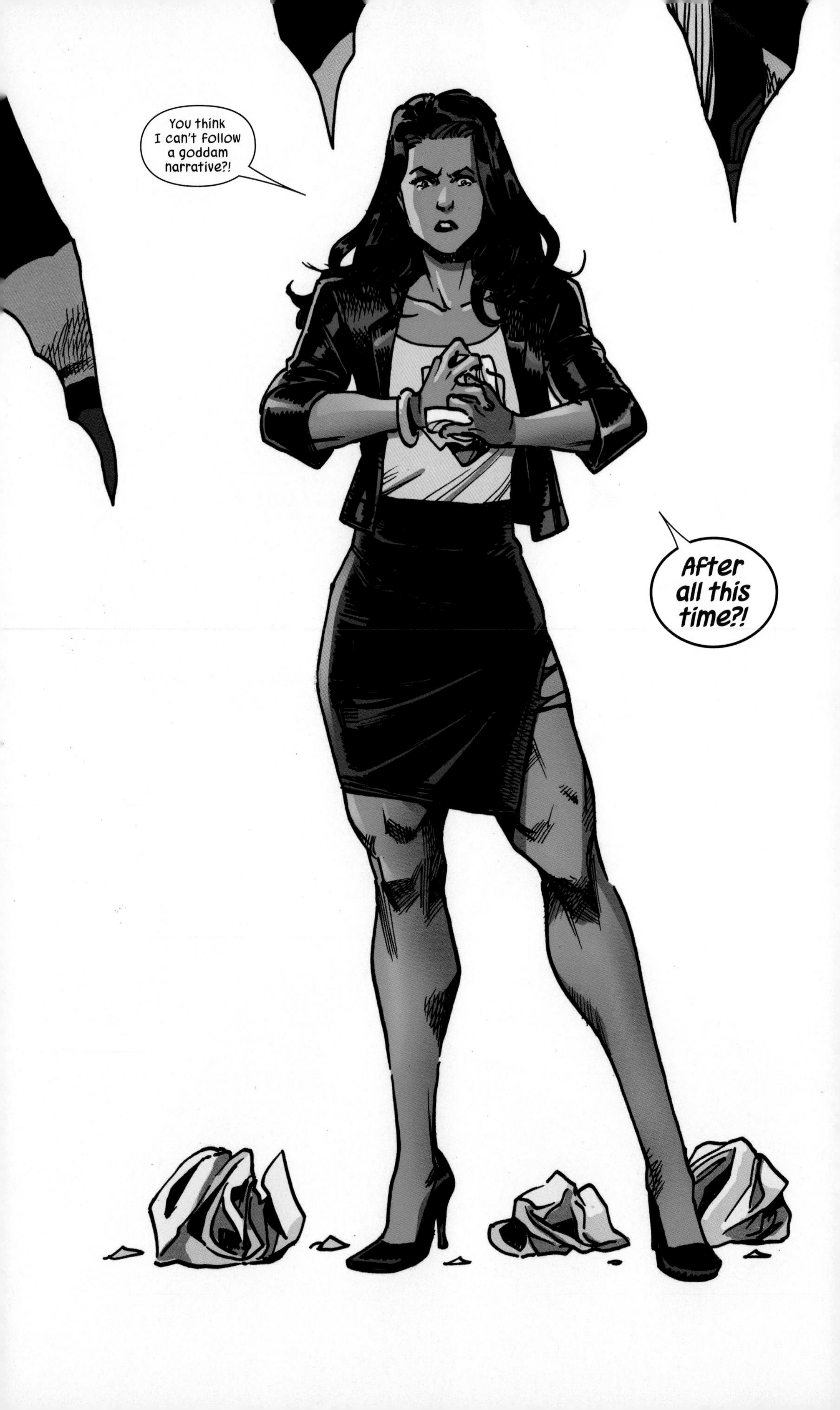
You think I can't follow a goddam narrative?!
After all this time?!

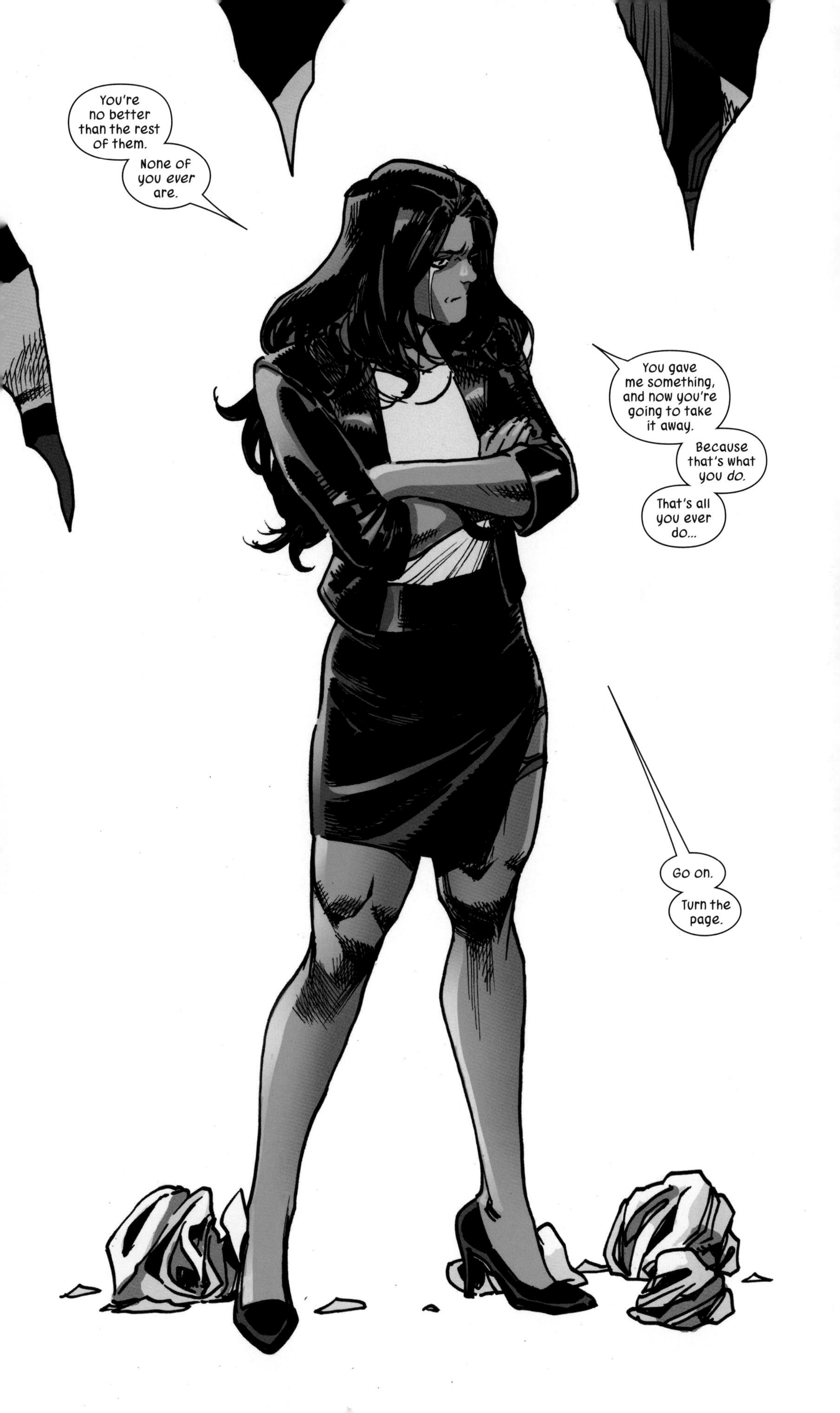
You're no better than the rest of them.
None of you ever are.
You gave me something, and now you're going to take it away.
Because that's what you *do*.
That's all you ever do...
Go on.
Turn the page.

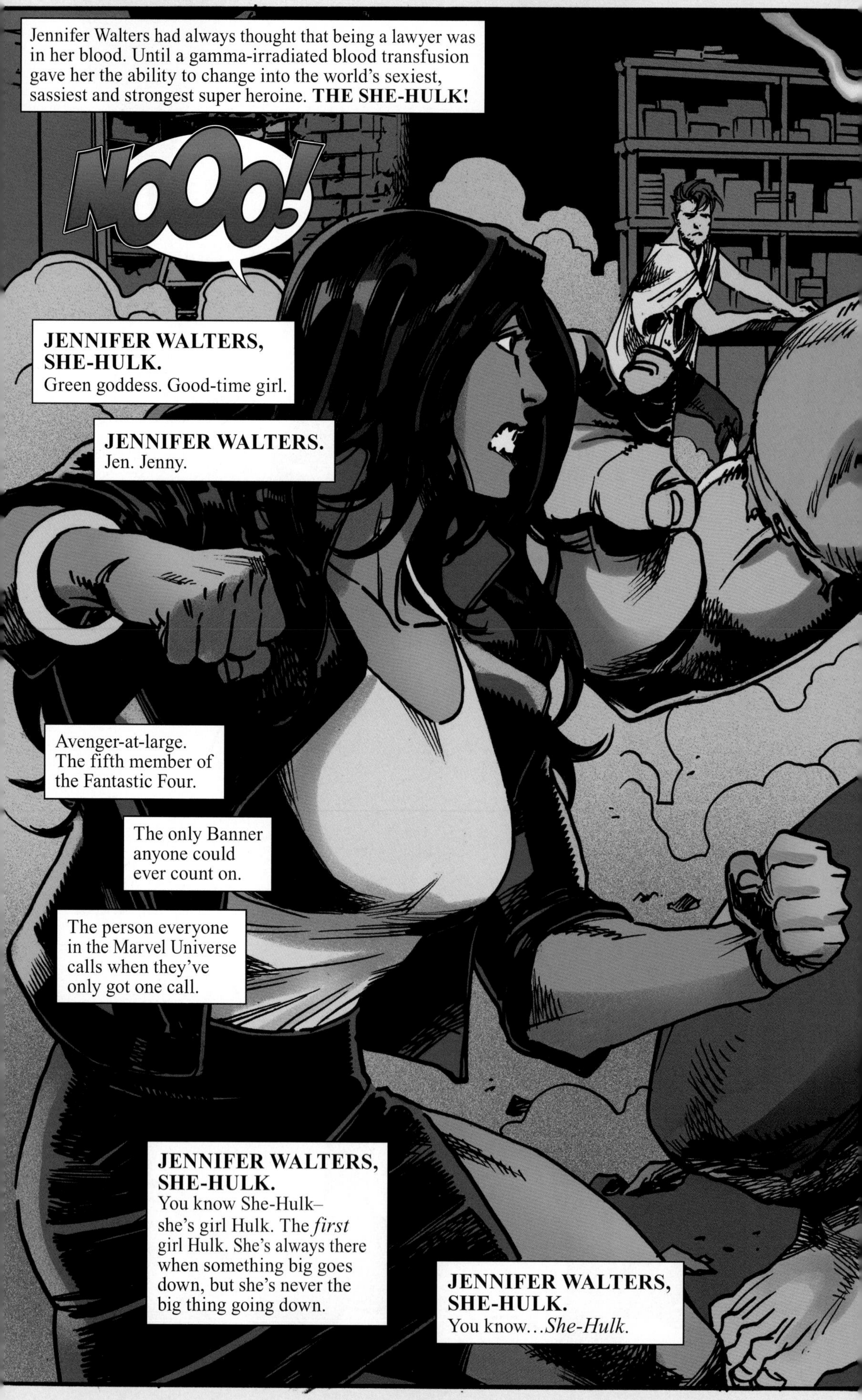
Jennifer Walters had always thought that being a lawyer was in her blood. Until a gamma-irradiated blood transfusion gave her the ability to change into the world's sexiest, sassiest and strongest super heroine. **THE SHE-HULK!**
NOOO!
JENNIFER WALTERS, SHE-HULK. Green goddess. Good-time girl.
JENNIFER WALTERS. Jen. Jenny.
Avenger-at-large. The fifth member of the Fantastic Four.
The only Banner anyone could ever count on.
The person everyone in the Marvel Universe calls when they've only got one call.
JENNIFER WALTERS, SHE-HULK. You know She-Hulk– she's girl Hulk. The *first* girl Hulk. She's always there when something big goes down, but she's never the big thing going down.
JENNIFER WALTERS, SHE-HULK. You know...*She-Hulk.*

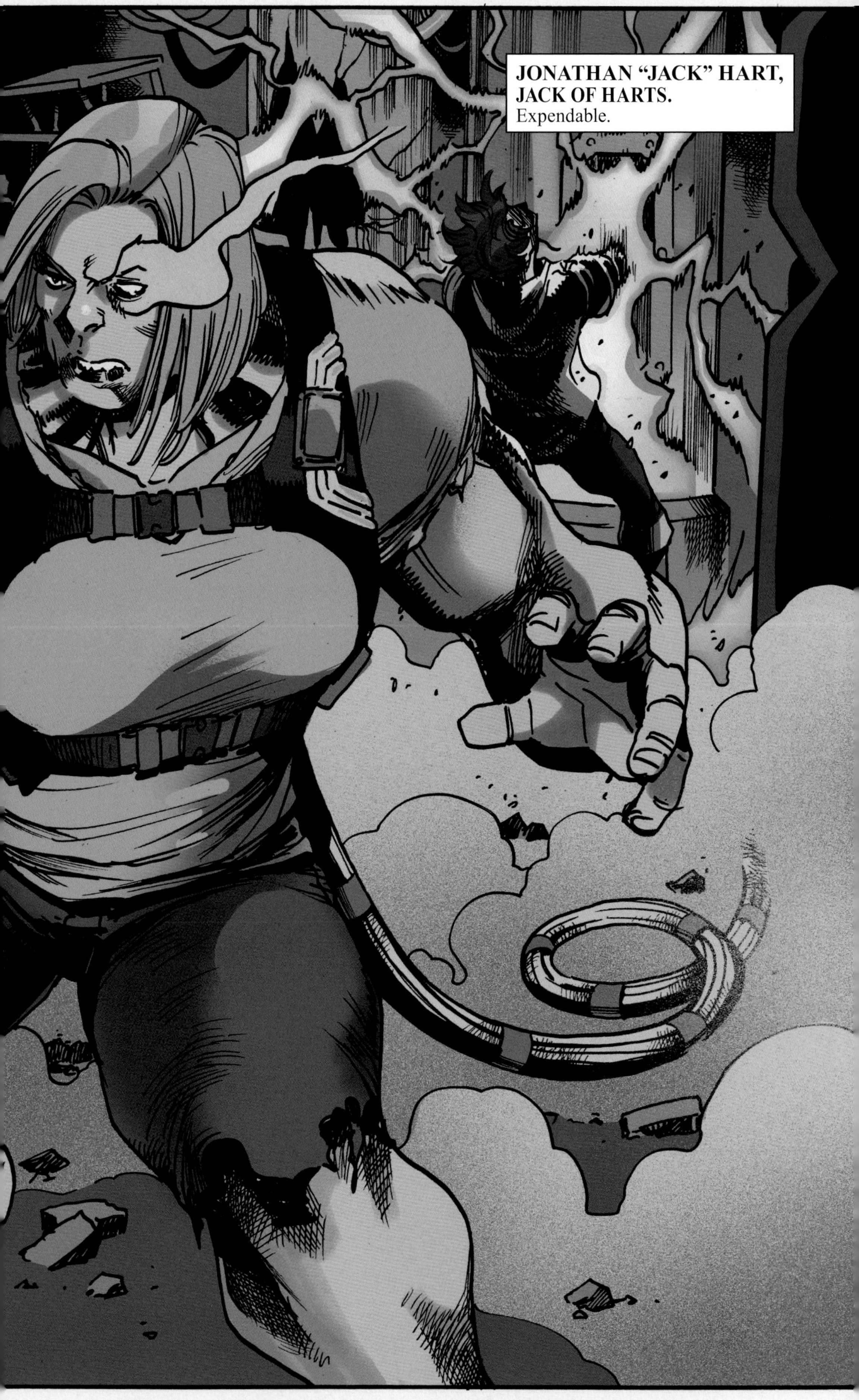
JONATHAN "JACK" HART,
JACK OF HARTS.
Expendable.

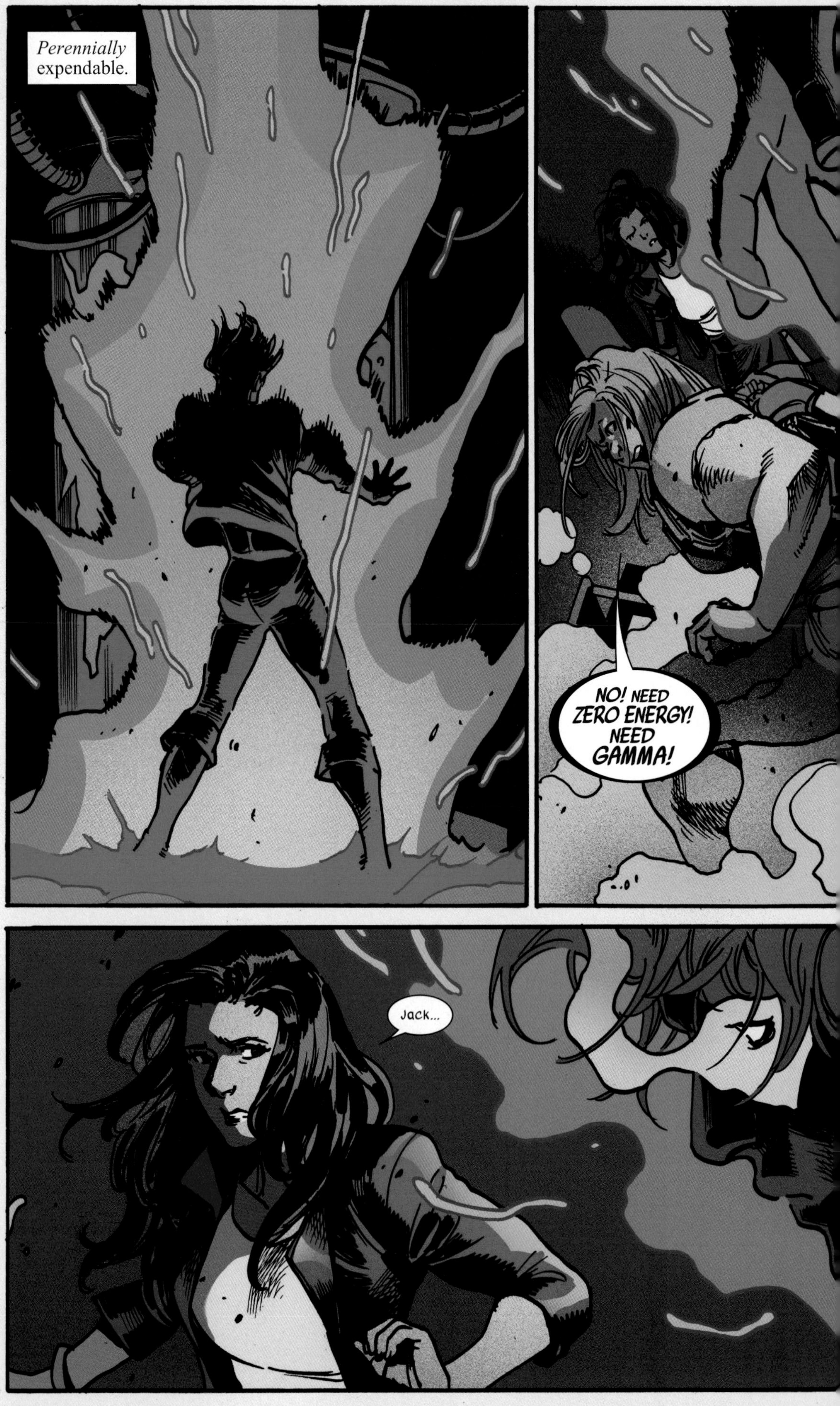
Perennially expendable.
NO! NEED ZERO ENERGY! NEED GAMMA!
Jack...

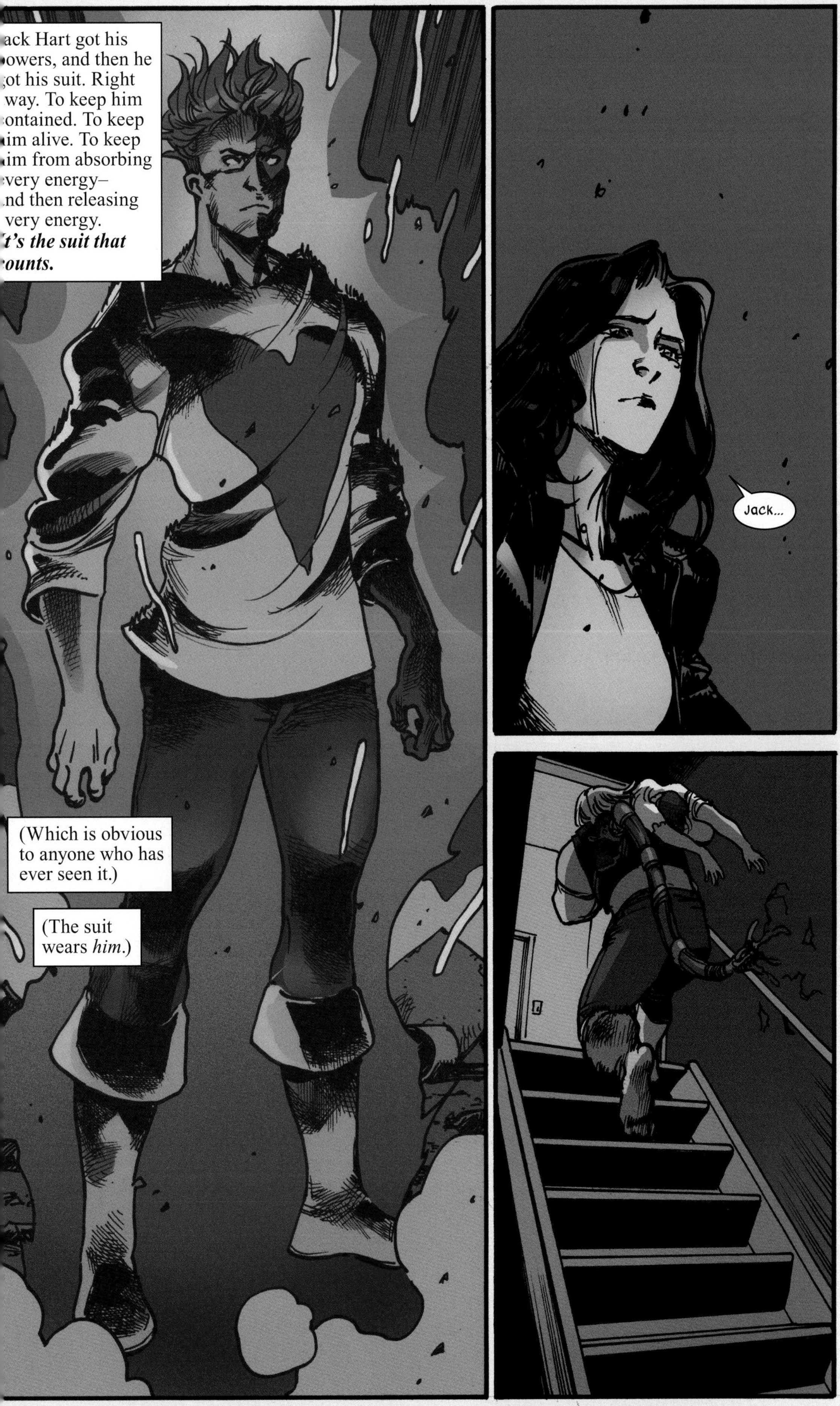
ack Hart got his owers, and then he ;ot his suit. Right way. To keep him ontained. To keep im alive. To keep im from absorbing very energy– nd then releasing very energy. *t's the suit that ounts.*
(Which is obvious to anyone who has ever seen it.)
(The suit wears *him*.)
Jack...

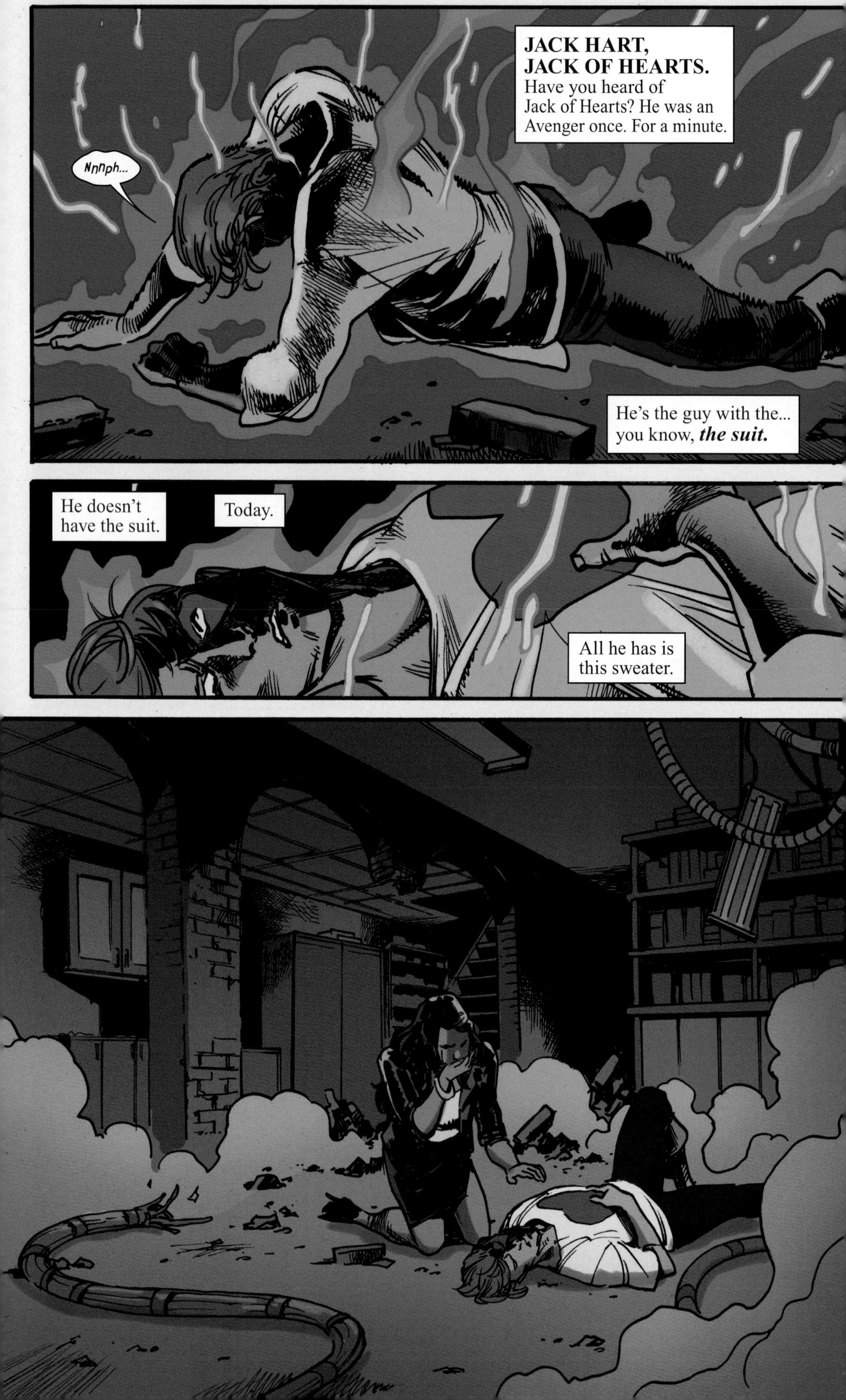
JACK HART,
JACK OF HEARTS.
Have you heard of Jack of Hearts? He was an Avenger once. For a minute.
Nnnph...
He's the guy with the... you know, *the suit.*
He doesn't have the suit.
Today.
All he has is this sweater.

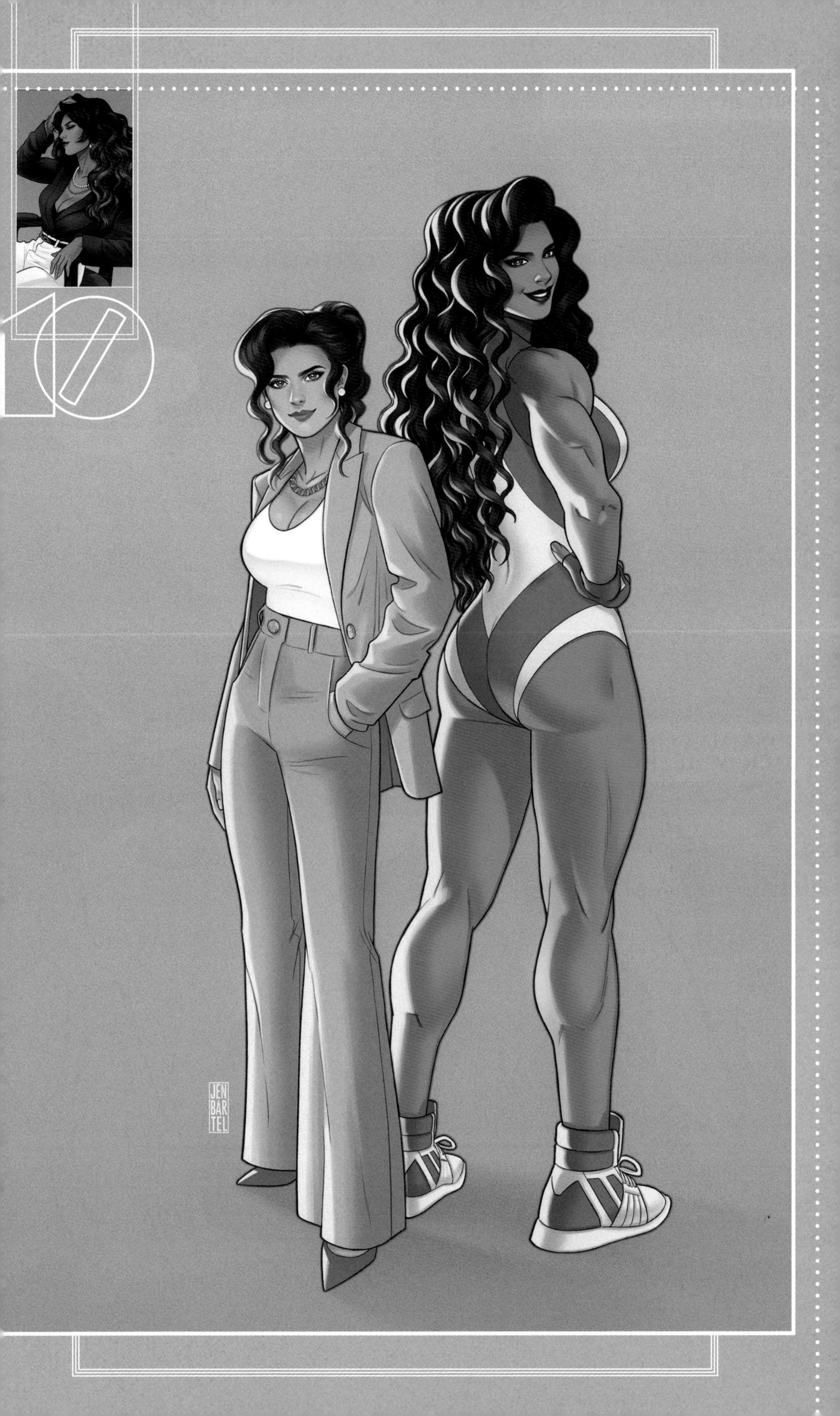
JEN
BAR
TEL

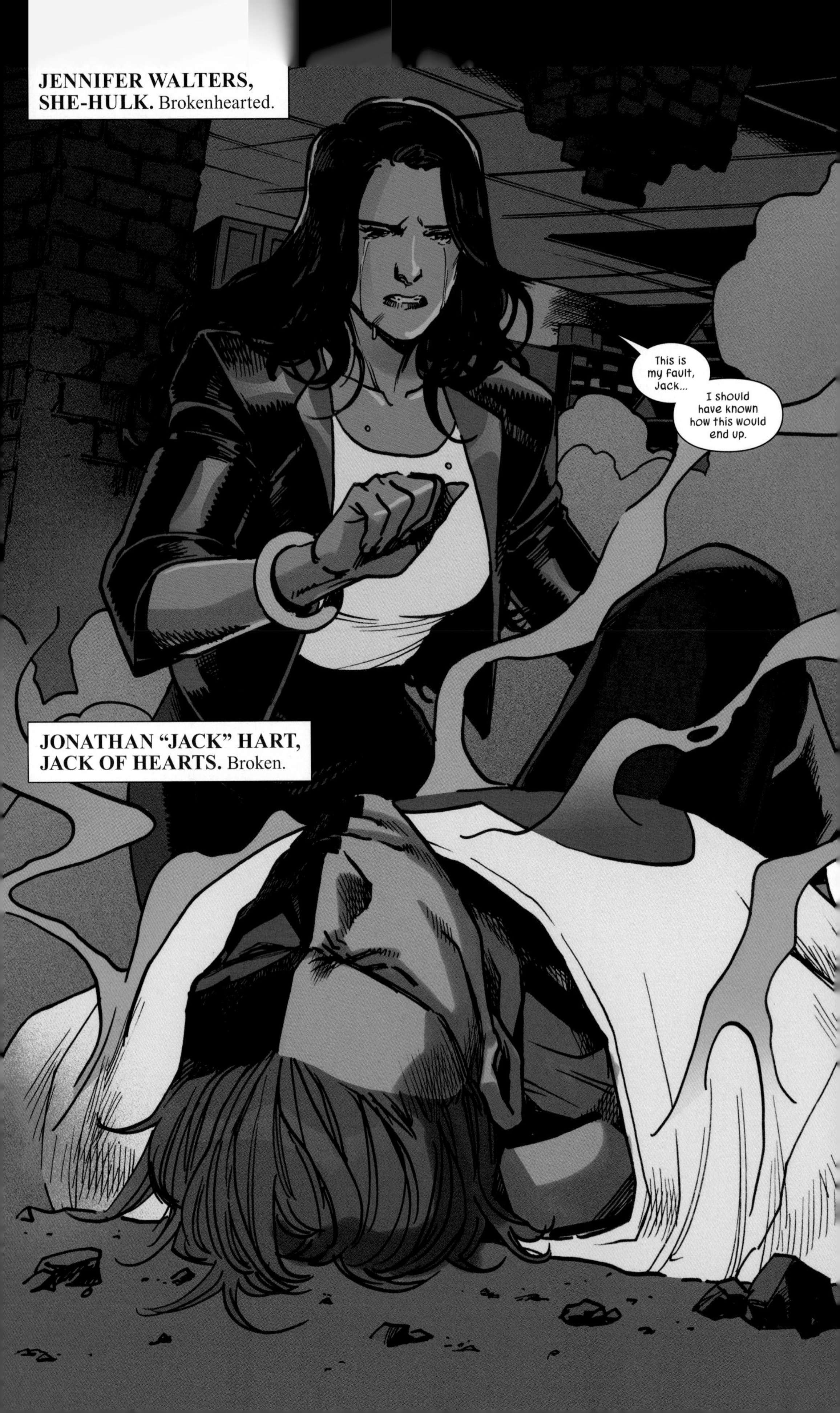
JENNIFER WALTERS, SHE-HULK. Brokenhearted.
This is my fault, Jack...
I should have known how this would end up.
JONATHAN "JACK" HART, JACK OF HEARTS. Broken.

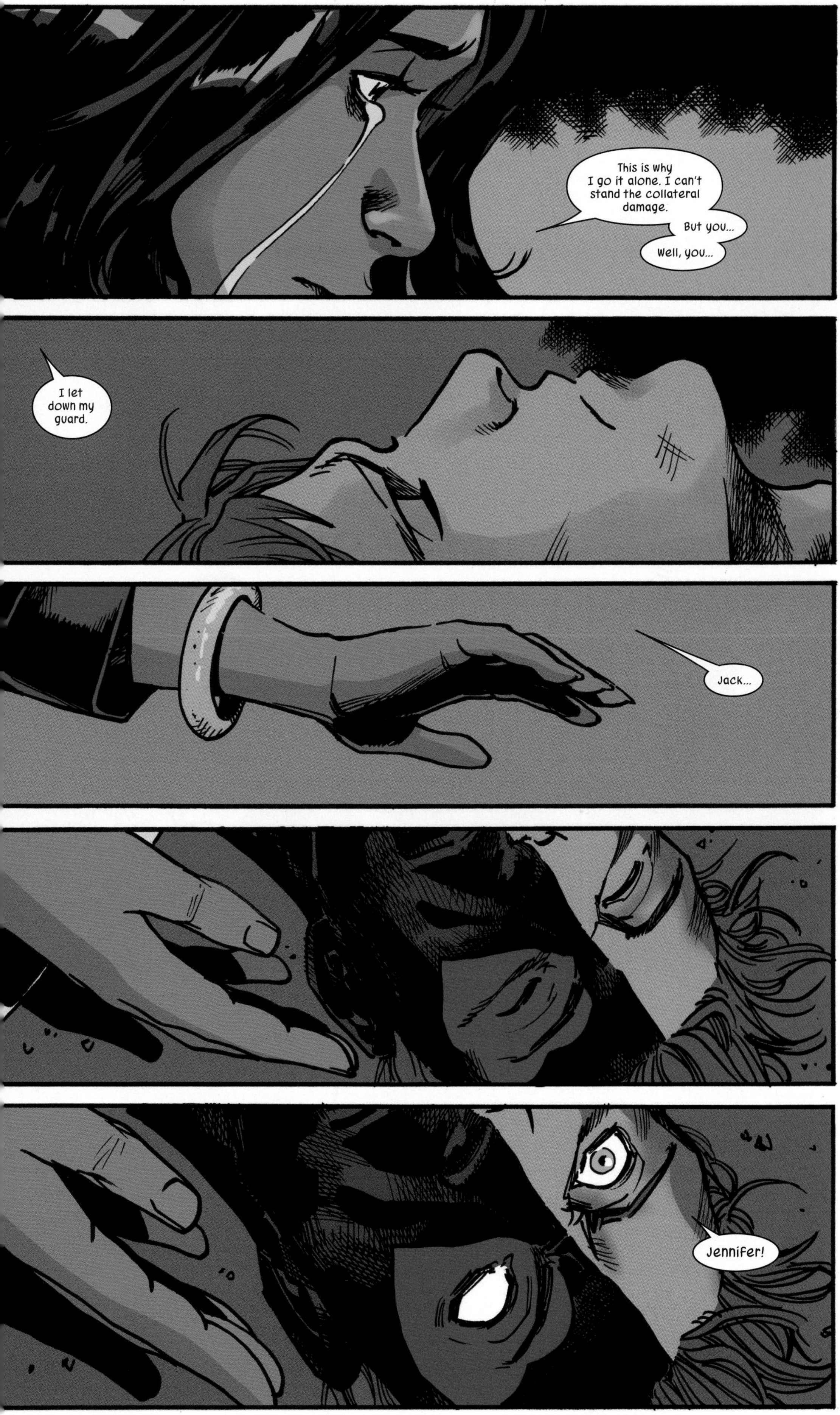
This is why
I go it alone. I can't
stand the collateral
damage.
But you...
Well, you...
I let
down my
guard.
Jack...
Jennifer!

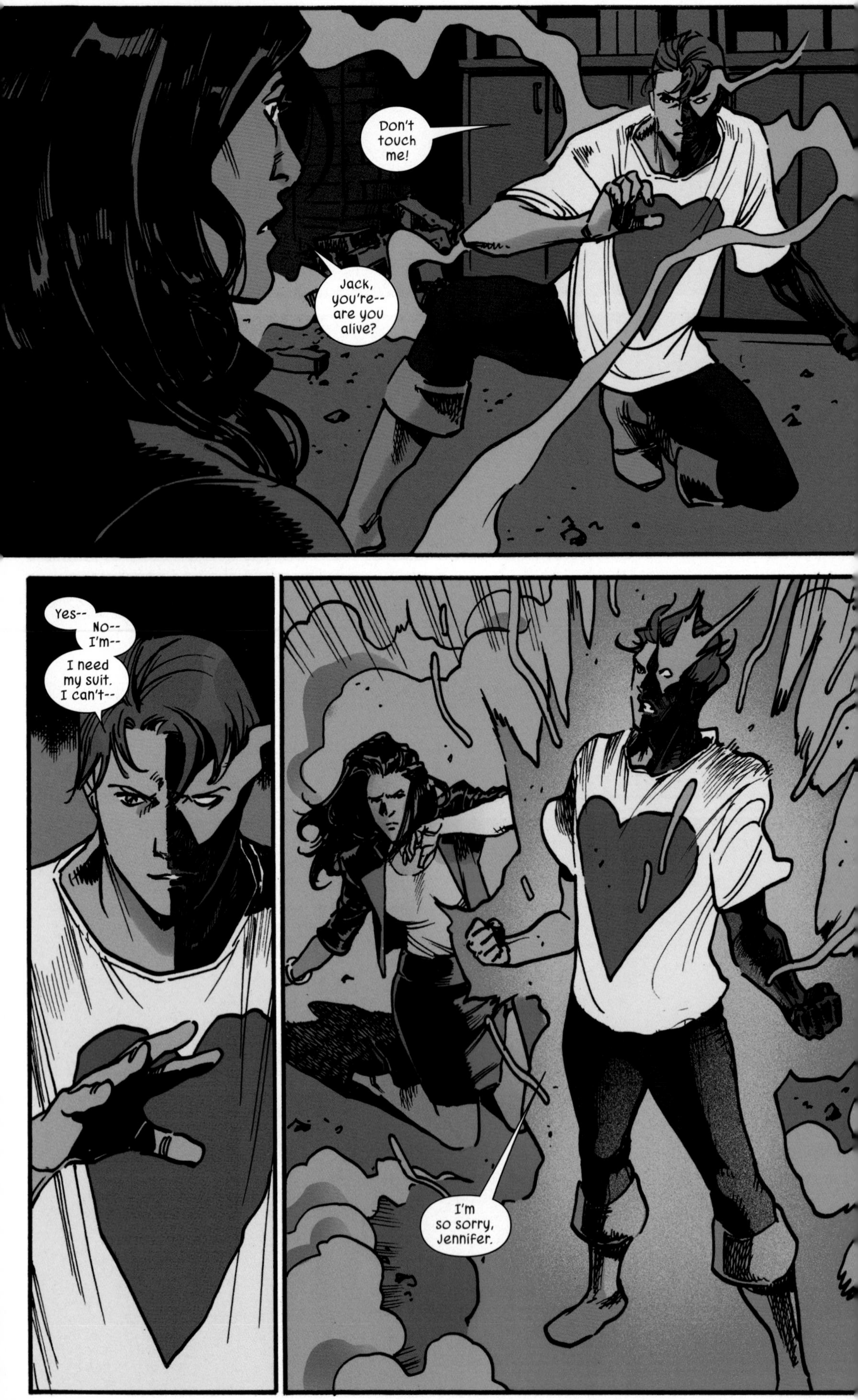
Don't touch me!
Jack, you're-- are you alive?
Yes--
No--
I'm--
I need my suit. I can't--
I'm so sorry, Jennifer.

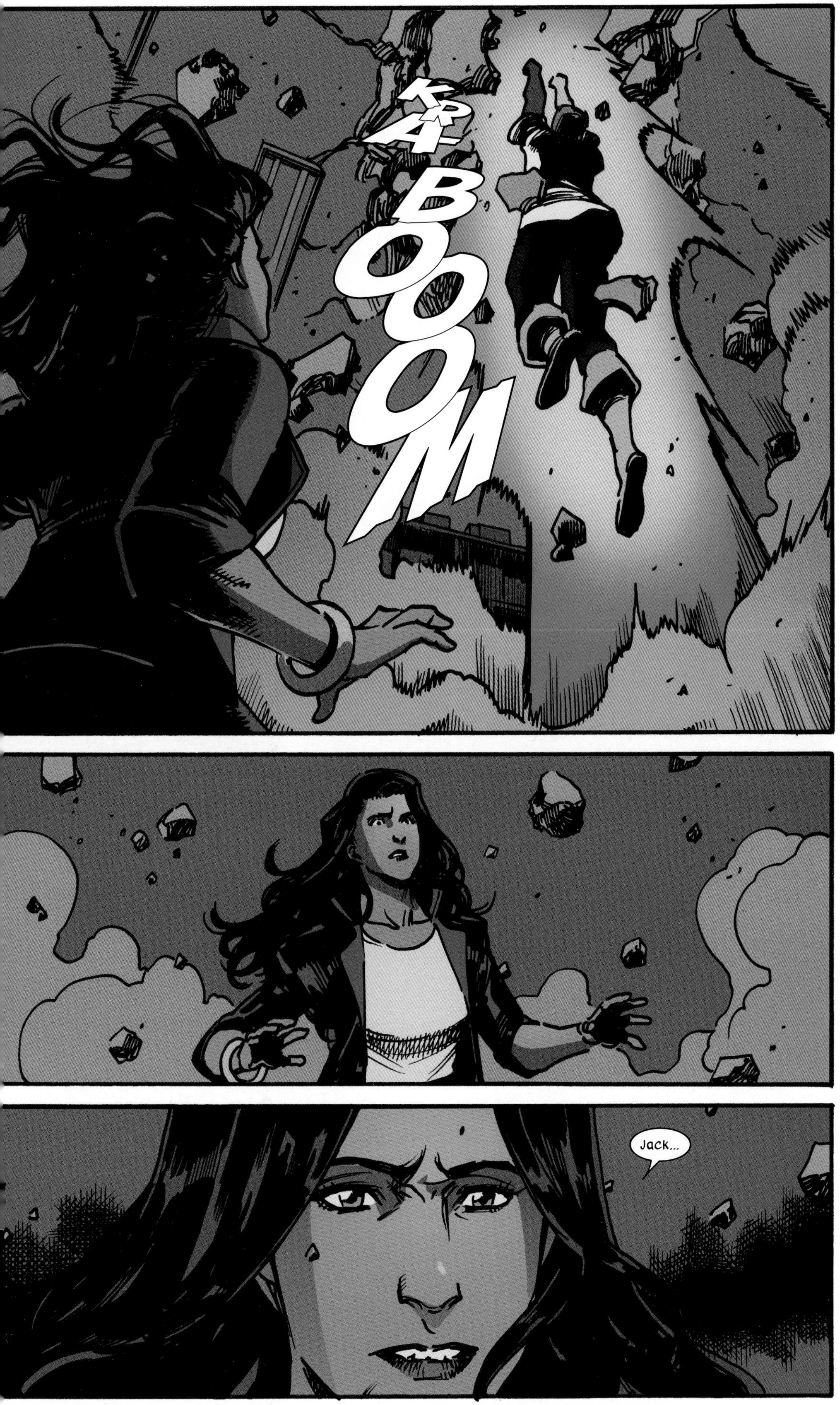
KRA-BOOOOM
Jack...

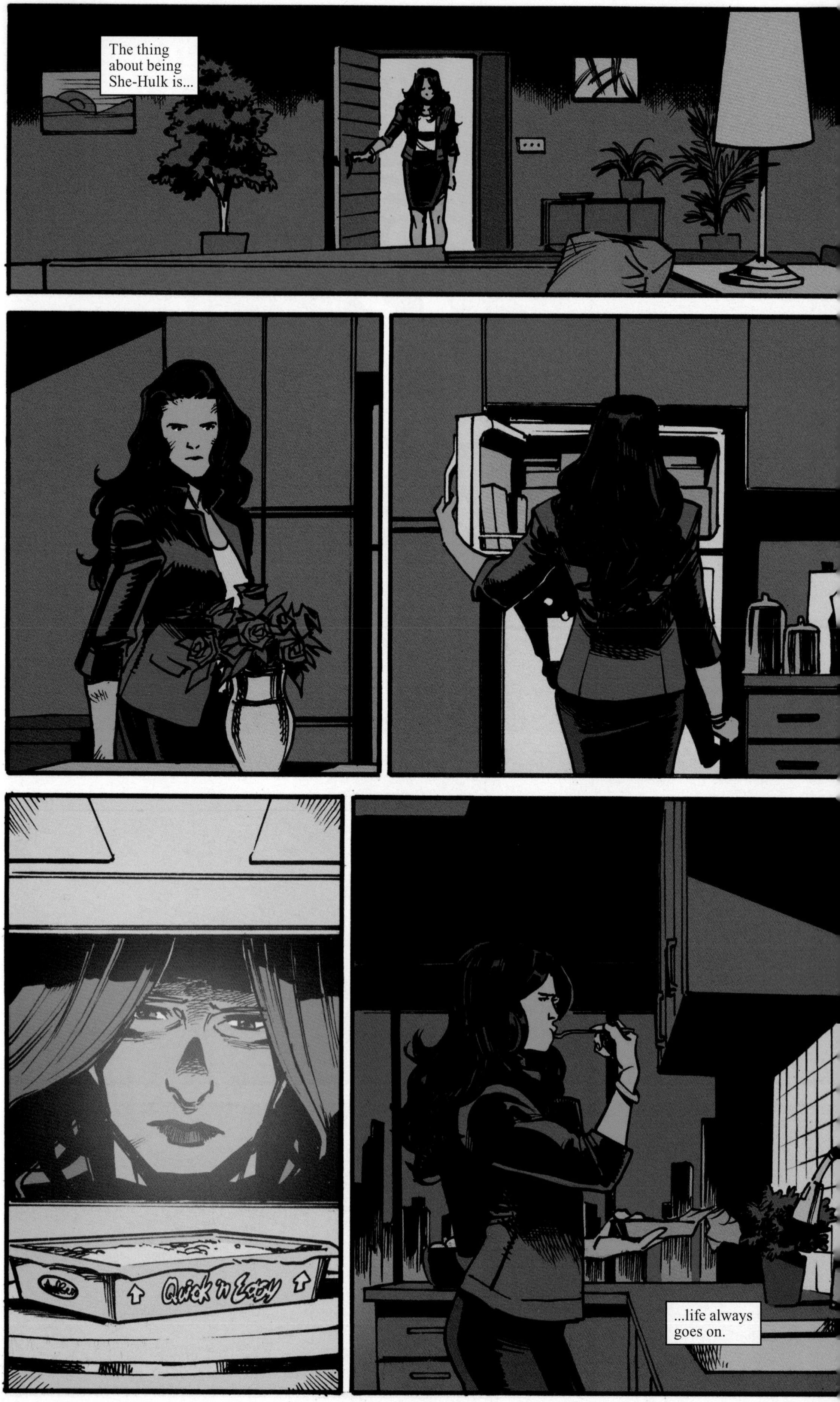

The thing about being She-Hulk is...
Quick 'n Easy
...life always goes on.

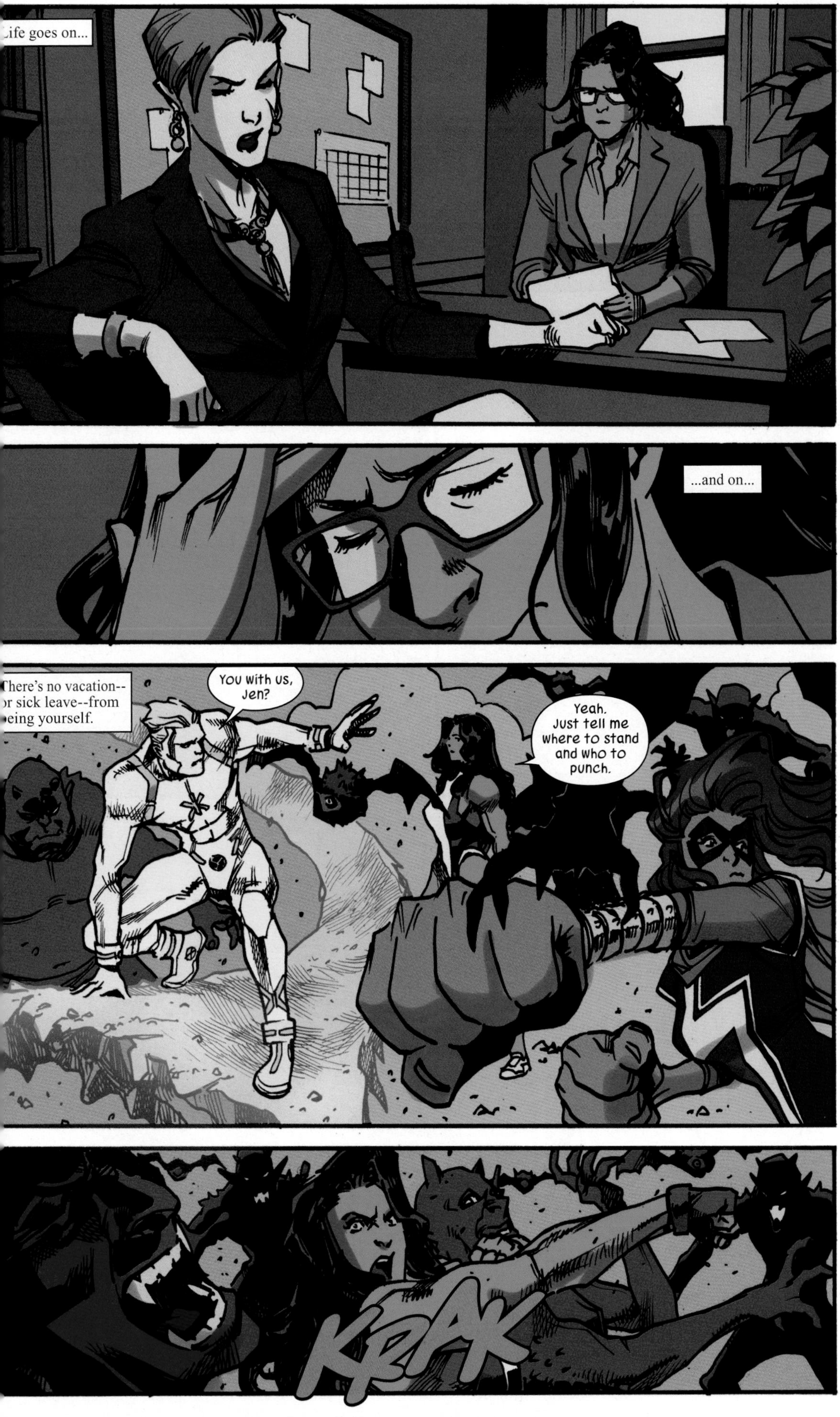
Life goes on...
...and on...
There's no vacation--or sick leave--from being yourself.
You with us, Jen?
Yeah. Just tell me where to stand and who to punch.
KRAK

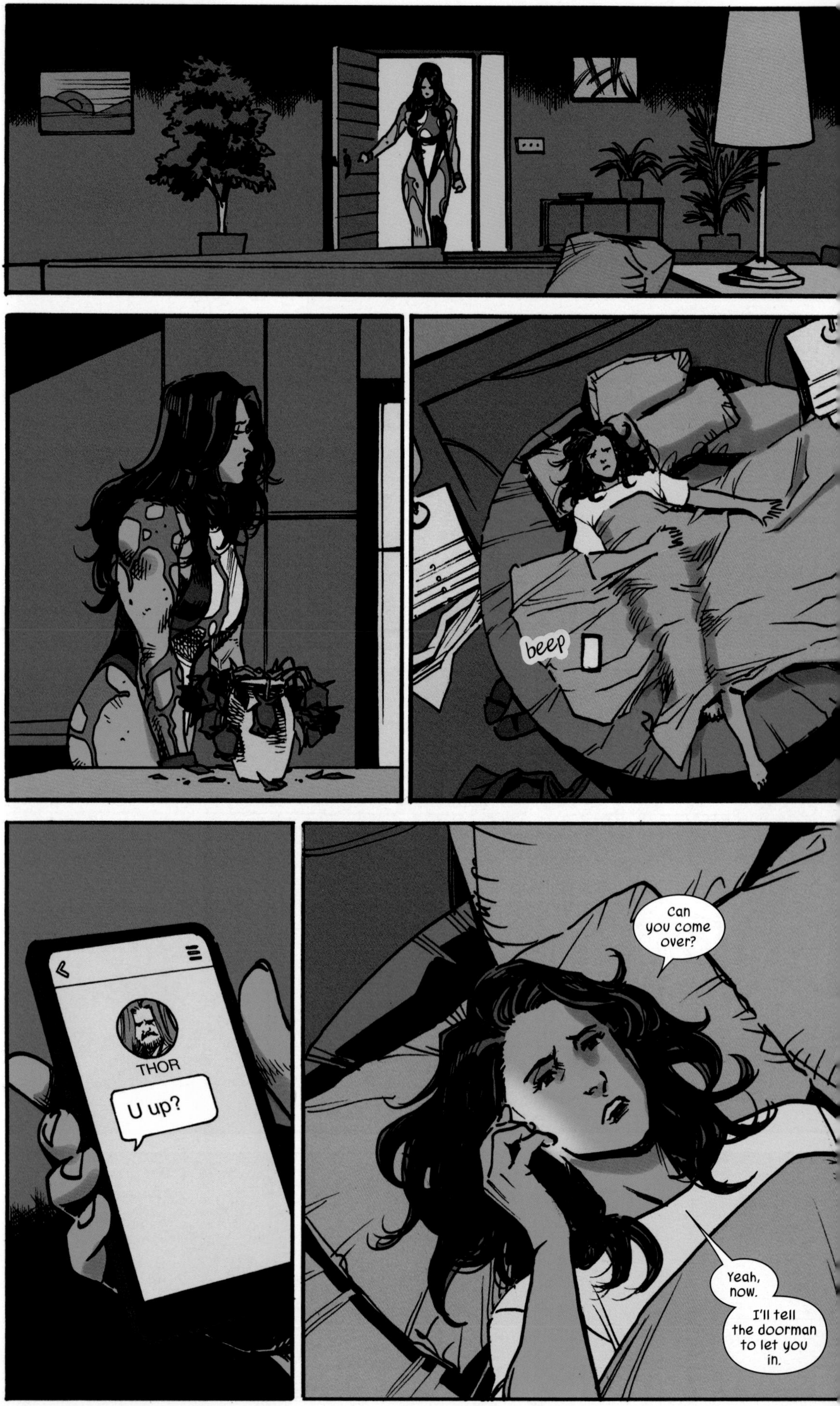
beep
THOR
U up?
Can you come over?
Yeah, now.
I'll tell the doorman to let you in.

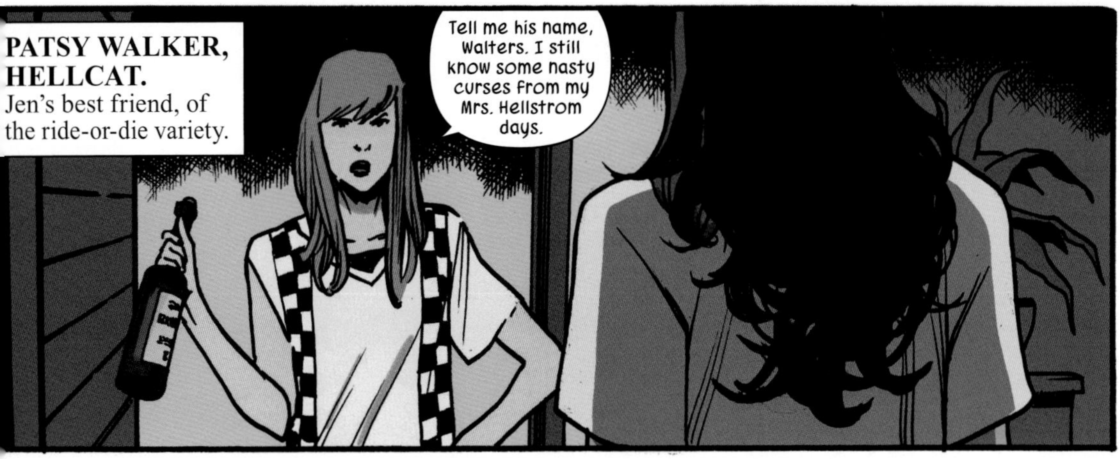
PATSY WALKER, HELLCAT.
Jen's best friend, of the ride-or-die variety.
Tell me his name, Walters. I still know some nasty curses from my Mrs. Hellstrom days.

A FEW MINUTES LATER...

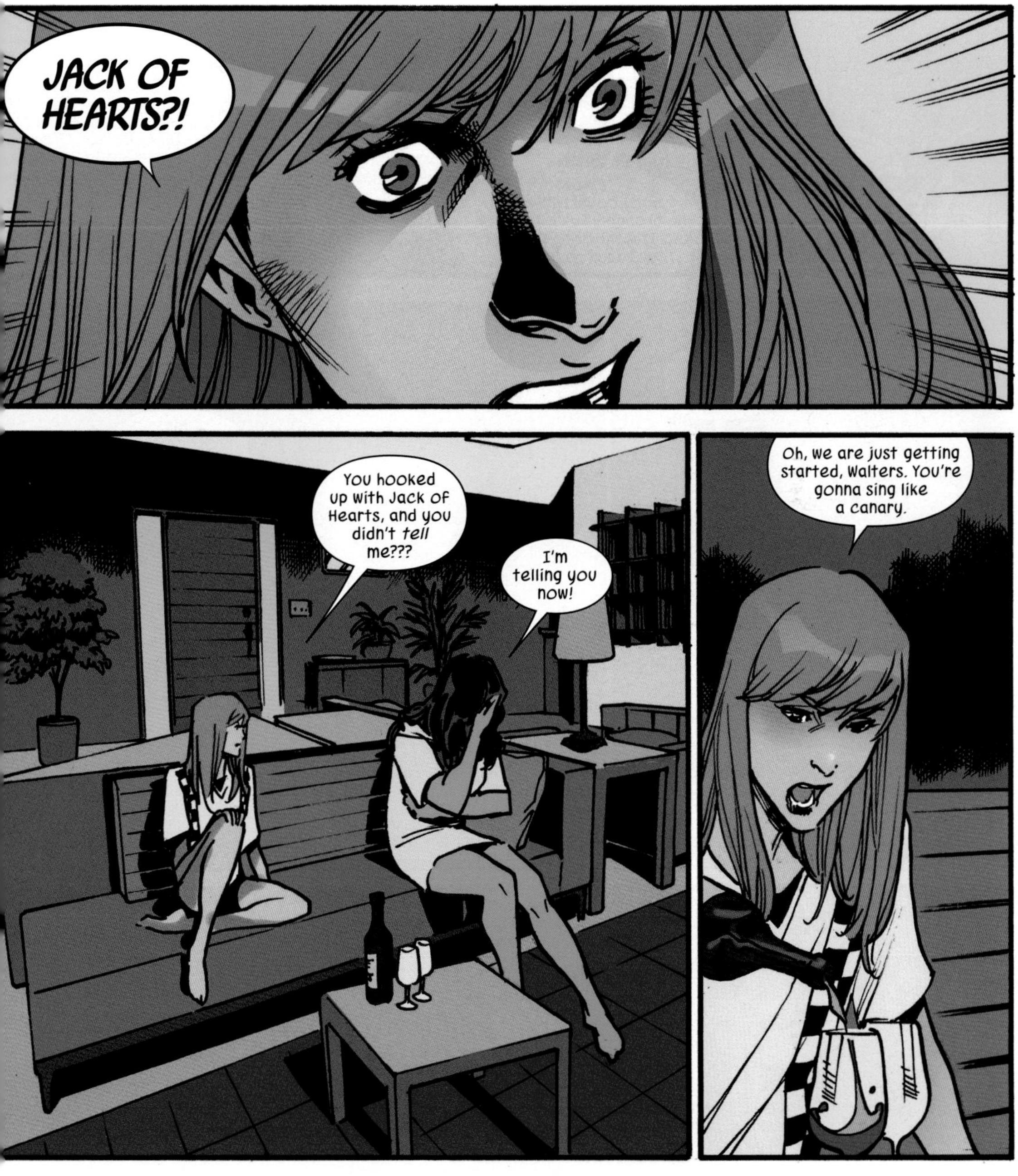
JACK OF HEARTS?!
You hooked up with Jack of Hearts, and you didn't *tell* me???
I'm telling you now!
Oh, we are just getting started, Walters. You're gonna sing like a canary.

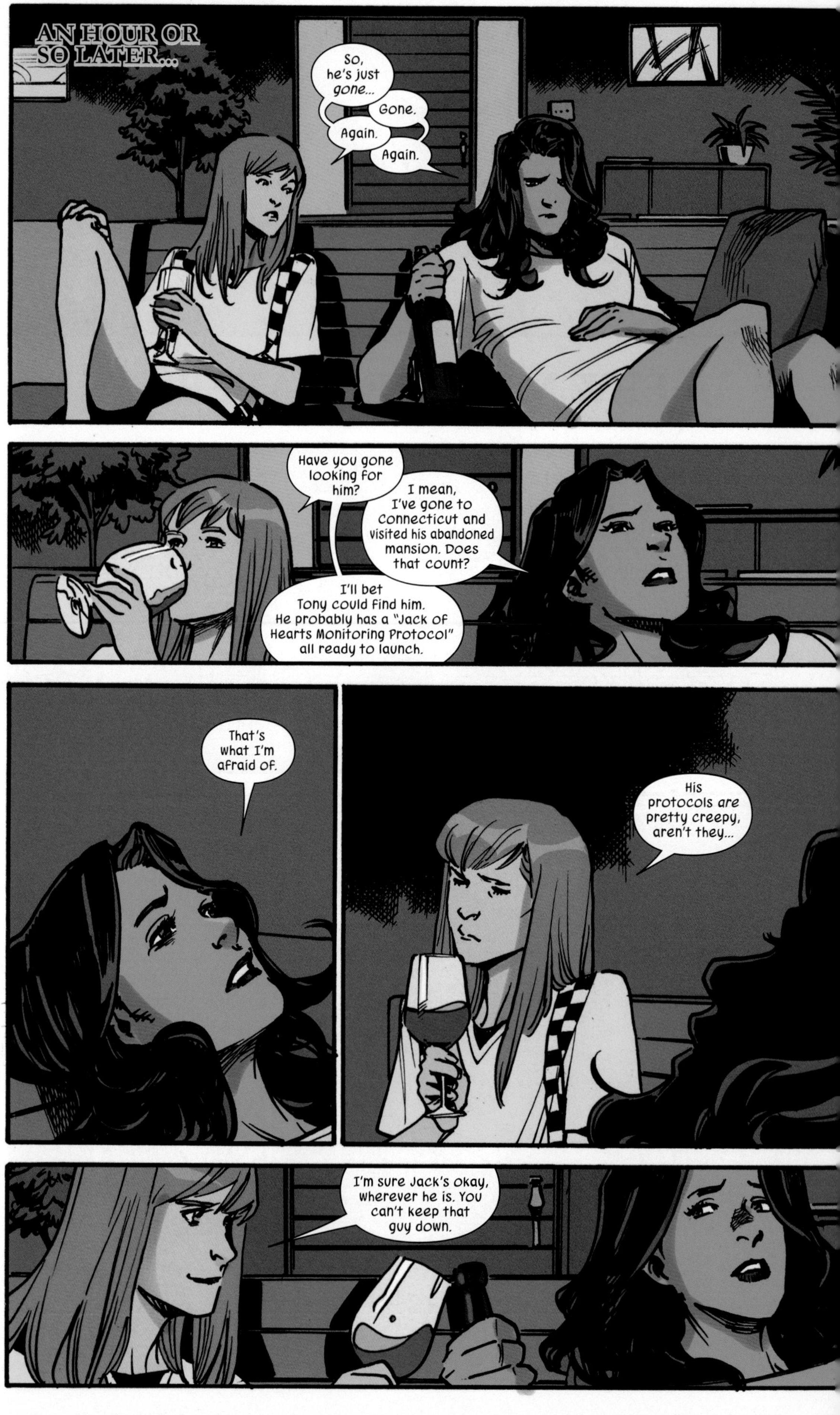
AN HOUR OR SO LATER...
So, he's just *gone*...
Gone.
Again.
Again.
Have you gone looking for him?
I mean, I've gone to Connecticut and visited his abandoned mansion. Does that count?
I'll bet Tony could find him. He probably has a "Jack of Hearts Monitoring Protocol" all ready to launch.
That's what I'm afraid of.
His protocols are pretty creepy, aren't they...
I'm sure Jack's okay, wherever he is. You can't keep that guy down.

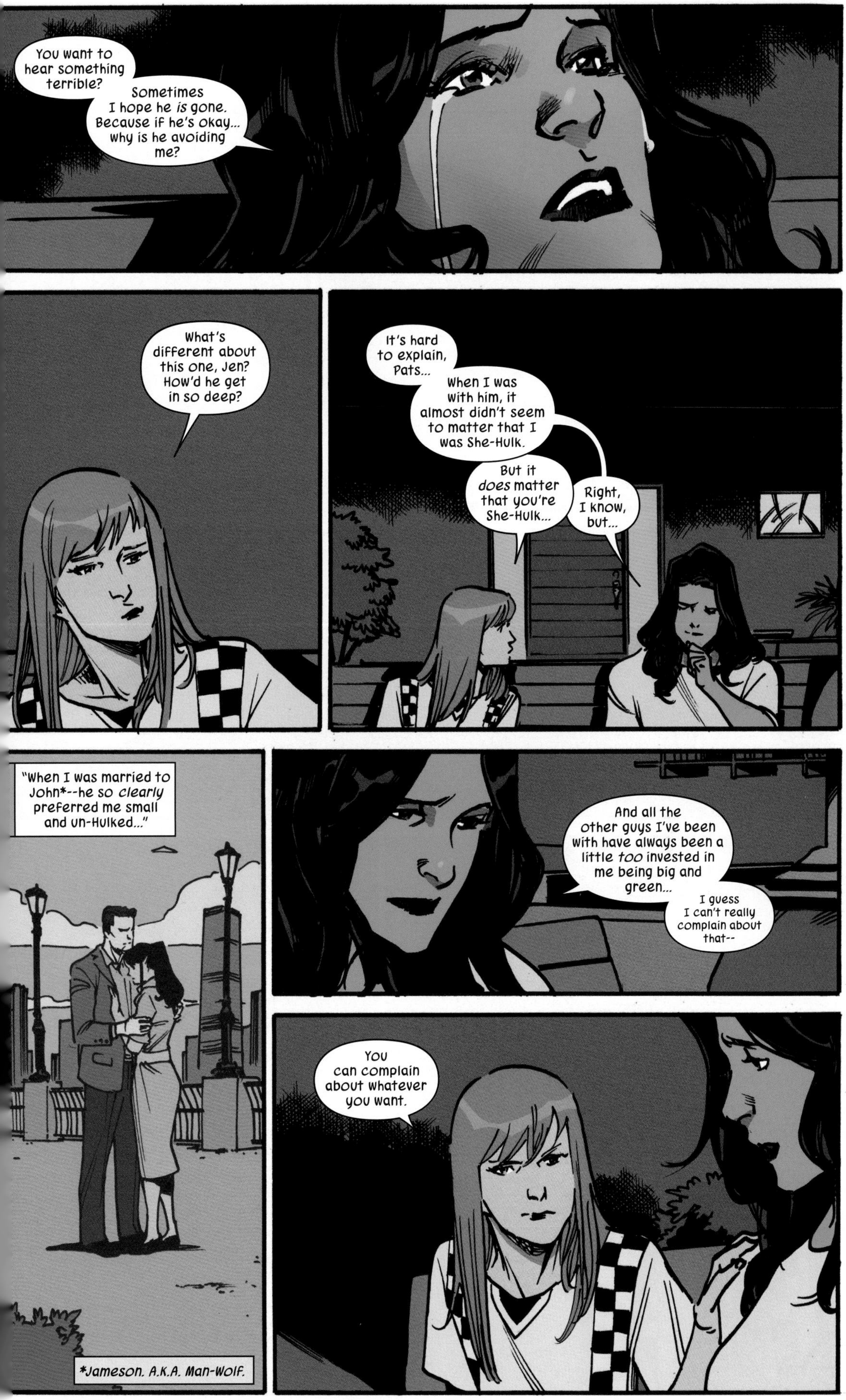
You want to hear something terrible?
Sometimes I hope he *is* gone. Because if he's okay... why is he avoiding me?
What's different about this one, Jen? How'd he get in so deep?
It's hard to explain, Pats...
When I was with him, it almost didn't seem to matter that I was She-Hulk.
But it *does* matter that you're She-Hulk...
Right, I know, but...
"When I was married to John*--he so *clearly* preferred me small and un-Hulked..."
*Jameson. A.K.A. Man-Wolf.
And all the other guys I've been with have always been a little *too* invested in me being big and green...
I guess I can't really complain about that--
You can complain about whatever you want.

I mean, Wyatt* was different.

But Wyatt took his responsibilities-- and mine--so seriously...

*Wingfoot. Jen's former fiancé and Johnny Storm's best friend.

"We were never really focused on each other for long."

And Jack?

Jack made me feel like I was Jennifer Walters again, the person I was before all of this started.

But also like I was Jennifer Walters, She-Hulk-- the person I am now.

Like I could be everything.

Babe, you are everything.

You're, like, the *most* everything.

I just really miss him, Patsy.

I know...

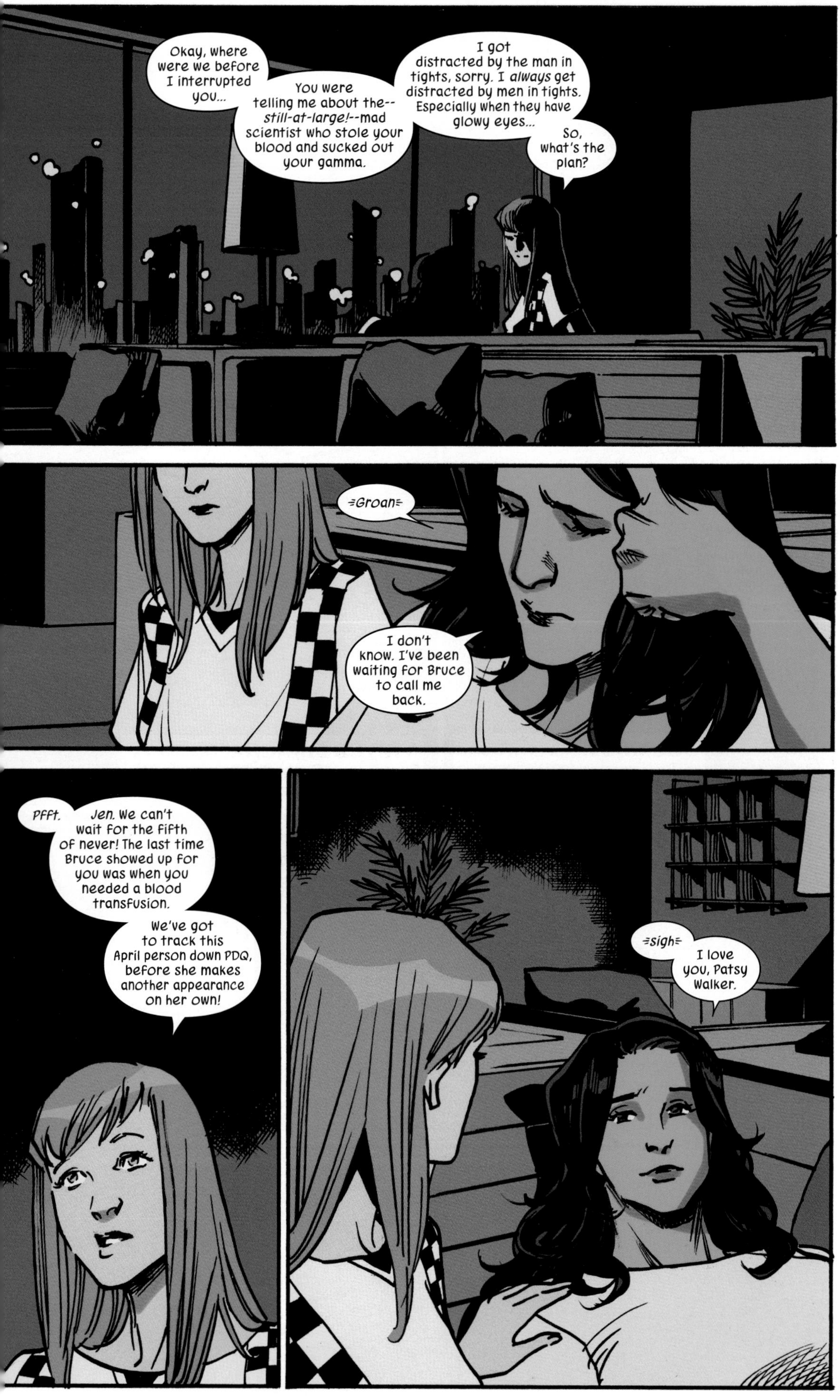

Okay, where were we before I interrupted you...
You were telling me about the-- *still-at-large!*--mad scientist who stole your blood and sucked out your gamma.
I got distracted by the man in tights, sorry. I *always* get distracted by men in tights. Especially when they have glowy eyes...
So, what's the plan?
=Groan=
I don't know. I've been waiting for Bruce to call me back.
Pfft.
Jen. We can't wait for the fifth of never! The last time Bruce showed up for you was when you needed a blood transfusion.
We've got to track this April person down PDQ, before she makes another appearance on her own!
=sigh=
I love you, Patsy Walker.

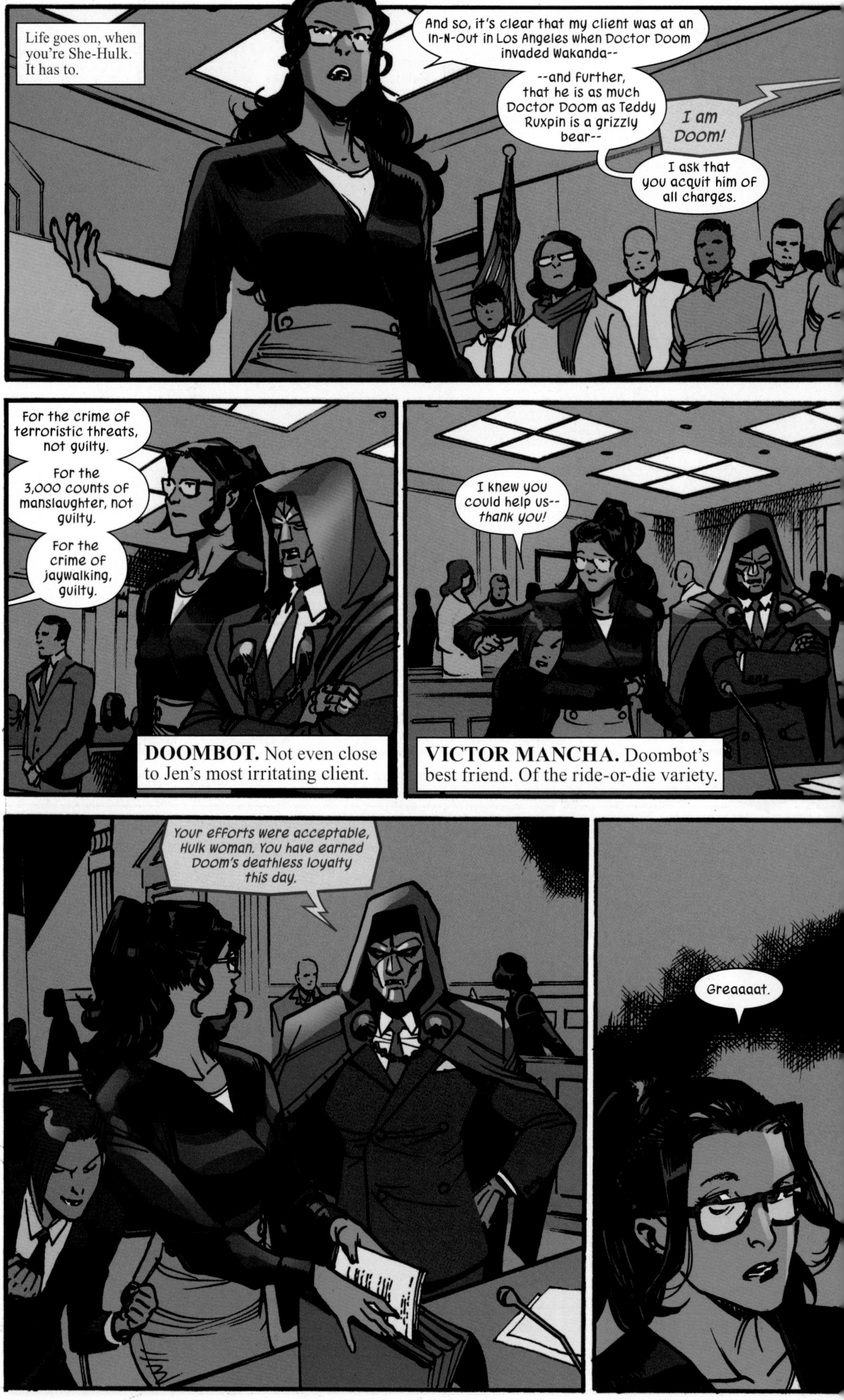
Life goes on, when you're She-Hulk. It has to.
And so, it's clear that my client was at an In-N-Out in Los Angeles when Doctor Doom invaded Wakanda--
--and further, that he is as much Doctor Doom as Teddy Ruxpin is a grizzly bear--
I am Doom!
I ask that you acquit him of all charges.
For the crime of terroristic threats, not guilty.
For the 3,000 counts of manslaughter, not guilty.
For the crime of jaywalking, guilty.
DOOMBOT. Not even close to Jen's most irritating client.
I knew you could help us--thank you!
VICTOR MANCHA. Doombot's best friend. Of the ride-or-die variety.
Your efforts were acceptable, Hulk woman. You have earned Doom's deathless loyalty this day.
Greaaaat.

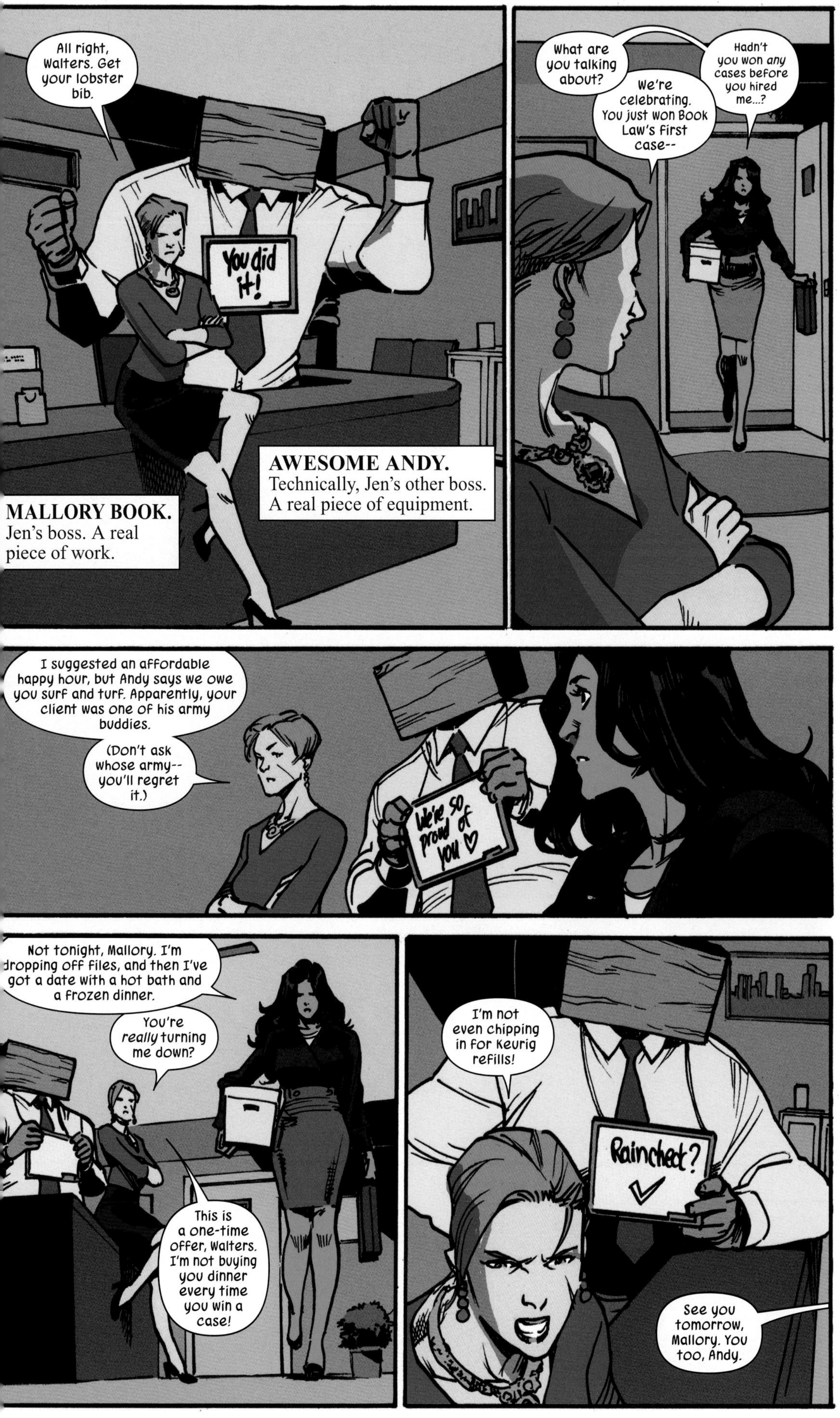
All right, Walters. Get your lobster bib.
You did it!
AWESOME ANDY. Technically, Jen's other boss. A real piece of equipment.
MALLORY BOOK. Jen's boss. A real piece of work.
What are you talking about?
We're celebrating. You just won Book Law's first case--
Hadn't you won any cases before you hired me...?
I suggested an affordable happy hour, but Andy says we owe you surf and turf. Apparently, your client was one of his army buddies.
(Don't ask whose army-- you'll regret it.)
We're so proud of you ♡
Not tonight, Mallory. I'm dropping off files, and then I've got a date with a hot bath and a frozen dinner.
You're *really* turning me down?
This is a one-time offer, Walters. I'm not buying you dinner every time you win a case!
I'm not even chipping in for Keurig refills!
Raincheck?
See you tomorrow, Mallory. You too, Andy.

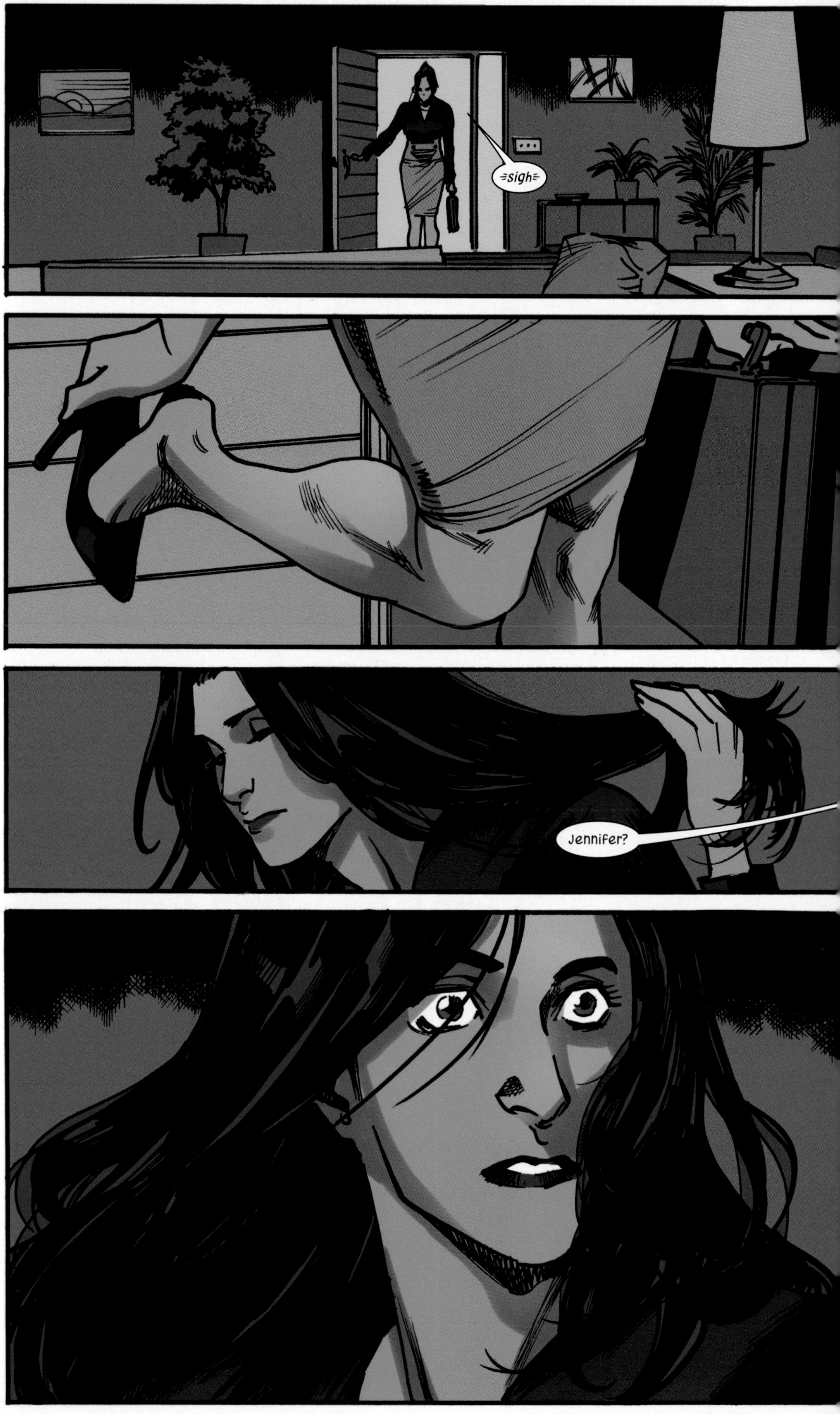
sigh
Jennifer?

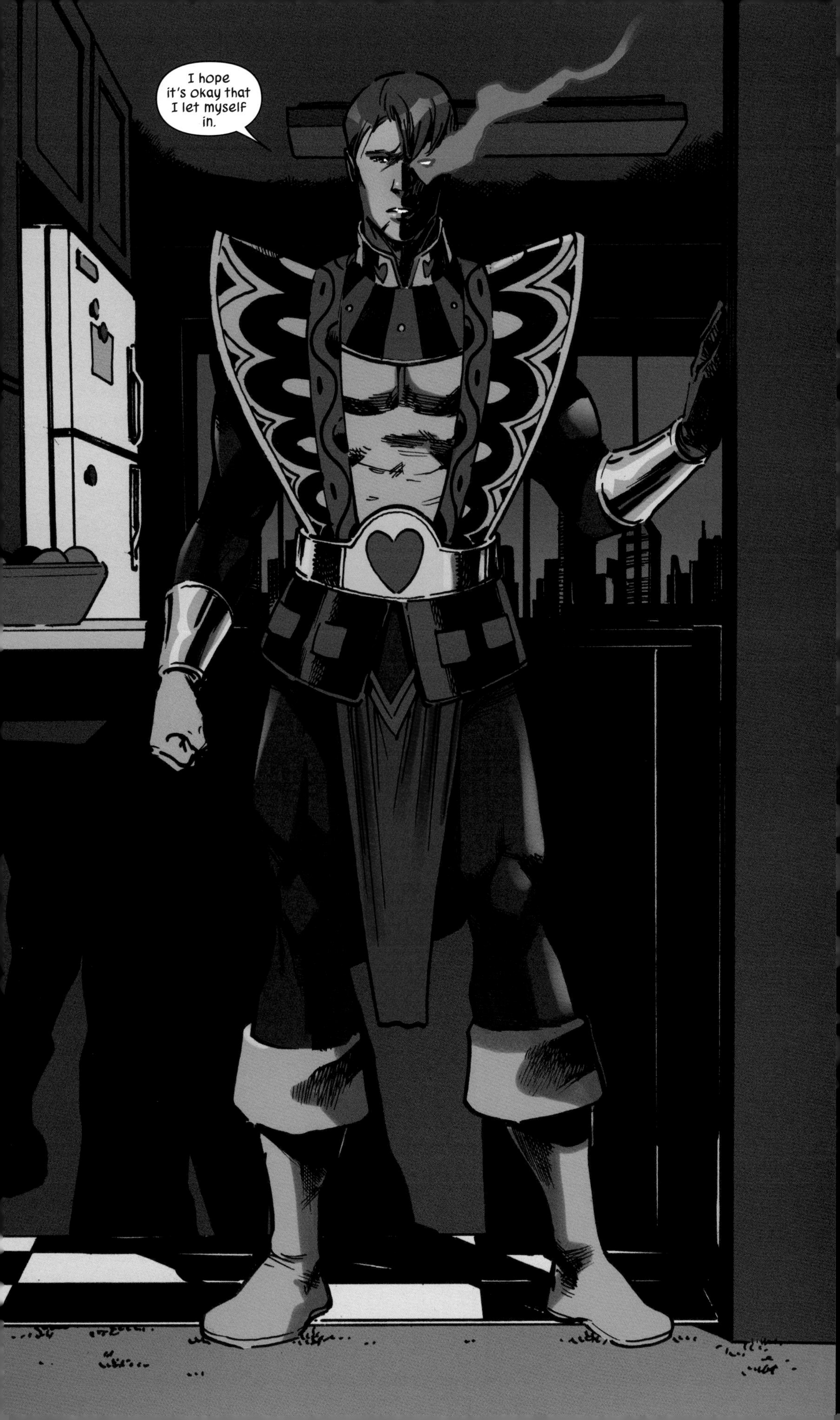
I hope it's okay that I let myself in.

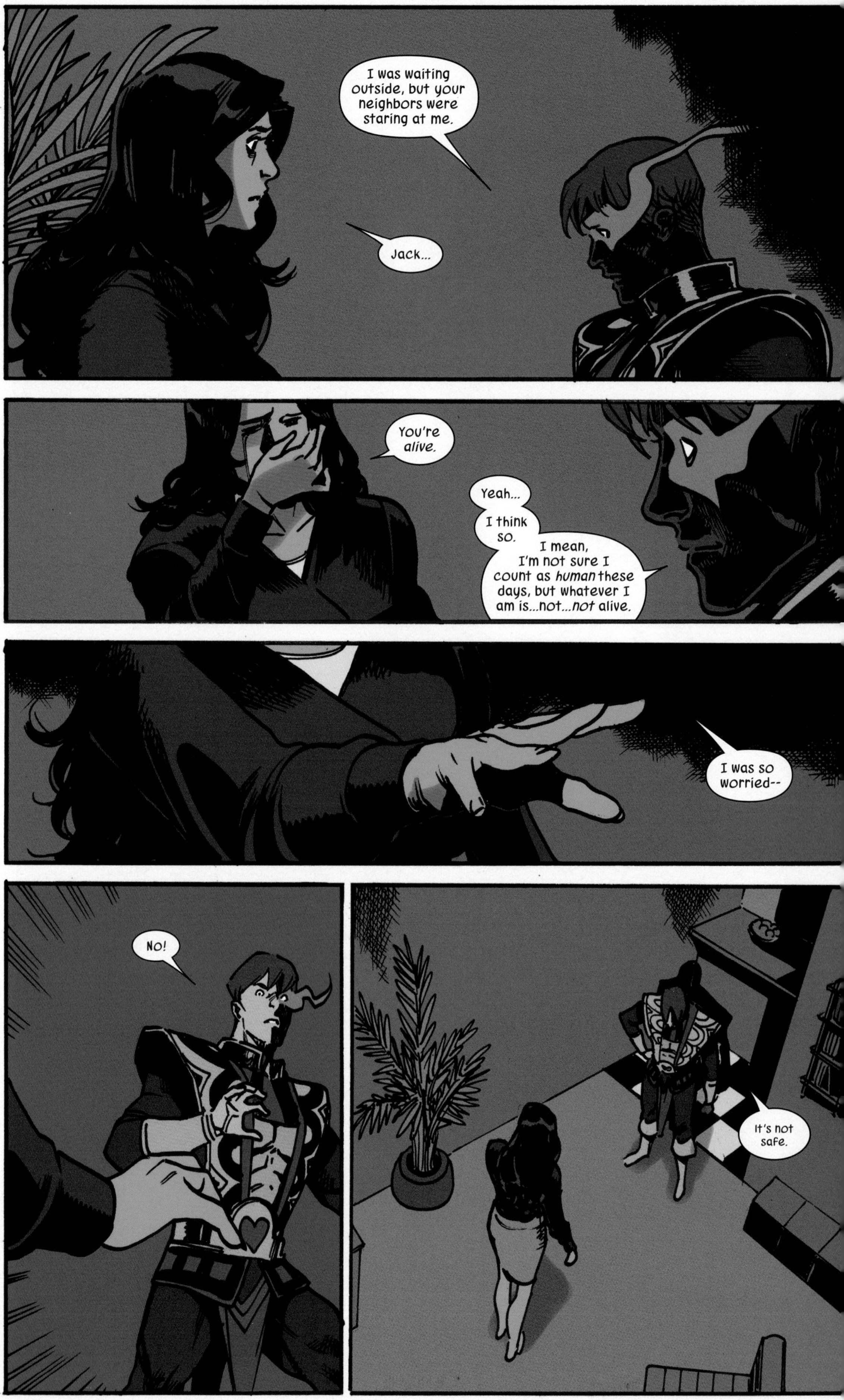
I was waiting outside, but your neighbors were staring at me.
Jack...
You're *alive.*
Yeah...
I think so.
I mean, I'm not sure I count as *human* these days, but whatever I am is...not...*not* alive.
I was so worried--
No!
It's not safe.

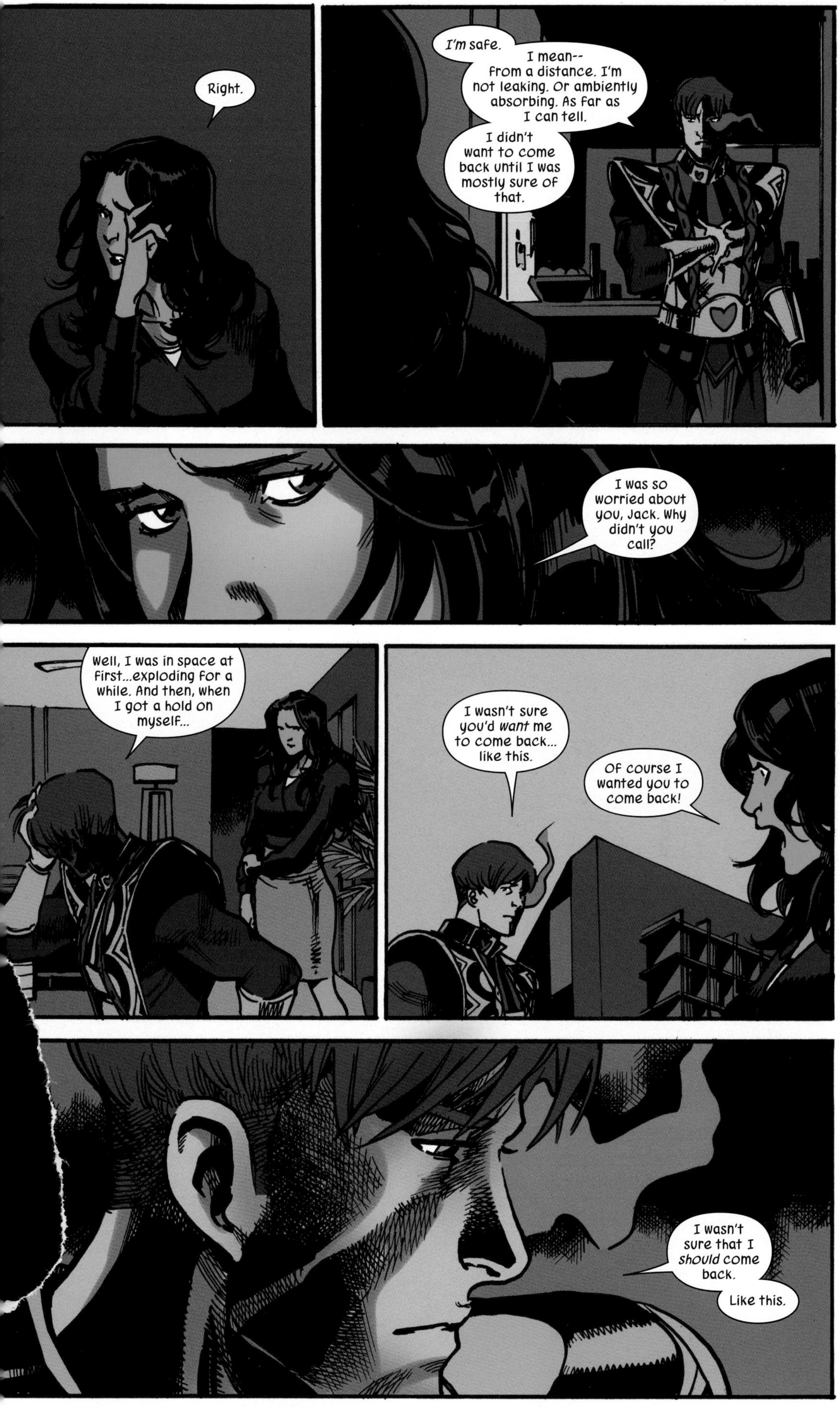
Right.
I'm safe.
I mean-- from a distance. I'm not leaking. Or ambiently absorbing. As far as I can tell.
I didn't want to come back until I was mostly sure of that.
I was so worried about you, Jack. Why didn't you call?
Well, I was in space at first...exploding for a while. And then, when I got a hold on myself...
I wasn't sure you'd *want* me to come back... like this.
Of course I wanted you to come back!
I wasn't sure that I *should* come back.
Like this.

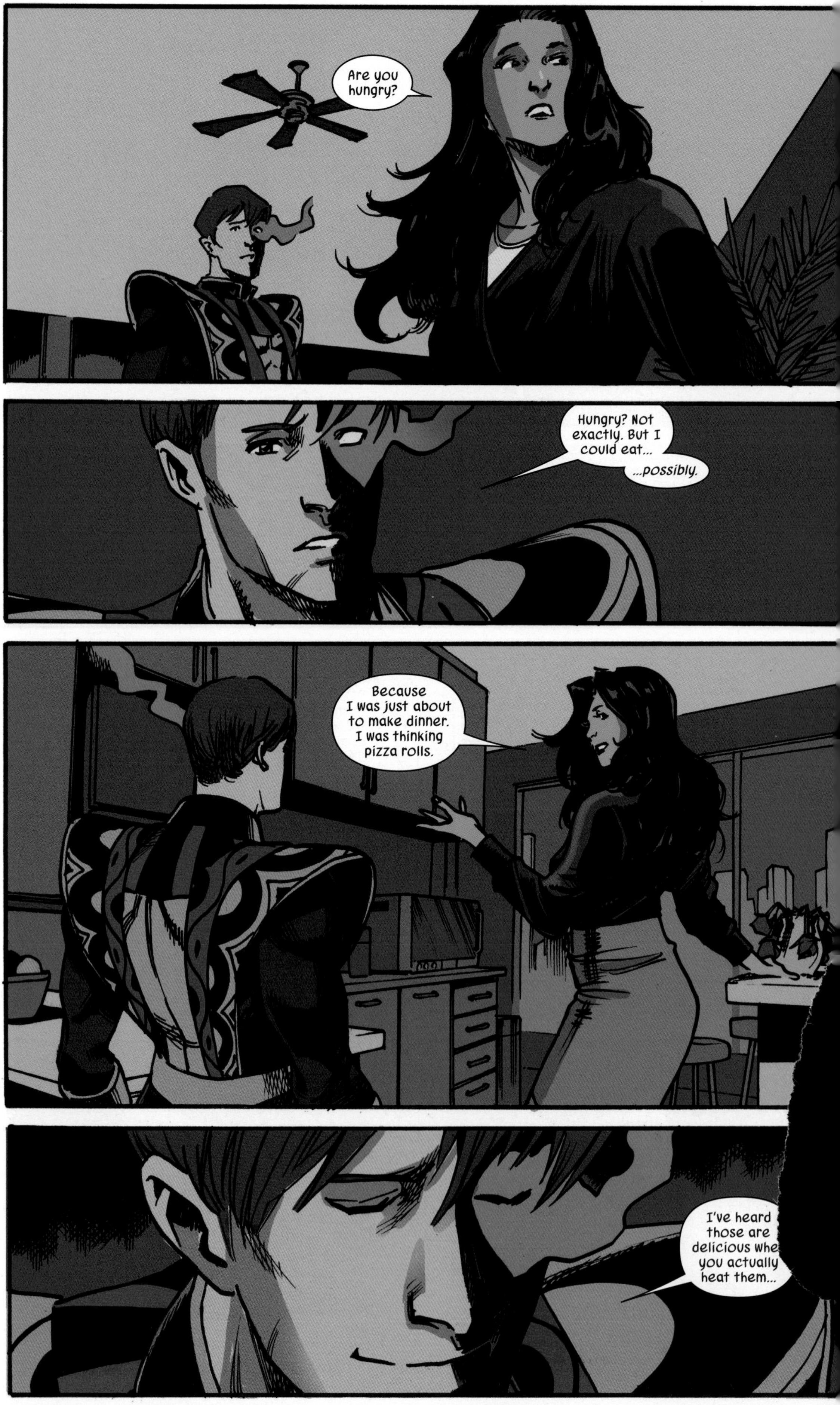

Are you hungry?
Hungry? Not exactly. But I could eat...
...possibly.
Because I was just about to make dinner. I was thinking pizza rolls.
I've heard those are delicious whe you actually heat them...

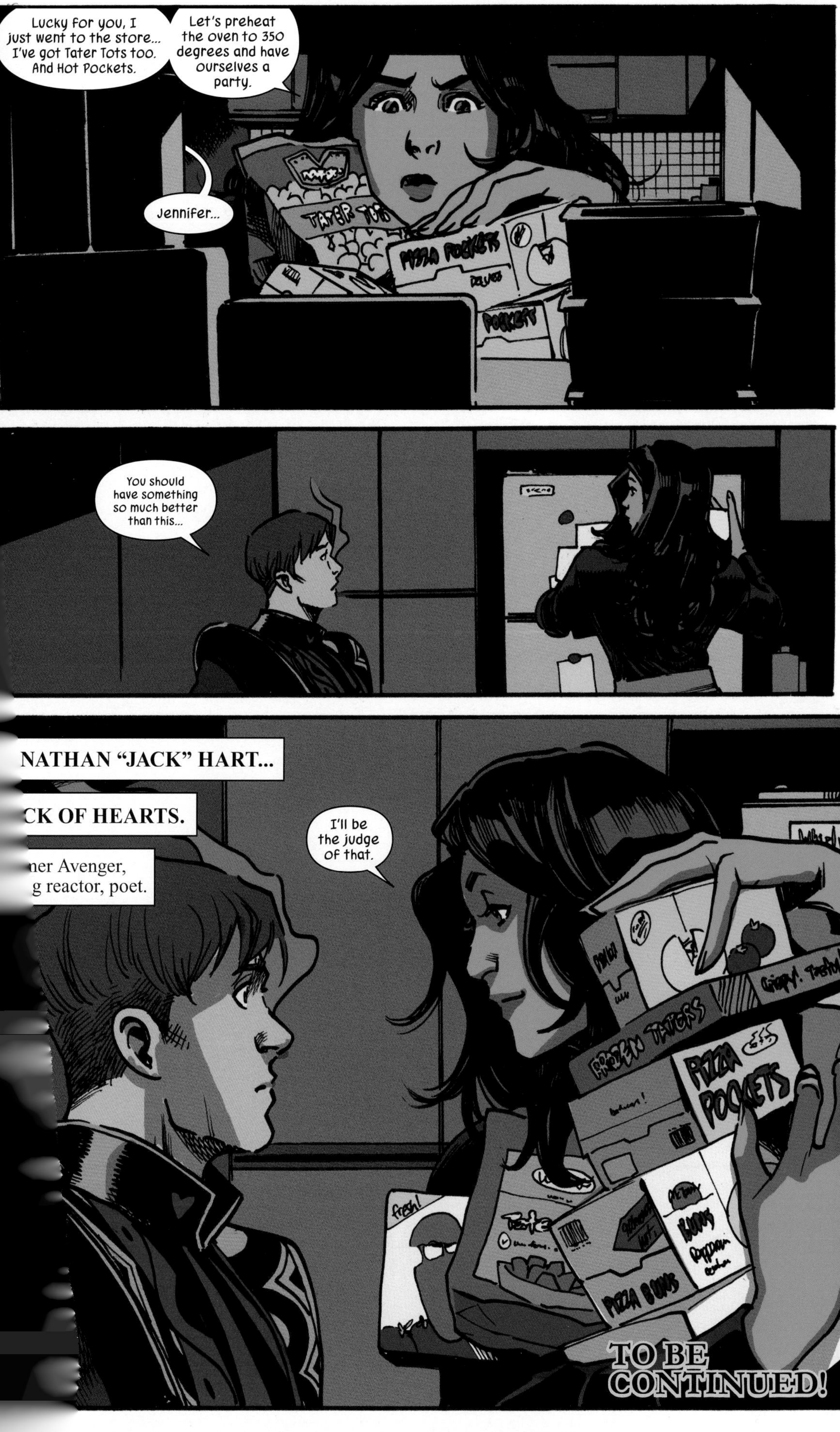

Lucky for you, I just went to the store... I've got Tater Tots too. And Hot Pockets.
Let's preheat the oven to 350 degrees and have ourselves a party.
Jennifer...
You should have something so much better than this...
NATHAN "JACK" HART...
CK OF HEARTS.
ner Avenger,
g reactor, poet.
I'll be the judge of that.
PIZZA POCKETS
TO BE CONTINUED!

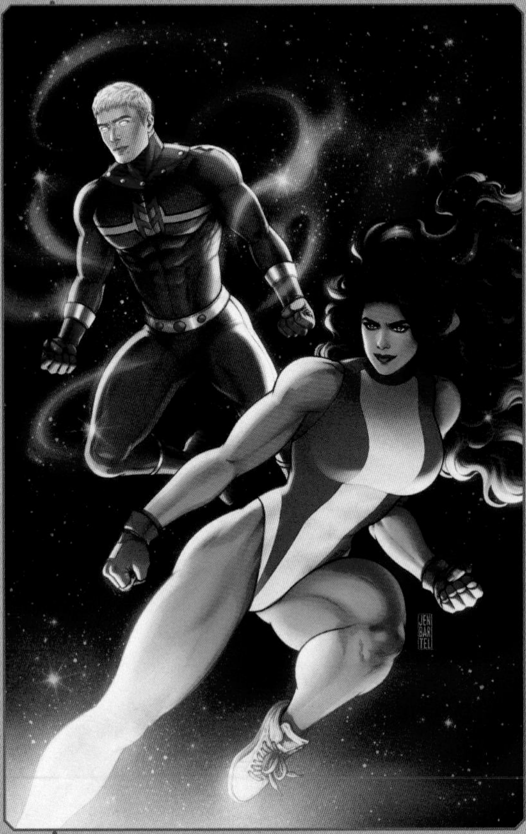
JEN BAR TEL

#7 MIRACLEMAN VARIANT BY **JEN BARTEL**

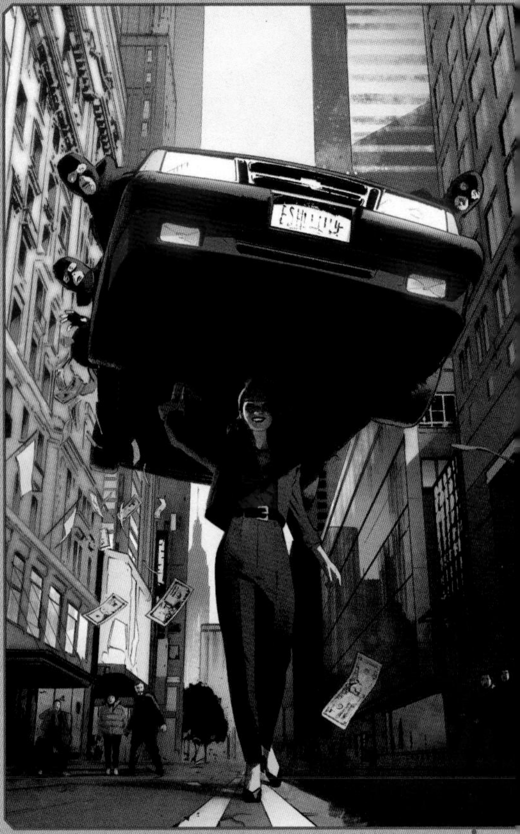

#8 VARIANT BY **MICHAEL DOWLING**

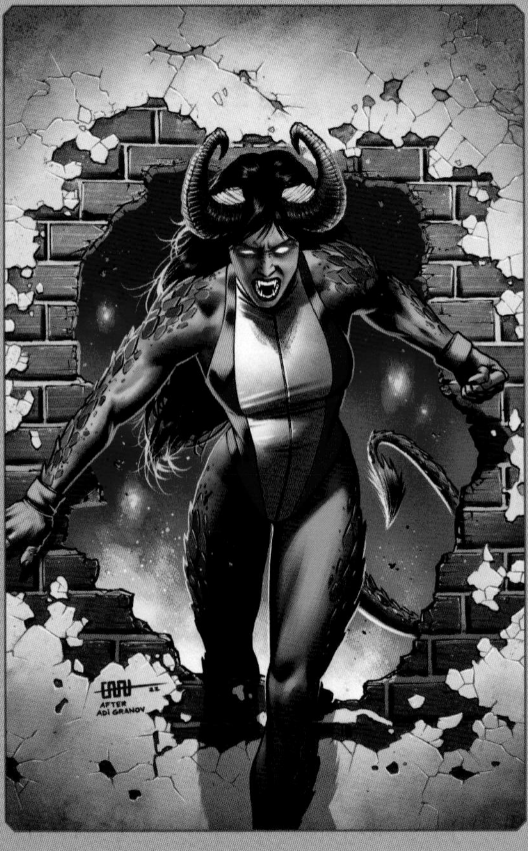
CAFU
AFTER ADI GRANOV

#9 DEMONIZED VARIANT BY **CAFU**

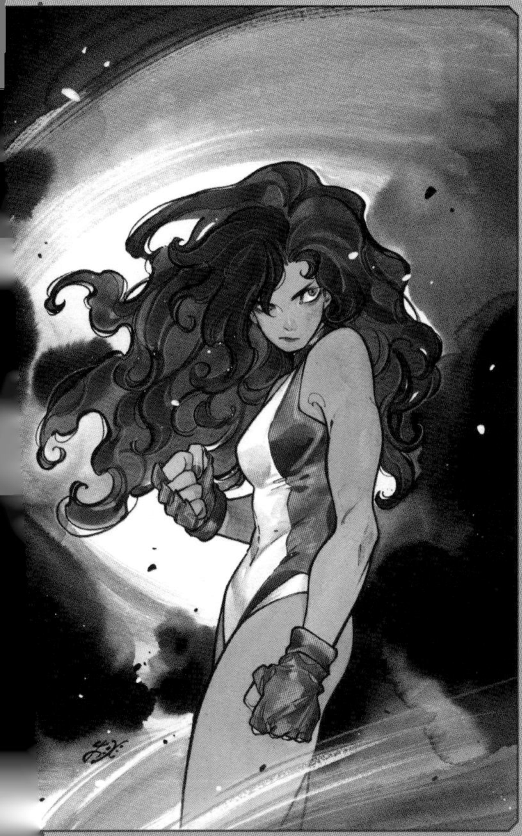

#9 MARVEL UNIVERSE VARIANT BY **PEACH MOMOKO**

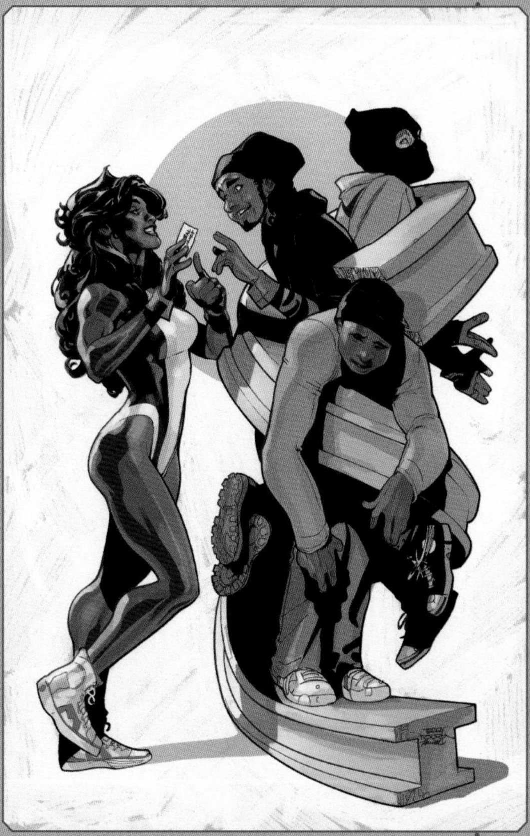

#9 VARIANT BY **TERRY DODSON** & **RACHEL DODSON**

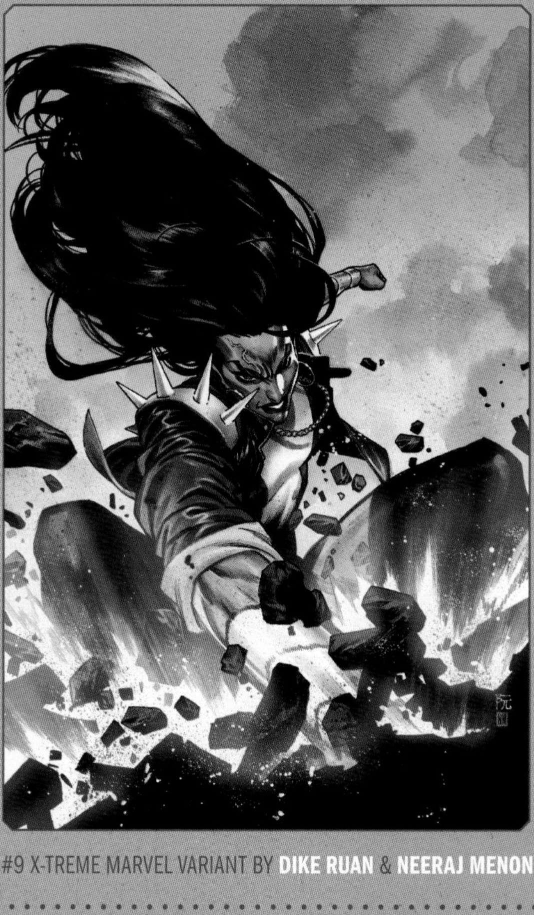

#9 X-TREME MARVEL VARIANT BY **DIKE RUAN** & **NEERAJ MENON**

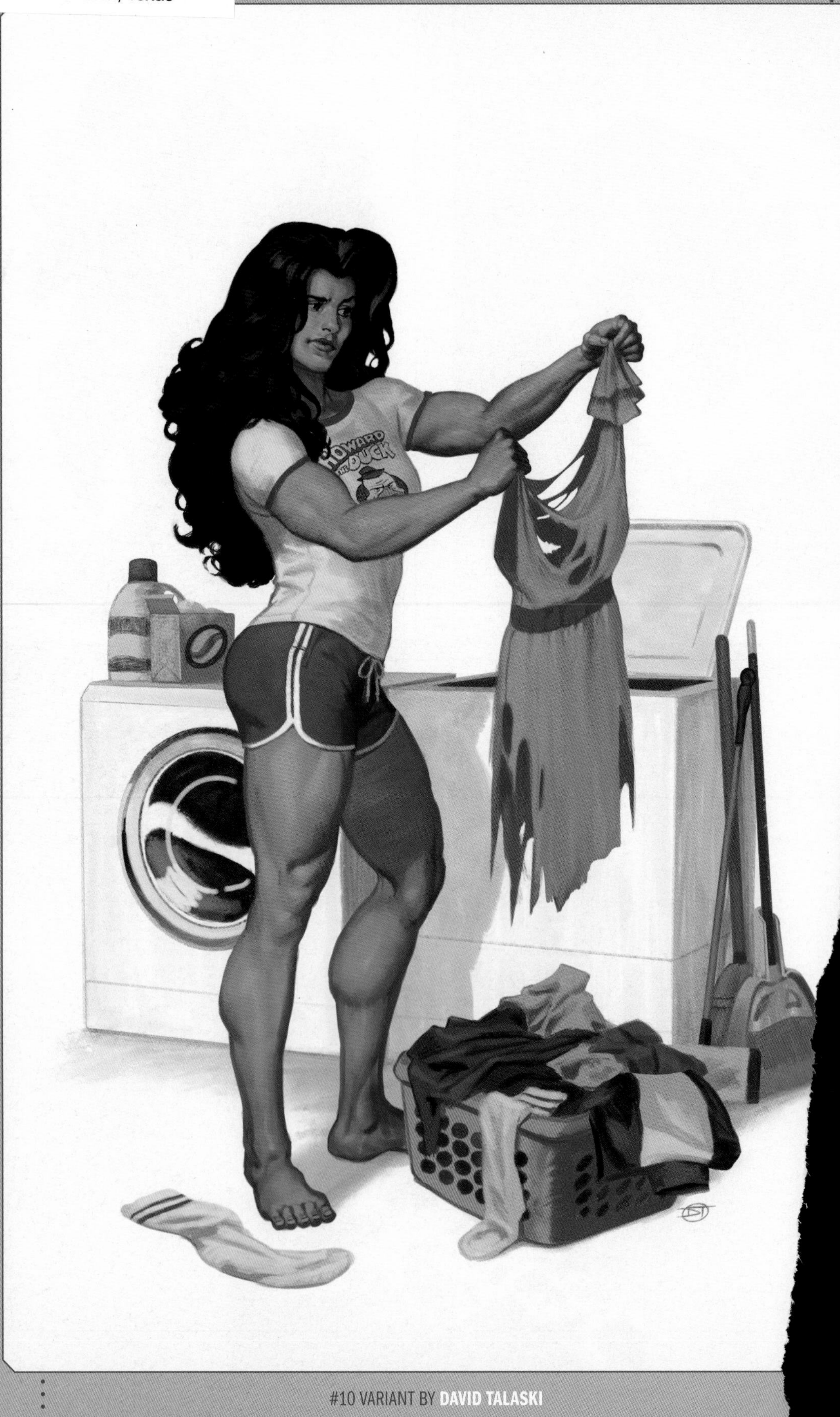
HOWARD THE DUCK

#10 VARIANT BY **DAVID TALASKI**